Anti-Democratic Thought

edited by

Erich Kofmel

imprint-academic.com

This collection copyright © Erich Kofmel (Editor) 2008
Individual contributions copyright © their authors 2008

The moral rights of the authors have been asserted.
No part of this publication may be reproduced in any form
without permission, except for the quotation of brief passages
in criticism and discussion.

Published in the UK by Imprint Academic
PO Box 200, Exeter EX5 5YX, UK

Published in the USA by Imprint Academic
Philosophy Documentation Center
PO Box 7147, Charlottesville, VA 22906-7147, USA

ISBN 9 781845 401245

A CIP catalogue record for this book is available from the
British Library and US Library of Congress

To Wits; Alexander W. Higgins (despite); and 'intellectual terrorists'

I saw slaves on horses and princes walking like slaves on the ground.

Qoheleth 10:7

Contents

Re-Introducing Anti-Democratic Thought
  Erich Kofmel 1

Is Plato's Political Philosophy Anti-Democratic?
  Thom Brooks 17

Reversing Plato's Anti-Democratism:
Castoriadis' 'Quirky' Plato
  Wendy C. Hamblet 35

J.S. Mill's Elitism:
A Classical Liberal's Response to the Rise of Democracy
  Andy Hamilton 49

The Rhetoric of False Appearances and True Essences:
Anti-Democratic Thought in France at
the Turn of the Twentieth Century
  Tuula Vaarakallio 67

Tolstoy's Anarchist Denunciation
of State Violence and Deception
  Alexandre J.M.E. Christoyannopoulos 85

'The Sovereign Disappears in the Voting Booth':
Carl Schmitt and Martin Heidegger on Sovereignty
and (Perhaps) Governmentality
  Thomas Crombez 101

The Criticism of Democracy in Rabbi E.E.M. Shach's Thought
  Moshe Hellinger 123

State(ments) of Emergency:
Anti-Democratic Narratives in Bangladesh
  Jalal Alamgir 141

From Democracy to Accountability
  Pauline C. Westerman 165

Fighting Capitalism and Democracy
  Erich Kofmel 187

Contributors 241

Erich Kofmel

Re-Introducing Anti-Democratic Thought

I

Introduction[1]

It is quixotic to fight *all* the people.

How to introduce this book? I cannot trust my readers to have an open mind. We live in democracies that purport to be tolerant and free-thinking, but that tolerance and freedom of thought stops at the boundaries of democracy.

There is honour in fighting a tyrant. There is honour in fighting unjust political rule. We applaud the few who dare to think—and act—against tyranny. Elsewhere.

The reason why the many do not fight tyranny is because they do not perceive tyranny as such. They do not see the tyrant as tyrant. They do not want to be made aware of him.

It is the same 'many' who refused to see Hitler for what he was, that—just a few years later—constituted the democratic people, the sovereign, of post-war Germany. Those refusing to see the tyrant and act against tyranny had become the tyrant themselves (for a second time, after the Weimar period), had established the tyranny of *all* the people over the

---

[1] This paper was first presented at the Second Global International Studies Conference of the World International Studies Committee (WISC) in Ljubljana, Slovenia, July 2008. Earlier extended versions of parts of the paper were presented at the Inaugural International Symposium of the Sussex Centre for the Individual and Society (SCIS) in Brighton, England, July 2006, and at the Jerusalem Seminar in the History of Political Thought at the Hebrew University of Jerusalem, Israel, February 2008. All papers collected in this volume were used for instruction and discussed at a Short Course 'Democracy and Its Critics: Re-Introducing Anti-Democratic Thought into the Syllabus' at the Annual Meeting of the American Political Science Association (APSA) in Boston, USA, August 2008.

individual and the few. Over the few exceptional souls who would fight tyranny wherever, and in whatever disguise, they encountered it.

The people of religious countries such as the United States (at a mechanical level, impaired by liberalism) and Iraq (at a deeper level) still retain an understanding of what the word 'honour' means. In western Europe, the term has lost its meaning.

If there is honour in you, you will fight against a tyrant and tyranny, even in the most totalitarian societies. We, here, in our democracies, will expect you to fight your tyrants. Elsewhere everywhere.

Only as a citizen of a liberal western democracy you are *not* expected to fight your government. You are not allowed to oppose democracy.

Would not, in any other circumstances, the fact that, under various legislation, we are forbidden from criticizing the form of government we are subjected to be taken as evidence that there is no freedom of speech in our countries? That we live under tyrannical rule?

That's the tyranny of democracy. The tyranny of everyone. There is honour in fighting a tyrant, but no honour to be gained from fighting democracy. Honour is bestowed by the people, by the admiration of the people. It is quixotic to fight *all* the people.

Or is it?

Only he will fight democracy who finds, like Don Quixote, honour and pride within himself, rather than through others. I am the proponent of a new engagement with anti-democratic thought. This paper outlines a positive agenda for the future.

The entire book marks the beginning of a daring new debate and re-introduces anti-democratic thought and practice to the academic discourse and into the syllabus. It wishes to offer a serious discussion of anti-democratic thought, rather than an apology of democracy.

We must begin to see the tyrant for what it is.

II

Anti-Egalitarianism

Francis Fukuyama, in his seminal work proposing that liberal democracy and capitalism might constitute the 'end point of mankind's ideological evolution' and the 'final form of human government' — in short, the 'end of history' (1992: xi) — left open the possibility of an alternative ending:

> The end of history will be a very sad time. The struggle for recognition, the willingness to risk one's life for a purely abstract goal, the worldwide ideological struggle that called forth daring, courage, imagination, and idealism, will be replaced by economic calculation, the

endless solving of technical problems, environmental concerns, and the satisfaction of sophisticated consumer demands. ... Perhaps this very prospect of centuries of boredom at the end of history will serve to get history started once again (1989: 18).

Fukuyama's 'last man' (who, in spite of constituting the second half of the title of the book, *The End of History and the Last Man*, seems to have escaped most readers' notice) — 'the victorious slave' (1992: 301) in Hegelian and Nietzschean terms — who is '[t]he man of desire, Economic Man, ... will perform an internal "cost-benefit analysis"', put up with it, and work 'within the system'. Western society 'has managed to contrive it so that its brightest and most privileged young people produce things that are neither beautiful nor useful, such as the mountains of litigation produced by lawyers every year' (309).

Fukuyama admits however that the system, come time, may be challenged by a man 'who feels that his worth is constituted by something more than the complex set of desires that make up his physical existence'. A 'man of anger who is jealous of his own dignity' (180) and wishes to be recognized 'not just as equal, but as superior to others' (xxiii). In short, a new 'master', a 'first man'. 'Does not the satisfaction of certain human beings depend on recognition that is inherently unequal?' (xxiii). A notion that leaves a wide opening for an ultimately anti-liberal development of world history and might doom democracy to the fatal destiny that so many writers from Plato (1941: 288–98) and Aristotle (1988: 1305a; see Fukuyama, 1992: 335) to Friedrich Nietzsche (1998a; 1998b) and Oswald Spengler (1971) prophesied.

Nietzsche, 'an open opponent of democracy' (Fukuyama, 1992: 313), in the last decades of the nineteenth century 'raised the question: is recognition that can be universalized worth having in the first place? Is not the *quality* of recognition far more important than its universality?', and 'what is the value of recognition that comes to everyone merely by virtue of being a human being?' (301–2; his emphasis). For Nietzsche,

> [t]he Christian religion originated in the realization that the weak could overcome the strong when they banded together in a herd, using the weapons of guilt and conscience. In modern times this prejudice had become widespread and irresistible, not because it had been revealed as true, but because of the greater numbers of weak people (Fukuyama, 1992: 301).

'[T]he *democratic* movement is Christianity's heir' (Nietzsche, 1998a: 89; his emphasis): 'Ye preachers of equality, the tyrant-frenzy of impotence crieth thus in you for "equality"' (1967: 151). Democratic man, for Nietzsche, is inherently unable 'to feel any shame in himself for being unable to rise above' his desire 'to satisfy a host of petty wants through the calculation of long-term self-interest' (Fukuyama, 1992: 301; see also 308–9 on Alexis de Tocqueville's similar view).

In a democracy, '[w]hen an individual's highest and strongest instincts break forth with a passion, driving him far above and beyond the average, beyond the lowlands of the herd conscience', 'the moral perspective now considers how harmful or harmless an opinion, an emotional state, a will, a talent is to the community, to equality'. 'Exalted, self-directed spirituality, a will to solitude, even great powers of reason are felt as a danger', *'Morality in Europe today is herd animal morality'* (Nietzsche, 1998a: 88–9; his emphasis).

'[T]he evils of extreme equality' for Fukuyama are 'creeping mediocrity or the tyranny of the majority' (1992: 295), the latter term being used first by de Tocqueville in 1835 (2000) and reprised by J.S. Mill in 1859 (1989: 8). Even such a man as Mill, often considered a liberal democrat, found harsh words (worth quoting at length) for what he called the 'collective mediocrity' of the modern masses:

> In sober truth, whatever homage may be professed, or even paid, to real or supposed mental superiority, the general tendency of things throughout the world is to render mediocrity the ascendant power among mankind. ... At present individuals are lost in the crowd. In politics it is almost a triviality to say that public opinion now rules the world. The only power deserving the name is that of masses, and of governments while they make themselves the organ of the tendencies and instincts of masses. ... I am not complaining of all this. I do not assert that anything better is compatible, as a general rule, with the present low state of the human mind. But that does not hinder the government of mediocrity from being mediocre government. No government by a democracy ..., either in its political acts or in the opinions, qualities, and tone of mind which it fosters, ever did or could rise above mediocrity, except in so far as the sovereign Many have let themselves be guided (which in their best times they always have done) by the counsels and influence of a more highly gifted and instructed One or Few. The initiation of all wise or noble things, comes and must come from individuals; generally at first from some one individual (66).

What then about democracy and equality? 'The honour and glory of the average man is that he is capable of following that initiative' of a superior man (66). (It bears pointing out that Spengler holds precisely liberalism responsible that '[n]oble ideas are no longer recognized, but only vocational interest. Hence it is that on the soil of burgher equality', where money and intellect reign supreme, everything is being rejected 'that cannot be rationally grasped': 1971: II/449.) It is superior man who 'seeks out struggle and sacrifice, ... tries to prove that the self is something better and higher than a fearful, needy, instinctual, physically determined animal' (Fukuyama, 1992: 304).

The German term used by Nietzsche, '*Übermensch*', should be translated as superior (or higher) human being, rather than as 'Superman'. For he is not talking about something that is more than human, but about what is best in humans—and given only a few in every age.

Not all anti-democratic thought is anti-egalitarian and not all anti-egalitarian thought is anti-democratic. However, anti-egalitarians have long held the strongest objections to democracy. Liberals in the seventeenth and eighteenth centuries, while demanding economic freedom, did not at all support democracy (Macpherson, 1977: 20), and liberal elitism persisted throughout the nineteenth century. Jeremy Bentham and James Mill, in the early nineteenth century, were among the first liberals to back universal male suffrage once they had become convinced that the poor would let themselves be guided by the property-owning classes (Macpherson, 1977: 37–43). What is called 'democratic' or 'anti-democratic' thought in any given context remains a matter of definition. To limit the franchise has been the practice of most democracies.

Much anti-democratic (and anti-egalitarian) thought has been expressed by means other than formal political theory or philosophy—be it aphorisms, novels, or sequences of dramatic dialogue—, and authors tend to write in a polemical rather than academic style (Nietzsche even called his *On the Genealogy of Morals* in the subtitle 'a polemic': 1998b). In his 1883 play *An Enemy of the People*, Henrik Ibsen lets his hero, Dr Stockmann, challenge an assembly of his fellow townsmen thus:

> The majority *never* has right on its side. Never, I say! That is one of these social lies against which an independent intelligent man must wage war. Who is it that constitutes the majority of the population in a country? Is it the clever folk or the stupid? I don't imagine you will dispute the fact that at present the stupid people are in an absolutely overwhelming majority all the world over. But, good lord!—you can never pretend that it is right that the stupid folk should govern the clever ones! [*Uproar and cries*] Oh yes—you can shout me down, I know! but you cannot answer me. The majority has *might* on its side—unfortunately; but *right* it has *not*. I am in the right—I and a few other scattered individuals (in Carroll, 1974: 139; Ibsen's emphases).

Superior men (and women) have 'not learned to submit' themselves, have 'not learned petty policy' and 'petty virtues' of 'petty people'. These petty people 'are the Superman's greatest danger! Surpass, ye higher men, ... the "happiness of the greatest number" —! And rather despair than submit yourselves' (Nietzsche, 1967: 326–7). It is important to understand that what Nietzsche says is 'a law only for mine own; I am not a law for all. He, however, who belonged unto me must be strong'.

> Ye higher men, learn *this* from me: On the market-place no one believeth in higher men. But if ye will speak there, very well! The rabble, however, blinketh: — "we are all equal."
>
> "Ye higher men," — so blinketh the rabble — "there are no higher men, we are all equal; man is man, before God — we are all equal!"
>
> Before God! — Now, however, this God hath died. Before the rabble, however, we will not be equal. Ye higher men, away from the market-place! (325; his emphasis)

It was Max Stirner who in 1845 said, preceding Nietzsche by almost half a century: 'Man has killed God in order to become now — "*sole* God on high"' (1971: 109; his emphasis). But Nietzsche would not submit: 'God hath died: now do *we* desire — the Superman to live' (1967: 326; his emphasis).

Ayn Rand, in her 1947 novel *The Fountainhead*, introduced the concept of 'creators' and 'second-handers'. According to her, what distinguishes the creators is that they are not concerned with how they are perceived by others. They just don't care. 'This is what I wanted because *I* wanted it, not because it made my neighbours gape at me' (1994: 593; her emphasis). Creators are interested solely in their work (this work might be politics, though), not in people (not even a *polis* or constituency) — for 'true master-natures ... the people is nothing but an object' (Spengler, 1971: II/455). They often have great difficulty connecting to people. 'We haven't even got a word for the quality I mean — for the self-sufficiency of man's spirit. It's difficult to call it selfishness or egotism, the words have been perverted' (Rand, 1994: 593-4).

Second-handers, by contrast, have appropriated the values of democratic society. They have gone through our educational system and, to speak in Foucauldian terms, been 'normalized' to the good life of a consumer and citizen. Already Plato knew that without 'superhuman' faculties no young man (or woman) will escape being pressed 'until he accepts all their notions of right and wrong, does as they do, and comes to be just such a man as they are' (1941: 199–200). Foucault, more recently, stressed that '[a]ny system of education is a political way of maintaining or modifying the appropriation of discourses, along with the knowledges and powers which they carry' (1981: 64). Of course, '[i]t is always possible that one might speak the truth in the space of a wild exteriority, but one is "in the true" only by obeying the rules of a discursive "policing" which one has to reactivate in each of one's discourses' (61). In this way, democracy, more effectively than any tyrant, exercises mind control over everyone. We indoctrinate ourselves, *of* the people's own accord and wish, *by* the people's consent and collaboration, and *for* the people's and our own best. Every citizen polices first himself and then every other. (Democracy may be about to bring this mechanism to perfection, having first accustomed us to exposing the still hidden, inner workings of our minds to the visibility of the Internet, and perfecting now the instruments, both technical and legal, to police and prosecute such involuntary exposure under the banners of 'anti-terrorism' and 'security'.) This is the real meaning of self-lessness — self-enslavement. Second-handers are their own master only as far as self-slavery is concerned: 'It's what I could not understand about people for a long time. They have no self. They live within others. They live secondhand' (Rand, 1994: 591). 'That's the emptiness I couldn't understand in people' (592).

> What would happen to the world without those who do, think, work, produce? Those are the egotists. You don't think through another's brain and you don't work through another's hands. ... I think your second-handers understand this, try as they might not to admit it to themselves. Notice how they'll accept anything except a man who stands alone. ... The independent man kills them because they don't exist within him and that's the only form of existence they know (592–3).

The relationship between Rand's lead character, the architect Howard Roark, builder of skyscrapers, and Nietzsche is intimate: 'Verily, he who here towered aloft his thoughts in stone, knew as well as the wisest one about the secret of life' which 'requireth elevation' (Nietzsche, 1967: 153). '[T]hat particular sense of sacred rapture men say they experience in nature — I've never received it from nature, only from ... skyscrapers' (Rand, 1994: 433). And as for the death of God:

> The sky over New York and the will of man made visible. What other religion do we need? ... Is it beauty and genius they want to see? Do they seek the sense of the sublime? Let them come to New York, stand on the Hudson, look and kneel. When I see the city from my window — no, I don't feel how small I am — but I feel that if a war came to threaten this, I would like to throw myself into space, over the city, and protect these buildings with my body (433).

Plato's philosopher republic, although not politically viable, is not far removed from Rand's ideas. Plato holds that '[w]hat is natural is that the sick man ... should wait at the door of the physician, and that all who need to be governed should seek out the man who can govern them; it is not for him to beg them to accept his rule, if there is really any help in him' (1941: 196).

Spengler, meanwhile, hails the future coming of 'Caesarism', a period in which capitalism and democracy will be challenged by, and ultimately defeated at the hands of, exceptional individuals of great mental strength, possessed of a piercing vision, strategic genius, ruthlessness and overwhelming endurance, who mean to gain political power without stooping to the base level of electoral prejudice (1971: II/420, 435). This final stage of western civilization will be preceded, according to Spengler, by ideologies, such as Marxism, and political concepts and theories losing their meaning ('and their end comes not from refutation, but from boredom': II/454), a general decline in the political condition of nations and widespread mistrust in democratic institutions, processes and performance, as well as a rekindling of religious sentiment he called the 'Second Religiousness' (II/435). The 'Caesarmen', he said, will reclaim politics by whatever means necessary and in doing so become once more 'the Destiny of an entire people or Culture' (II/418).

Reinterpreting the term 'Caesarism' in a profoundly postmodern sense, though, it may seem questionable whether the wars Spengler foresaw for the end time of western civilization will still be decided on a battlefield (see II/420, 435, 465, 506). 'Caesars' — under this designation or another — will yet again be great individuals seizing the opportunity to creatively carve political power for themselves, and on their own terms, out of the formless remains of history. The ancient values that Spengler expected to reaffirm themselves may not be 'blood' and 'soil' though, but honour, mastery, and the willingness to political experimentation. While the 'Caesars'-to-come may not as easily as in the past be able to disregard the populace, the preceding or immediate failure of democracy will open up new realms of unpredicted political possibility before them.

In Nietzsche's words a different, yet similar expectation reads:

> *But true philosophers are commanders and lawgivers*. They say, "This is the way it *should* be!" Only they decide about mankind's Where to? and What for? and to do so they employ the preparatory work of all philosophical workers, all subduers of the past. With creative hands they reach towards the future, and everything that is or has existed becomes their means, their tool, their hammer. Their "knowing" is *creating*, their creating is law-giving, their will to truth is—*will to power* (1998a: 105; his emphases).

The next step will be to *do* it. 'Thus wilt thou learn also from me; only the doer learneth' (Nietzsche, 1967: 307). 'Great man never want experience'. It is 'for a creative mind less than nothing' (Disraeli, 1962: 137). On 'spirits that are strong and original enough …, on forerunners, on men of the future, who in the present will forge the necessary link to force a thousand-year-old will onto *new* tracks' (1998a: 90; his emphasis), Nietzsche remarked, 'surely they will be men who experiment. By the name that I have dared to call them I have already expressly underlined their acts of experimenting and their joy in experimenting' (103).

III

A Positive Agenda for Anti-Democratic Thought

Anti-democratic thought may be directed against a particular form of democracy only or against every form of democracy imaginable. Wherever a form of 'democracy' arose or was proposed, it also found its critics and opponents. Historically, anti-democratic thought directed against abstract democratic principles and ideals most often originated from supporters of competing political systems such as guardianship, absolute monarchy, aristocratic government, collectivist anarchism, socialism, communism, fascism, or theocracy (besides contributions to this book, see Femia, 2001; Roberts, 1994; Spitz, 1949; DeLorme and McInnis, 1969; Dahl, 1989). Parliamentarism has thus been criticized by thinkers as diverse as the Catholic conservative Carl Schmitt, 1922 in *Political Theology* (1985), the communist revolutionary Vladimir Lenin, 1917 in *The State and Revolution* (1975), and the popular science-fiction author H.G. Wells, who noted in *After Democracy* (1932) the need to 'replace the dilatory indecisiveness of parliamentary politics' with a liberal-fascist 'competent receiver' along the lines of Plato's *Republic* (in Coupland, 2000: 543).

Many anti-democratic individualists on the other hand have felt coerced by majority decisions regardless of democracy's claim to be the political system least obstructive to individual liberty — as evidenced for example by Stirner's individualist anarchism in *The Ego and His Own* (1971) and much of the anti-egalitarian writings outlined above.

Criticisms of democracy purporting to propose ways of improving democratic processes and performance and/or the political participation of the people over against liberal democracy have arisen chiefly within the context of particular countries and their singular experience with democracy. Recently proposed measures to address democratic disenchantment and what has been called the 'post-democratic' condition (see, for example, Crouch, 2004; Baofu, 2004) include selection of office bearers by lot (so-called sortition; see Dowlen, 2008; Goodwin, 2005; Sutherland, 2008; Gataker, 2008), re-localization of decision making to the community level (see, for instance, Starr, 2000: xi, 111; Danaher and Burbach, 2000: 10), as well as emergent forms of electronic direct democracy. All alternative (that is, non-liberal) forms of 'democracy' that have been proposed — while professing to capture the true essence of democracy — seem virtually indistinguishable from both anti-democratic thought and non-democratic forms of government.

In a historical and cross-cultural perspective the fact cannot be denied that most democracies failed. Many formerly democratic countries do not have a democratic government now. Many countries have never known democracy.[2] Only western democracies for a short while — maybe to be dated from the fall of Soviet communism to the rise of radical Islam — believed themselves invincible. It may therefore seem expedient to think about political alternatives once more and to study threats to democracy from within and without as well as common modes of failure of democracy across times and cultures.

Will people's disillusion with democratic practices (such as the impact money has on campaigning), mass politics, and the equal inconsequence of everyone's vote ultimately terminate democracy? Duncan Black clad common-sense observations in the scientific terms of 'median voter theory' when claiming that all political parties and candidates will have to play to the centre in order to win votes (1948). Computer models, survey techniques and market research help parties and politicians 'penetrating into the hearts and minds of ordinary [voters] to learn *precisely* which combinations of myth and greed might work to generate support from key voting groups' (Ackerman and Fishkin, 2003: 10; their emphasis), and political psychologists predict voters' behaviour with eighty percent accuracy, based on emotions and passions, with little regard to the policy questions under consideration (Westen, 2007: 115) — 'people vote for the candidate who elicits the right feelings, not the candidate who presents the best arguments' (125). Asked for the main parties' stance on contentious policy issues, voters' replies will tend to be slightly worse than if tossing a coin to determine the correct answer (Luskin, 2002: 230–1). Even during the Cold War, a majority of Americans was not able to say whether the Soviet Union was a member of Nato (Erickson and Luttberg, 1973: 25). Electorates today are by no means better informed. A possible explanation of voter ignorance is that the voters have nothing to lose:

> Today, a person is deemed to be politically "represented" no matter what, i.e., regardless of his own will and actions or that of his representative. A person is considered represented if he votes, but also if he does not vote. He is considered represented if the candidate he has voted for is elected, but also if another candidate is elected. He is represented, whether the candidate he voted or did not vote for does or does not do what he wished him to do. And he is considered politically represented, whether "his" representative will find majority support among all elected representatives or not (Hoppe, 2001: 283–4).

---

2   On anti-democratic thought in contemporary China, see Nathan (2008).

In a democracy, '[h]aving the liberty to cast [a vote] is roughly as valuable as having the liberty to cast a vote on whether the sun will shine tomorrow' (Hardin, 2003: 179). The consequence is political apathy among the population even of the most democratic countries, resulting in a drop in party membership as well as voter turn-out. The 2005 Labour victory in Britain — dubbed a 'landslide' by some commentators — was in sober truth owed to thirty-five percent of the votes cast, or a miserly twenty-one percent of the total electorate.[3] Spengler said: 'As then sceptre and crown, so now peoples' rights are paraded for the multitude, and all the more punctiliously the less they really signify' (1971: II/464; see also Graham, 2002; Rancière, 2006; Gilley, 2006; Kaplan, 1997; Hoppe, 2001).

Still, all known political alternatives may have discredited themselves. The competing political systems of the twentieth century lost their struggle for world domination. This raises the question whether anti-egalitarian thought whose time had not come in the nineteenth and twentieth centuries will provide the basis for a *post*-postmodern political theory?

As Spengler knew, there are world-historic developments that will happen if we like it or not,

> our direction, willed and obligatory at once, is set for us within narrow limits, and on any other terms life is not worth the living. We have not the freedom to reach to this or to that, but the freedom to do the necessary or to do nothing. And a task that historic necessity has set *will* be accomplished with the individual or against him (1971: II/507; his emphasis).

I do not believe that all political systems have been tried yet. Our world is changing rapidly. Will the technological innovations of recent decades, and those to come, make possible political forms that never existed (nor could be imagined) in history — or will we have to fall back, post democracy, into the abyss of authoritarian despotism, as envisaged by Plato and Aristotle?

Spengler said that money would finally lose its value, its meaning, and politics would reclaim its rightful place.

That is the challenge of our time: reclaiming politics.

This book marks the beginning of a daring new debate. It is not satisfied with studying the historical dimensions of anti-democratic thought — as were so many of our predecessors —, but wishes to study its future too.

This (re-)introduction approaches anti-democratic thought from an angle different from that of earlier authors such as, most recently, Joseph

---

[3] I owe these references to Keith Sutherland (see Sutherland, 2008).

Femia (2001). Rather than focusing on discourse analysis and similarities in the arguments advanced by various strands of anti-democratic thought, the focus here lies on anti-egalitarianism and the underlying causes that led individuals to thinking and taking up arguments against democracy in the first place.

These reasons have not changed.

Exceptional men and women still are dissatisfied with democracy and the rule of everyone-else over the individual and unwilling to accept at face value the old tendentious and partisan adage that, despite its admitted shortcomings, no better political system is imaginable.

There are many difficulties in trying to make valid statements about anti-democratic thought. That should not stop us. We have to navigate the difficulty that anti-democratic thinkers may contradict each other. So too do democratic thinkers. Anti-democratic thought as much as democracy theory is not a coherent body of work. We need to understand the context in which anti-democratic thought arose and arises. Anti-democratic thought resulting from support for alternative political systems should be kept separate from anti-democratic thought directed against more fundamental principles of democracy, such as equality.

Anti-democratic thought can be—must be—re-invented as a positive project for the twenty-first century. In doing so, we need to avoid making claims that are obviously wrong. To distinguish ourselves from earlier polemical attacks on democracy, we need to phrase each word, each sentence, our whole argument carefully and in a manner that is simple and straightforward and cannot easily be refuted. We need to submit anti-democratic polemics, plays and novels to academic study and turn what we find into scientific knowledge and political resources.

Much nineteenth- and early twentieth-century anti-democratic thought suffered from unfamiliarity with the practical workings of democracy. Criticism was often unsophisticated, repetitive and superficial. It will be the challenge of twenty-first-century anti-democratic thought to criticize democracy, with hindsight, in a more sophisticated manner, to develop and formulate more subtle expressions of anti-democratic thought, to move away from cheap stereotypes and become as analytical and diverse as pro-democratic thought. Different traditions and strands of anti-democratic thought must be allowed to compete freely with each other and with democracy. Intellectuals need to lose the unjustified prejudice in favour of democracy—now just as unjustified as the largely prejudicial anti-democratic thought two-hundred years ago.

We need to confront those who call 'anti-democratic' everything they don't like about democracy, and whatever kind of social and political thought they do not understand or approve of, by giving anti-democratic thought clearer contours and new substance.

The contributions joined together here will be seen as a turning point. The book in its entirety, more than in its parts, is a milestone on the way from democracy to a post-democratic order. It will be perceived as exemplary for a category of writings. Anti-democratic thought is no longer to be treated as an inconsequential appendage to democracy theory. University and college courses on 'Democracy and Its Critics', may their teachers be in favour or critical of democracy, will benefit from the serious discussion of anti-democratic thought on offer here, more than from any apology of democracy.

IV

Conclusion

Liberal political theorists like de Tocqueville and J.S. Mill warned against 'the tyranny of the majority', and when Fukuyama perceived the danger of 'creeping mediocrity' that comes with general equality he only echoed Mill who lamented 'collective mediocrity' that could not help but lead to 'mediocre government'. Both Mill and Spengler deplored the influence of the press (and those who own it) on public opinion. It bears pointing out that Spengler and others held precisely liberalism responsible for the deterioration of the political and mental condition of western civilization.

'To-day Parliamentarism is in full decay', Spengler wrote (1971: II/456). In 'the final battle between Democracy and Caesarism' (II/435) — yet to come—, '[a]fter a long triumph of world-city economy and its interests over political creative force, the political side of life manifests itself after all as the stronger of the two', though, 'the master-will subdues again the plunderer will' (II/506).

'To make a revolution and create an entirely new society requires remarkable individuals with greater than usual hardness, vision, ruthlessness, and intelligence' (Fukuyama, 1992: 304–5). They will lead us to a *post*-postmodern world in which values and morals will once more have attained meaning, will give people back 'ideals by which to live and die' (314). In our society this may mean to create real *values* for the first time.

> The problem with the present-day self-esteem movement is that its members, living as they do in a democratic and egalitarian society, are seldom willing to make choices concerning what should be esteemed. They want to go out and embrace everybody, telling them that no matter how wretched and degraded their lives, they still have self-worth, that they are *somebody*. They do not want to exclude any person or any act as unworthy. ... [I]n a democracy we are fundamentally averse to

saying that a certain person, or way of life, or activity, is better and more worthwhile than another (303; his emphasis).

But, according to Ayn Rand, 'our soul has a single basic function—the act of valuing. "Yes" or "No," "I wish" or "I do not wish"' (1994: 525).

'Good and evil, and rich and poor, and high and low, and all names of values: weapons shall they be, and sounding signs, that life must again and again surpass itself' (Nietzsche, 1967: 153), must overcome '[t]he idiosyncratic democratic prejudice against everything which dominates and wishes to dominate' (1998b: 59). Nietzsche called this the 'will to power' (Fukuyama, 1992: 189).

As for the leaders who would achieve such a development of history, to 'ye who make the soul giddy, ye preachers of *equality*' (Nietzsche, 1967: 151),

> [a]n ice-cave to their bodies would our happiness be, and to their spirits!
> And as strong winds will we live above them, neighbours to the eagles, neighbours to the snow, neighbours to the sun: thus live the strong winds.
> And like a wind will I one day blow amongst them, and with my spirit, take the breath from their spirit: thus willeth my future (150).

We will not succumb. We will endure. We believe that none of us was 'born to be a second-hander' (Rand, 1994: 594).

We were born to be paradigm shifters.

This book re-introduces anti-democratic thought and practice to the academic discourse and into the syllabus. The present paper outlined a positive agenda for the future.

It is easier for a true individual to accept that another individual should rule, rather than to accept that a faceless mass should rule over oneself and that a majority of mediocrity should be placed higher than one's own best judgement.

Thought collected in this volume opens the way for all things to come—it shows us the way to overcome the democratic and egalitarian bias that hinders humankind from progress in so many fields.

Let us be quixotic. We will not be disillusioned. We will not be deceived.

The tyrant has been laid bare.

For everyone to stare at—and wonder.

Honour and Pride.

References

Ackermann, B., and J.S. Fishkin (2003), 'Deliberation day', in *Debating deliberative democracy*, eds. J.S. Fishkin and P. Laslett (Malden, MA: Blackwell).
Aristotle (1988), *The politics*, ed. S. Everson/trans. B. Jowett and J. Barnes (Cambridge: Cambridge University Press).
Baofu, P. (2004), *Beyond democracy to post-democracy: conceiving a better model of governance to supercede democracy* (2 vols.; Lewiston, NY: Edwin Mellen Press).
Black, D. (1948), 'On the rationale of group decision-making', *Journal of Political Economy*, 56 (1): 23–34.
Carroll, J. (1974), *Break-out from the Crystal Palace: the anarcho-psychological critique: Stirner, Nietzsche, Dostoevsky* (London and Boston: Routledge & Kegan Paul).
Coupland, P. (2000), 'H.G. Wells's "liberal fascism"', *Journal of Contemporary History*, 35 (4): 541–58.
Crouch, C. (2004), *Post-democracy* (Cambridge: Polity).
Dahl, R.A. (1989), *Democracy and its critics* (New Haven: Yale University Press).
Danaher, K., and R. Burbach, eds. (2000), *Globalize this! The battle against the World Trade Organization and corporate rule* (Monroe, ME: Common Courage Press).
DeLorme, R.L., and R.G. McInnis, eds. (1969), *Antidemocratic trends in twentieth-century America* (Reading, MA: Addison-Wesley).
Disraeli, B. (1962), *Coningsby or The new generation* (New York: New American Library).
Dowlen, O. (2008), *The political potential of sortition: a study of the random selection of citizens for public office* (Exeter and Charlottesville: Imprint Academic).
Erickson, R.S., and N.R. Luttberg (1973), *American public opinion: its origin and impact* (New York: Wiley).
Femia, J.V. (2001), *Against the masses: varieties of anti-democratic thought since the French Revolution* (Oxford: Oxford University Press).
Fukuyama, F. (1989), 'The end of history?', *The National Interest*, 16: 3–18.
Fukuyama, F. (1992), *The end of history and the last man* (New York: The Free Press).
Gataker, T. (2008), *The nature and uses of lotteries*, ed. C. Boyle (Exter and Charlottesville: Imprint Academic).
Gilley, B. (2006), 'The new antidemocrats', *Orbis*, 50 (2): 259–71.
Goodwin, B. (2005), *Justice by lottery* (2nd ed.; Exeter and Charlottesville: Imprint Academic).
Graham, G. (2002), *The case against the democratic state: an essay in cultural criticism* (Exeter and Charlottesville: Imprint Academic).
Hardin, R. (2003), 'Street-level epistemology', in *Debating deliberative democracy*, eds. J.S. Fishkin and P. Laslett (Malden, MA: Blackwell).
Hoppe, H.-H. (2001), *Democracy: the god that failed* (New Brunswick: Transaction Publishers).
Kaplan, R.D. (1997), 'Was democracy just a moment?', *Atlantic Monthly*, 280 (6): 55–80.
Lenin, V.I. (1975), *The state and revolution: the Marxist theory of the state and the tasks of the proletariat in the revolution*, trans. not named (Moscow: Progress Publishers).
Luskin, R.C. (2002), 'Political psychology, political behavior, and politics: questions of aggregation, causal distance, and taste', in *Thinking about political psychology*, ed. J.H. Kuklinski (Cambridge: Cambridge University Press).

Macpherson, C.B. (1977), *The life and times of liberal democracy* (Oxford, London, New York: Oxford University Press).
Mill, J.S. (1989), *On liberty and other writings*, ed. S. Collini (Cambridge: Cambridge University Press).
Nathan, A.J. (2008), 'China's political trajectory: what are the Chinese saying?', in *China's changing political landscape: prospects for democracy*, ed. C. Li (Washington, DC: Brookings Institution Press).
Nietzsche, F. (1967), *Thus spake Zarathustra: a book for all and none*, trans. T. Common (London: George Allen & Unwin).
Nietzsche, F. (1998a), *Beyond good and evil: prelude to a philosophy of the future*, trans. M. Faber (Oxford: Oxford University Press).
Nietzsche, F. (1998b), *On the genealogy of morals: a polemic*, trans. D. Smith (Oxford: Oxford University Press).
Plato (1941), *The republic of Plato*, trans. F.M. Cornford (Oxford: Oxford University Press).
Rancière, J. (2006), *Hatred of democracy*, trans. S. Corcoran (London and New York: Verso).
Rand, A. (1994), *The fountainhead* (London: HarperCollins Publishers).
Roberts, J.T. (1994), *Athens on trial: antidemocratic traditions in western thought* (Princeton: Princeton University Press).
Schmitt, C. (1985), *Political theology: four chapters on the concept of sovereignty*, trans. G. Schwab (Cambridge, MA, and London: MIT Press).
Spengler, O. (1971), *The decline of the west*, trans. C.F. Atkinson (London: George Allen & Unwin).
Spitz, D. (1949), *Patterns of anti-democratic thought: an analysis and a criticism, with special reference to the American political mind in recent times* (New York: Macmillan).
Starr, A. (2000), *Naming the enemy: anti-corporate movements confront globalization* (London and New York: Zed Books).
Stirner, M. (1971), *The ego and his own*, ed. J. Carroll/trans. S.T. Byington and J. Carroll (London: Jonathan Cape).
Sutherland, K. (2008), *A people's parliament* (Exeter and Charlottesville: Imprint Academic).
Tocqueville, A. de (2000), *Democracy in America*, ed./trans. H.C. Mansfield and D. Winthrop (Chicago and London: University of Chicago Press).
Wells, H.G. (1932), *After democracy: addresses and papers on the present world situation* (London: Watts & Co.).
Westen, D. (2007), *The political brain: the role of emotion in deciding the fate of the nation* (New York: Public Affairs).

Thom Brooks

Is Plato's Political Philosophy Anti-Democratic?

I

Introduction[1]

Perhaps one of the most controversial figures in political philosophy is Plato. Today, he is both a leading figure of political philosophy's canon and yet he has virtually no defenders of his political philosophy. While his works, such as the *Republic*, are amongst the most celebrated texts in the field, his theory of the state garners little, if any, support. This essay is an attempt to help rehabilitate Plato's theory of the state.

Of the many reservations against this theory, the central problem today concerns Plato's rejection, even perhaps 'hatred', of democracy (Mackie, 2003: 2). Contemporary political philosophers argue that Plato accepts 'Guardianship' whereby all political power is controlled by a small elite in virtue of their superior knowledge of governance and, thus, the common citizenry are denied all political power. Plato's theory of the state is objectionable not simply because it is anti-democratic, but because the people lack any political power.

The structure of this essay is as follows. First, I will begin by examining Plato's rejection of democracy. I will argue that this rejection concerns Athenian democracy only and that 'modern democracy' overcomes his primary objections.[2] Thus, Plato's widely understood rejection of all forms of democracy may be overstated and inaccurate. Secondly, I will turn to the common objection to Plato's theory of the state that it defends

---

1   An earlier, more extensive version of this essay was published in the *Bulletin of the Hegel Society of Great Britain* (Brooks, 2006b). My sincere thanks to Peter Jones, Harry Lesser, Alan Matthews, Ian O'Flynn and Bob Talisse for helpful comments on previous drafts.
2   Throughout, I refer to what we normally call democracy today as 'modern democracy'.

Guardianship. My strategy will be to cast some doubt on this view, especially given his changing views on politics in the *Laws*. Therefore, the Guardianship objection has limited force because Plato's mature theory of the state is different from the view of Guardianship attributed to him. Finally, I conclude with a general defence of Plato's anti-democratic theory of the state whereby power is neither controlled solely by unelected experts nor the citizenry. Instead, political power is held by both the citizenry and unelected experts who work together in concert, although the citizenry can overrule experts.

II

Plato's Rejection of Democracy

It is important to first recognize that Plato's critique of 'democracy' is a critique of 'Athenian democracy' and not democracy as we understand it today. In fact, most, if not all, of his criticisms of democracy do not create specific problems for modern democracy precisely for this reason. In this section, I will examine four different arguments put forward by Plato against democracy. These arguments are:

(A) Democracies are actually anarchic societies that lack any kind of coherent unity.

(B) Democracies are more likely to follow their citizens' impulses and desires, rather than any concern for the common good.

(C) Larger democracies fail to permit sufficient voice for their citizens, offering disincentives to citizens to participate.

(D) Democracies are essentially governments run by fools: it would be best to have those with expertise in statecraft take command, as the citizens are unable to govern well because they simply do not know what they are doing.

I will now examine each of these arguments in turn. My purpose will be to demonstrate both that Plato offers these four arguments against democracy and also to demonstrate how modern democracy can accommodate his arguments against Athenian democracy.

A. *Democracies are actually anarchic societies*

Plato's first criticism of democracies is that they are characterized by anarchy. For example, he attacks democratic governments for being essentially libertarian societies, whereby each citizen can 'arrange his own life in whatever manner pleases him': 'anarchy' is mistaken as 'freedom' (*Republic*:

557b, 560e; see also Annas, 1981: 300).[3] The share and scope of power held and exercised by each citizen is much greater than that held by democratic citizens today. But it is also not without its own problems. The thought is that if people can live however they please, they may choose a form of life that imposes restrictions on someone else's well-being. This gives us reason to reject democracies as an attractive form of political organization. Whilst these worries may be well placed with regard to classical democracies, no one today would think modern democracies function similarly.

Plato's second criticism is that democracies lack any kind of unity on account of their being essentially anarchic societies. Democracies lack unity in one of two ways. First, democracies lack political structure (*Republic*: 562b–c). Democracies are more akin to a collection of individuals occupying a common space, rather than a form of political organization. For example, Plato says:

> In this city, there is no requirement to rule, even if you're capable of it, or again to be ruled if you don't want to be, or to be at war when the others are, or at peace unless you happen to want it. And there is no requirement in the least that you not serve in public office as a juror, if you happen to want to serve, even if there is a law forbidding you to do so (*Republic*: 557e–558a).

The society lacks any rules beyond whatever its citizens see fit. One democracy might differ radically from another, depending upon the varieties of people who happen to compose it. Secondly, Plato accuses democracies of lacking leadership. If everyone rules and everyone has equal political voice, then no one can speak for anyone else and, it is thought, not for the community as a whole as well. In a society where all are equal, that society, in effect, 'lacks rulers' (*Republic*: 558c).

From these criticisms, Plato proposes a form of government that is not anarchical and has a clear political decision-making structure in place. This structure ensures that the community will avoid slipping into anarchy and it helps foster a coherent political unity. For Plato, one possible structure is a society where each person pursues tasks that they are naturally well-suited to perform. He believes that there exists a natural division of labour, forming a natural unity, whereby some are best suited to work as cobblers, others as medical doctors, and a chosen few as philosopher-kings. A second possible and related structure, in the *Laws*, holds that a legislator creates laws and educates the public about their necessity, while a democratically elected body has the task of enforcing these laws.

---

[3] All Plato quotations come from Plato (1997).

In this way, political unity is fostered by pursuing the moderation of 'the mixed wine of freedom' (see Brooks, 2006a).

At first glance, Plato's claims seem far off the mark. It is certainly not obvious in which respects, if any, modern democracies are mere aggregates rather than unified societies. Perhaps modern democracies are more aggregative — that is, perhaps they give a certain priority to individual rights above any variety of group rights[4] — than Plato would prefer, but there is an identifiable unity present nonetheless. We have clear institutional structures, as well as political leaders, such as generals, prime ministers, presidents, and the like, in our modern democracies and, indeed, they do know their remits, duties, and obligations as set out in public laws, all things considered.

These criticisms of Athenian democracy then do not stick to modern democracies today, because modern democracies can address them. We then satisfy Plato's general worries about democracy because, well, we're not that kind of democracy after all. In fact, we actually come much closer to addressing their concerns than either they or we might have imagined.

B. Democracies are more likely to follow their citizens' impulses and desires, rather than any concern for the common good

A second argument against democracies is that they are more likely to follow their citizens' impulses and desires, rather than any concern for the common good of all. If democracies are essentially anarchic societies, then, on this view, each person is free to choose whatever ends for the community and him- or herself that he or she wants. Not only might these choices clash, but the problem is that all will be disposed to think of themselves ahead of others. The common good will be lost in the wild pursuit of individual desires. Moreover, these individuals are pursuing their passions, rather than reason, because reason is inapplicable: the citizenry do not know how to rule and, thus, cannot have reason as their guide (see *Republic*: 561b–c, and Irwin, 1977: 229). Any democratically elected officials are then little more than 'servants' dedicated to the satisfaction of 'the city's appetites' (Plato, *Gorgias*: 517b).

For example, in a memorable passage from the *Republic*, we are told that the common people 'always look down at the ground like cattle, and, with their heads bent over the dinner table, they feed, fatten, and fornicate ... their desires are insatiable ... like a vessel full of holes' (586a–b). Democratic citizens are like 'people groping in the dark' because they simply do not know how to govern (Plato, *Phaedo*: 561b–c; see also *Republic*: 520c–d).

---

4   On group rights, see Jones (1999), reprinted in Brooks (2008).

The only guide the citizenry have is the pursuit of their individual passions. Worse still, citizens lack any means of choosing amongst competing passions, apart from whatever takes their fancy at a given time. Plato says: 'And so [the democrat] lives, always surrendering rule over himself to whichever desire comes along, as if it were chosen by lot. And when that is satisfied, he surrenders the rule to another, not disdaining any but satisfying them all equally' (*Republic*: 561b). As a result, a democracy is ruled by the pursuit of the passions of its members and not the pursuit of their common good (*Republic*: 559d–561c).

In addition, Plato identifies two further difficulties. First, a great number of people falsely believe they possess sufficient political expertise, which would justify their involvement in political affairs (*Philebus*: 48c–49a). Citizens are untroubled with the thought that they deserve an equal political voice with one another on account of their having political status (e.g. being a citizen). Their lack of knowledge of which ends are best pursued by the state never enters their minds as a serious concern. Secondly, the people are more keen to win arguments, rather than pursue truth, when engaged in a philosophical investigation with one another (see *Gorgias*: 457c–d). Thus, even if the citizens held sufficient political knowledge, it is thought that they would be unable to manage it effectively.

The solution to this problem is to constrain popular participation in politics, creating room for those with some particular expertise in governance to guide political decision making. The thought is that those who know best how to govern are those best able to detect the common good of the community and enable its pursuit to the good of all.

It is worth pointing out that representative modern democracy takes stock of Plato's worries again here. As Joseph Schumpeter notes, modern democracy is not characterized best as 'rule of the people'; but, instead, '[d]emocracy means only that the people have the opportunity of accepting or refusing the men who are to rule them .... [T]his may be expressed by saying that democracy is the rule of the politician' (1942: 284–5). The general public do not directly vote for anything nor anyone other than those who govern them, save in the occasional referenda. We limit access to participation in such a way that all the vicariousness that exists in the greater society is put under some control. In addition, our elected political leaders cannot work alone, but must often work amongst themselves and compromise with one another. They cannot be moved solely by whatever whim takes their fancy and they have the opportunity to rationally reflect upon potential policy options before deciding on any course of action. This is not to say that our politicians always make the best judgements or that democracy today lacks a need for further development. Instead, my point here is only that it can actually accommodate this second worry of Plato's in a positive manner.

C. *Larger democracies fail to permit sufficient voice for their citizens*

Plato proposes a third, more specific objection to democracy which may be stated briefly. This objection is that democracies with larger populations fail to permit sufficient voice for their citizens. The thought here is that in large democracies, 'democracy', as such, is essentially meaningless. This is because the so-called 'voice' each person has is particularly minute. That is, my vote is worth far more in decisions involving three or maybe a dozen people than in a polity of three hundred million people. My share in decision making, my 'voice', depreciates when the polity expands its number of citizens. Political participation, thus, becomes relatively worthless, even if democracy could be justified on a much smaller scale. Instead, we should opt for a form of political decision-making that takes citizens more seriously, where the decisions of key stakeholders matter.

While I would not want to deny the attractiveness of this argument, we can accept this view and at the same time accept that this is not an argument to *deny* political participation. The fact that my vote might count less—however we might determine this—in one polity versus another is not an argument to avoid participating at all. This objection does not warrant a rejection of democracy.

D. *Democracies are essentially governments run by fools*

Perhaps the primary and most often highlighted, as well as criticized, problem for Plato concerns his objection to democracy on the grounds that democracies make decisions without any coherent notion of what they are doing. Democracies are essentially governments run by fools. Instead of democracies, it would be best to have those with expertise in statecraft take command, as the citizens are unable to govern well because they simply do not know what they are doing. Thus, in Aristotle's words, we should endorse the view that 'they should rule who are able to rule best' (1984, *Politics*: 1273b5–6 [Book II]).

As we have seen, the problem with democracies is that they allow all citizens to possess an equal voice in political decision making, without regard to the citizenry's lack of knowledge or ability. All members are treated equally despite the fact that some are more capable of good governance than others (see *Republic*: 558c). Therefore, the cobbler and the medical doctor each have an equal say regarding governance, both equal to the person with particular expertise in governance. One result is that political judgements will be based by and large upon mere guesswork, as expert legislators are not in full command. Democracies are generally poorly governed as a consequence.

Plato argues that judgements based upon true knowledge carry a certain epistemic authority that judgements based upon right or wrong opinion lack. Every person possesses some degree of true knowledge, or expertise, in one type of 'craft' *(technē)*.[5] Plato says that justice is 'doing one's own work and not meddling with what isn't one's own' (*Republic*: 433a–b, 441e). The right to rule is not conferred via majority approval nor material wealth, but expertise in statesmanship (see *Euthydemus*: 291c–292c; *Republic*: 426d, 477d–e; *Statesman*: 292c). Only a few or, perhaps, just one individual will possess this knowledge in any given state (*Statesman*: 297b–c; see also *Republic*: 494a). Furthermore, Plato claims, it is a common fact of life that people properly seek counsel solely from experts in a particular field. For example, in the *Theaetetus*, Plato says:

> In emergencies—if at no other time—you see this belief. When they are in distress, on the battlefield, or in sickness or in a storm at sea, all men turn to their leaders in each sphere as to God, and look to them for salvation because they are superior in precisely this one thing—knowledge. And wherever human life and work goes on, you find everywhere men seeking teachers and masters, for themselves and for other living creatures and for the direction of all human works. You find also men who believe that they are able to teach and to take the lead. In all these cases, what else can we say but that men do believe in the existence of both wisdom and ignorance among themselves? (170a–b)

As a consequence, whenever we discern those who possess expert knowledge in *governance*, it is right that they should rule as this is the craft they naturally pursue best—just as those with expertise in trade skills ought to work as manual labourers (*Statesman*: 266e). The expert statesman alone transforms the naturally bestowed authority from certitude all naturally have of their given craft to an authority that is *political* (see Vlastos, 1983: 503).

Plato's ideal monarchical city-state, found in his *Republic*, is to be ruled by philosopher-kings: men (and women) who rule neither for the sake of honour nor wealth, seeking only the advantage of the citizens they serve (347c–d, 412d–e). Only they should rule the state as only they have the necessary expertise, given that ruling is their exclusive craft.

Plato's political vision in the *Republic* is oft criticized, but I do not believe he was unaware of difficulties with it and, in fact, he comes to reject parts of this vision in favour of his more mature view in the *Laws* (Brooks, 2006a). The reasons for this change of heart are present already in the *Republic*. For

---

5 On *technē,* see Reeve (1988).

example, after he suggests that much of the discussion of the *Republic* has been a theoretical sketch, Plato tells us that 'the nature of practice' is to attain truth less well than in theory (472e–473a). The way forward entails making the smallest possible change to bring this theory into being: philosophers must rule as kings or kings rule as philosophers (473c–d; see also 499a–d).

Indeed, Plato admits that 'it is not impossible for this to happen', but 'it is *difficult* for it to happen' (499d; emphasis given; see also 502b–c, 540d). Furthermore, he says:

Glaucon: You mean that [the philosopher-king] will be willing to take part in the politics of the city we were founding and describing, the one that exists in theory, for I don't think it exists anywhere on earth.

Socrates: But perhaps, I said, there is a model of it in heaven, for anyone who wants to look at it and to make himself its citizen on the strength of what he sees. It makes no difference whether it is or ever will be somewhere, for he would take part in the practical affairs of that city and no other (592a–b).

Thus, the ideal state's existence as an earthly, political practice may be compromised by its heavenly and ideal nature. The philosopher-king will *only* come to rule the ideal model 'in heaven' and in 'no other'. Plato offers some additional evidence in the *Republic* and elsewhere to support the view that only a god or someone with a divine nature can actually serve as the philosopher-king ideal type. As an example, he tells us that (a) the 'gods are our guardians' (*Phaedo*: 62b), (b) philosophers become 'as divine and ordered as a human being can' (*Republic*: 500c–d), and (c) the philosopher-king has 'a divine ruler within himself' (*Republic*: 590c).

There is, however, an additional reason to think Plato was aware of the impossibility of implementing his *Republic*. For instance, we are unable to know the true nature of others with absolute certainty. The implications then are that the *Republic* will fail, as we will be unable to prevent the breeding of philosophically-natured persons with others, perhaps producing no offspring who might grow into philosopher-kings (*Republic*: 546a–b). This problem is compounded by the fact that Plato believes persons who are perfectly matched for breeding will naturally produce a given number of children with a lesser nature anyway (see Jenks, 2002). As a result, centralized restriction of sexual relationships is doomed to fail from the very start, aspiring to little more than a staving off of the inevitable.

Ultimately, Plato comes to endorse a mixture of expert rule with popular consent (see *Laws*: 693d–e). This form of government is a compromise 'between a monarchical and a democratic constitution' fusing a 'moderate authoritarianism' with 'moderate freedom', enjoying both 'freedom and friendship applied with good judgement' (*Laws*: 756e, 701e, 693d–e).[6] As we have seen, Plato believes democracies resemble anarchical societies (see *Republic*: 462c). The main problem with democratic governance is that the citizenry are completely unscrupulous as to who should make political judgements, allowing all citizens to participate equally at a task where some people perform much better than others (*Republic*: 557e–558a, 560b). If we are to incorporate popular participation into a just form of government, then it becomes necessary to ensure we will be governed by responsible leadership. Plato says:

> I suppose that, when a democratic city, athirst for freedom, happens to get bad cupbearers for its leaders, so that it gets drunk by drinking more than it should of *the unmixed wine of freedom*, then, unless the rulers are very pliable and provide plenty of that freedom, they are punished by the city and accused of being accursed oligarchs (*Republic*: 562c–d; emphasis added).

Democracies pursue freedom for its own sake, without any regard for corresponding responsibilities or the common good. Keeping in mind the common ancient Greek practice of always mixing wine with water prior to consumption, Plato opposes an 'unmixed wine of freedom' — a freedom to do whatever one pleases — perhaps for the reason that freedom is intoxicating: the citizens are more liable to become drunk and irresponsible. Plato does not forbid the consumption of wine — in this case synonymous with freedom — but he does forbid excessive consumption of it. Freedom is a good to be cultivated within one's own state, so long as it is constrained by 'good judgement' (*Laws*: 693d–e). With leaders capable of good judgement, a state is in possession of good cupbearers and will be ruled with principled moderation, but yet enjoy widespread, popular freedoms.

Plato's mature political vision is one where popular participation meets responsible leadership. A legislator creates laws, makes them publicly known, and attempts to convince the public they are justified. He is educated for this task and knowledgeable about governance. The people elect members to a representative body whose task is to enforce the community's laws. In this way, Plato believes he can account for democratic representation without falling prey to democracy's many pitfalls.

To conclude this part of the discussion, Plato offers four criticisms of democracy, as well as solutions to these worries. Plato's mixed government is a government where reason dominates and the arbitrariness of

---

6 Plato's 'moderate authoritarianism' has much in common with the notion of 'sceptical authoritarianism' I have defended elsewhere (see Brooks, 2002).

popular decision making is tempered. Importantly, modern democracy can accommodate these criticisms as well despite the fact that Plato's mixed government is not a democracy.[7] In virtue of the fact that modern democracy can withstand Plato's professed rejection of democracy for the four primary arguments stated above, we should not conclude that Plato's theory of the state is entirely hostile to democracy, even if he endorses a non-democratic state. In fact, the view that Plato is opposed to *all* forms of democracy is overstated and probably incorrect.

III

Is Plato an Advocate of Guardianship?

We have now seen that Plato's major criticisms of (Athenian) democracy can all be addressed by modern democracy and, thus, it can withstand his objections. However, even if it were true that modern democracy can accommodate most, if not all, of Plato's concerns, there remains reason for modern democrats to reject Plato's theory of the state. I will take up this challenge of Plato's theory in this section.

The most common objection to Plato's theory of the state is that it defends 'Guardianship'. This objection focuses specifically on Plato's *Republic*. In this work, Plato argues that philosopher-kings must possess full political power because only they possess 'the expert knowledge of kingship' (see *Republic*: 426d, 477d–e; *Euthydemus*: 291c–292c; *Statesman*: 292c, e, 308e, 311c). Thus, according to George Klosko, 'the central motif of the political theory of the *Republic* is putting philosophical intelligence in control of the state' (1986: 172).

The objection to Plato's support for Guardianship is stated forcefully by Robert Dahl (1998: 69–74; see also Talisse, 2005: 78–80, 100–1; Wolff, 1996: 75, 77). Dahl says:

> [A]lmost all of us do rely on experts to make crucial decisions that bear strongly and directly on our well-being, happiness, health, future, even our survival, not just physicians, surgeons, and pilots but in our increasingly complex society a myriad of others. So if we let experts make decisions on important matters like these, why shouldn't we turn *government* over to experts? Attractive as it may seem at times, the argument for Guardianship rather than democracy fails to take sufficient account of some crucial defects. ... *To delegate certain subordinate decisions to experts is not equivalent to ceding final control over major decisions.* ... The fundamental issue ... is not whether as individuals we must sometimes put our trust in experts. The issue is who or what

---

7 A further reason may be that Plato might recognize 'modern democracy' as an 'oligarchy'. I must thank Harry Lesser for suggesting this view.

group should have the final say in decisions made by the government of a state (1998: 70–1; emphasis given).

Dahl concedes that we regularly and quite rightly place our trust in experts of all kinds. He does not deny that experts can be useful in our lives. What Dahl disputes is that experts should have final control. Thus, the objection to Guardianship is rooted in at least two understandings of Plato's theory of the state. First, Plato puts all political power in the hands of an unelected elite and no power in the hands of the common citizenry. Secondly, Plato justifies political power solely in terms of political expertise, so that those who rule justifiably govern because they alone possess political expertise. A consequence of this understanding of Plato's theory is that it is objectionable primarily because the people lack final say on political decisions affecting the polity.

Dahl's objection to Plato's Guardianship has been taken up by others. For example, David Estlund — renaming Plato's Guardianship 'epistocracy' (Estlund, 2008: 30–2, 206–9) — argues that the problem with Plato's position is that unelected experts 'have all political authority, in virtue of their wisdom' (208). Similarly, Robert Talisse — who renames Plato's Guardianship 'epistemarchy' — rejects Plato's position on the grounds that it is 'politically untenable' as no one possesses the knowledge necessary to become a Guardian in Plato's state. Thus, Plato's view fails and power should be held by the people, rather than unelected political experts (Talisse, 2007: 92–3). Finally, Henry Richardson rejects Plato's Guardianship because it is a form of unjustified domination over citizens. In other words, this domination is unjustified primarily because the people would lack final approval on public policy (Richardson, 2002: 7–9). Thus, Dahl's objection to Plato's Guardianship is widely accepted as a damning criticism of Plato's theory of the state.

I do not believe this objection succeeds. It is true in Plato's *Republic* that the philosopher-kings do have this final control, but it is *not* the case in Plato's *Laws* which he wrote toward the end of his life and best reflect his most considered views on the state. In the *Laws*, Plato's views on the state change in significant respects. For example, he no longer defends political rule by unelected experts alone. Instead, he endorses a government fusing monarchy with democracy in a new political form. Plato says:

> Listen to me then. There are two mother constitutions, so to speak, which you could fairly say have given birth to all the others. Monarchy is the proper name for the first, and democracy for the second. The former has been taken to extreme lengths by the Persians, the latter by my country; virtually all the others, as I said, are varieties of the two. *It is absolutely vital for a political system to combine them,* if (and this is of course the point of our advice, when we insist that no state formed

without these two elements can be constituted properly) — if it is to enjoy freedom and friendship applied with good judgement (*Laws*: 693d–e; emphasis added; see also Plato, *Eighth Letter*: 353d–e).

He calls this compromise between monarchy and democracy 'moderate authoritarianism', 'which is precisely the sort of compromise a constitution should always be' (*Laws*: 701e, 756e).

The compromise works in the following way. We might understand a monarchy as rule by a king who issues and enforces all laws, whereas democracy is rule by the people who themselves issue and enforce all laws. Plato's *Laws* strikes a middle ground bringing the two together. First, we have a legislator who is a trained expert and unelected to his post. He is responsible for making all laws, as well as making a genuine effort to persuade the public that the laws he enacts are just laws (see *Laws*: 823a). The legislator represents the 'monarchy' half of the compromise. The second, 'democracy', half of the compromise are the Guardians of the Laws. These Guardians are vetted in a scrutiny process prior to competing in elections. The scrutiny process is meant to ensure that elected Guardians will perform well if elected (see *Laws*: 752d–754e, 755a–c). Other public offices are also filled through popular elections, including those of 'generals' and 'cavalry-commanders' (see *Laws*: 755c–d, 756a–b). The role of the Guardians of the Laws is to enforce the laws of the state. Thus, while they do not have the ability to propose and enact new laws, they do have the final say on the enforcement of laws as they may decide against enforcing particular laws in some circumstances.[8] While Plato does incorporate elections and democratic elements into his more considered and mature political vision, we are left with something far removed from anything we might consider to be a 'democracy' in any obvious sense.

We can now see that Plato is able to overcome the objection to Guardianship. The objection has two related sides. One side is that Plato places full political power in unelected philosopher-kings. The second side of the objection is that Plato denies the people a final say over political decisions.

Plato's mature and most considered theory of the state resists the objection to Guardianship because he, too, rejects Guardianship. First, in the *Laws*, Plato does not place full political power in the hands of unelected persons. Political power is shared between an unelected legislator and an elected body, the Guardians of the Laws. Together, the legislator and the Guardians of the Laws possess political power. Secondly, Plato does not deny the people a final say over political decisions. Instead, the elected

---

8   We might best understand the refusal of Guardians of the Laws to enforce laws enacted by the legislator as akin to acts of jury nullification. On jury nullification, see, for example, Brooks (2004).

Guardians of the Laws must accept the laws issued by the unelected legislator: if they do not accept these laws, then the legislator is unable to enforce the laws he enacts. Thus, the final say over the implementation of laws rests with an elected body.

Moreover, it is equally the case that Plato always took seriously the significance of winning the support of the public. For example, in the *Second Letter* attributed to Plato and addressed to Dionysius II, Plato tells us that he travelled to Syracuse in part so 'philosophy might gain favour with the multitude' (*Second Letter*: 312; see also *Seventh Letter*: 325d–e). This view is not confined only to the various letters attributed to him, but also in the *Republic*: part of the necessity of making the transition to philosopher rule in any state is to convince the majority of the people elsewhere that this project is a practical possibility (see *Republic*: 498d–499a). Therefore, the need for winning public support for public policy is a position Plato consistently holds all along, including in the *Republic*.

The great mistake of arguing that Plato's theory of the state may be objected to as a form of Guardianship rests on an inaccurate view that the *Republic* represents Plato's most considered theory of the state. It does not. Furthermore, as we have already seen, Plato had many reasons to doubt the soundness of the *Republic* within the *Republic* itself. Plato's most considered views are found in the *Laws* and here he does not advocate Guardianship. Thus, Plato can overcome the Guardianship objection.

IV

Plato's Moderate Authoritarianism

In this final section, I would like to consider the general plausibility of Plato's mature theory of the state. Principally, I will not defend a view of the state whereby we have a legislator and the Guardians of the Laws selected in a particular way and working together in a common project. Thus, my aim here is *not* to defend the full, specific details of Plato's mature theory of the state.

On the contrary, I believe that the main structural features of Plato's so-called moderate authoritarianism are defensible. These features are primarily two-fold. First, Plato clearly recognizes that the work of government should not be performed exclusively by elected officials. There is a need for specific expertise in good governance. Politicians may win votes and command the public, but they must be able to rely on professional civil servants composing the bureaucracy that can lend their expertise in assisting popularly elected officials in a greater appreciation of what laws would benefit the public, the proper drafting of laws, and the knowledge to understand how best to implement the policies that the public and their politicians desire. Together, the bureaucracy and popularly elected representatives bring into unity what Plato saw as monarchical and democratic elements. That the work of government should be performed by unelected experts alongside elected officials is then but one main structural feature of Plato's moderate authoritarianism.

The second main structural feature is that the unelected experts do not have the final say on what laws or policies should be implemented. Instead, the final say rests with popularly elected representatives. Indeed, this is precisely the scenario we find ourselves in today. No matter the tremendous benefit that the professional, unelected bureaucracy brings to good governance, they lack final say on all matters. Final say rests with popularly elected representatives.

We should be surprised if we found any fourth century BC text acceptable in its entirety. This is certainly not true with Plato's *Laws* and I nowhere want to claim anything so strong. Instead, I would only argue for a far more modest, perhaps even too modest, position that within this text, now nearly 2,500 years old, we find two main structures that are the root of proper governing today. This fact may be highly surprising.

In his *Democratic Autonomy*, Henry Richardson says:

> Democracy is everywhere triumphant, yet no one truly believes in its existence. In all parts of the world, the trappings of democracy abound, yet nowhere is it credible to believe that the people rule. ... Instead of ruling ourselves, it is thought, we are ruled by politicians, bureaucrats, and the special interests that hold the politicians and bureaucrats together (2002: 3).

This picture recognizes the centrality of a professional bureaucracy, while also wary of its potential threat to democracy. Richardson then offers a new account of democratic reasoning that can help us better understand the crucially important role of the bureaucracy in sound democratic governance, while setting out the framework and limits constraining bureaucratic activity so that the bureaucracy helps enable democratic governance without dominating or even suffocating it. This framework consists in public participation in, and control of, the bureaucracy (see Richardson, 2002: 250). This picture is not entirely opposite Plato's. Both recognize the importance, even necessity, of expert participation in governance. Yet, both also recognize the need for the popularly elected representatives to have the final say on all matters of government. The relevance of Plato's view here for contemporary democratic theory is perhaps surprisingly significant.

And, yet, is this about *democracy* or something else? When we examine arguments relating to Guardianship they seem to move in only two directions. Guardianship entails full political control in the hands of the unelected; democracy entails full political control in the hands of the elected. Plato's *Laws* offer us a philosophical halfway house in between Guardianship and this view of democracy. The popularly elected may have final say, but they do not possess *full* political control. For example, some political control is held by the courts that ensure that basic rules of fairness and constitutional protections are upheld. Unelected bureaucrats may also exercise a degree of political control, even if momentarily, when they act as whistle blowers regarding government plans.

If a 'moderate authoritarian' system of government is one where the popularly elected have the final say, but where political power is held, in part, by unelected experts that assist in governing, then this system of government may have much to recommend it.[9] More importantly, it appears to best capture the true nature of modern governance today. Indeed, perhaps this is why, as Richardson notes above, democracy appears so 'triumphant', while few believe it exists 'truly'. The heart of Plato's anti-democratic theory of the state may appear more compelling than we may have previously thought.

V

Conclusion

I have argued for several positions. I began by examining Plato's rejection of democracy. I demonstrated that his rejection centres on an understanding of Athenian democracy alone and that modern democracy is left relatively unscathed by his criticisms. I next discussed whether Plato's theory of the state is vulnerable to the objection that it is a form of Guardianship. I argued that, in fact, Plato also rejects Guardianship. This is demonstrated clearly in his later political thought, such as in his *Laws*. Only those making the error of taking his *Republic* to represent his most considered views on the state might be misled to believe Plato's theory fails to overcome the Guardianship objection. Finally, I demonstrated that his theory as presented in the *Laws* has at its heart two main structural features that are highly defensible. These features are, first, that proper governance should involve unelected experts working with elected representatives and,

---

9   The arguments in favour of moderate authoritarianism are largely prudential, rather than moral. Plato's views might have even greater appeal if they could be supplemented by additional moral reasons. My thanks to Bob Talisse for suggesting this view to me.

secondly, that the elected representatives should have the final say even if not complete control of all political decisions. These features seem readily born out in the importance of the professional bureaucracy and the judiciary, both unelected bodies where members are chosen on the basis of their expertise.

Together, these features spell out the main structural characteristics of Plato's moderate authoritarianism. As we have seen, this authoritarianism is not entirely opposed to modern democracy. However, I hope that I have shown that, even in this age of democracy, we should clearly defend the place of unelected experts in good governance without whom no government — authoritarian, democratic, or otherwise — can succeed.

References

Annas, J. (1981), *An introduction to Plato's Republic* (Oxford: Clarendon).
Aristotle (1984), *The complete works of Aristotle*, ed. J. Barnes/revised Oxford trans. (Princeton: Princeton University Press).
Brooks, T. (2002), 'A defence of sceptical authoritarianism', *Politics*, 22 (3): 152–62.
Brooks, T. (2004), 'A defence of jury nullification', *Res Publica*, 10 (4): 401–23.
Brooks, T. (2006a), 'Knowledge and power in Plato's political thought', *International Journal of Philosophical Studies*, 14 (1): 51–77.
Brooks, T. (2006b), 'Plato, Hegel, and democracy', *Bulletin of the Hegel Society of Great Britain*, 53/54: 24–50.
Brooks, T., ed. (2008), *The global justice reader* (Oxford: Blackwell).
Dahl, R.A. (1998), *On democracy* (New Haven: Yale University Press).
Estlund, D. (2008), *Democratic authority: a philosophical framework* (Princeton: Princeton University Press).
Irwin, T.H. (1977), *Plato's moral theory: the early and middle dialogues* (Oxford: Clarendon).
Jenks, R. (2002), 'The machinery of the collapse: on Republic VIII', *History of Political Thought*, 23 (1): 22–9.
Jones, P. (1999), 'Group rights and group oppression', *Journal of Political Philosophy*, 7 (4): 353–77.
Klosko, G. (1986), *The development of Plato's political thought* (New York: Methuen).
Mackie, G. (2003), *Democracy defended* (Cambridge: Cambridge University Press).
Plato (1997), *Complete works*, ed. J.M. Cooper/various trans. (Indianapolis: Hackett).
Reeve, C.D.C. (1988), *Philosopher-kings: the argument of Plato's Republic* (Princeton: Princeton University Press).
Richardson, H.S. (2002), *Democratic autonomy: public reasoning about the ends of policy* (Oxford: Oxford University Press).
Schumpeter, J.A. (1942), *Capitalism, socialism, and democracy* (New York: Harper & Row).
Talisse, R.B. (2005), *Democracy after liberalism: pragmatism and deliberative politics* (London: Routledge).
Talisse, R.B. (2007), *A pragmatist philosophy of democracy* (London: Routledge).

Vlastos, G. (1983), 'The historical Socrates and Athenian democracy', *Political Theory*, 11 (4): 495–516.
Wolff, J. (1996), *An introduction to political philosophy* (Oxford: Oxford University Press).

Wendy C. Hamblet

Reversing Plato's Anti-Democratism
Castoriadis' 'Quirky' Plato

I

Introduction[1]

Cornelius Castoriadis was a man of tremendous import on the European continent. A seminal social and political thinker and radical anti-communist, Castoriadis co-founded the legendary activist bloc *Socialisme ou Barbarie* and helped launch their famed journal of the same name. Many of his dedicated supporters credit him with single-handedly inspiring the May 1968 rebellion in France. Castoriadis worked as a professional economist at the Organization for Economic Cooperation and Development, and was a practicing psychoanalyst and distinguished Sovietologist. He constituted the critical conscience of the international Left for decades until his death in December 1997, in Paris, at the age of seventy-five.

Nevertheless, Castoriadis' pioneering ideas are better known than his name, since his ideas were so radical as to necessitate his writing under pseudonyms to avoid deportation, until he finally gained French citizenship in 1970.[2] Among his most radical ideas is the unwavering conviction that common people can manage their lives, their communities, and their countries by instituting self-governance. Kings, managers, professional politicians, priests, therapists, and all other 'experts' and rulers, for Castoriadis, can neither guarantee people's success nor rescue them from their

---

1   This paper was first presented at the Winter Symposium on Castoriadis in Akureyri, Iceland, March 2008.
2   Castoriadis was born (1922) in Constantinople and raised in Athens. In the radically polarized atmosphere of wartime Greece, the young Castoriadis joined the most left-wing Greek Trotskyite faction, and from his youth faced threat of death from both fascists and communists.

folly, if they refuse to manage themselves with vision, self-discipline, and resourcefulness.

This conviction constitutes a radical break with the tradition of philosophical ideas about commoners. Since its inception in ancient Greece two and a half millennia ago, philosophy has tended to pose itself over against the common people of their societies, with their *doxa*, their petty, shallow concerns, and their unappeasable appetites. Socrates says repeatedly that he cares not at all what the common man thinks; his true judges are reasonable truth-loving men—philosophers. The ancient Greek term *hoi polloi* translates literally as 'the many' but its connotation retains the archaic prejudice against commoners as ignorant, base, and morally barren. Ancient Greek philosophers, in keeping with this prejudice, tend to remain anti-democratic, favouring for rule those with merit over the mediocre many. Both Plato and Aristotle, at their most sympathetic, consider democracy to be the worst of the best, and the best of the worst, of all political forms.

Castoriadis' love for the ancient Greek philosophers is undeniable. His treatment of Plato in his lectures on the *Statesman*, even at their most critical, evidence that deep affection. Castoriadis names Plato the first to move beyond philosophical opinion, challenging us to choose between the bad (demagogues and sophists who deceive and lead people astray) and the good who represent justice. He also names Plato the first philosopher of suspicion, pressing sophists and other deceivers to explain *why* they are saying what they do say, seeking the subjective reasons for their deceitful practices (Castoriadis, 2002: 4). Castoriadis sees the 'quirky' Plato providing a 'second foundation' for philosophy, philosophy's 'second creation', reconfiguring philosophy as research, an endless questioning of crucial things (48, 49, 52, 53).

However, as a fervent socialist and political critic, Castoriadis has an equally ardent love for common people. For him, the best state is the one in which the least of the citizens has a significant share, the greatest opportunity to partake in 'explicit self-creation' and to contribute to the evolving forms of the 'imaginary institution of society' (Vidal-Naquet, 2002: xviii). Plato and Castoriadis are opposed at fundamental levels.[3] Castoriadis must resolve the contradiction if he is to maintain his simultaneous

---

3   Pierre Vidal-Naquet highlights the fundamental opposition between Plato and Castoriadis, in his foreword to Castoriadis' book on the *Statesman* (Vidal-Naquet, 2002). He notes that Castoriadis celebrates the immortal contribution of the Athenians as their integration of historicity into their political forms, over against Plato, for whom the statesman's most crucial task is to block the historical process.

loves — for the anti-democratic Plato and for the shoemaker, the carpenter, and other common folk.

Plato's *Statesman* is often taken as Plato's clearest statement of his elitist political convictions; here we see ideal governance reduced most radically from the (*Republic*'s and the *Laws*') elite esoteric few to an elite mysterious one, the royal man. The guardian class has disappeared, no auxiliaries help to distribute or balance power, no nocturnal council oversees or advises. Ostensibly, in this dialogue Plato endorses dictatorship. Castoriadis' lectures on the *Statesman* offer a convenient opportunity to analyze how he deals with Plato's anti-democratism. Castoriadis presses Plato hard on his political elitism at every turn of the dialogue, but ultimately offers a new sympathetic interpretation from which Plato emerges more compromising, more democratic. Whether this reading is legitimate or coloured by his desire to resolve his contradictory loves is the overriding question of this paper.

II

Castoriadis' Quirky Plato

Castoriadis opens his lectures on Plato's *Statesman* with his evolutionary interpretation of the Platonic corpus; four phases of Plato's evolving thought situate the *Statesman* in the final phase, acting as a 'bridge' to the *Philebus* where Plato is seen to abandon crucial theories of his youth (Castoriadis, 2002: 17-9). Castoriadis reads in the *Statesman* a new metaphysics which appreciates earthbound realities, a new politics for the people and by the people, and a new logic that reconfigures the question of justice from the *who* of fitness for rule to the *how* of just distribution.

Let us examine how Castoriadis harvests a radical democrat from the Plato concealed in the *Statesman*. The dialogue is a continuation of the earlier exercises in *diaīresis*, begun in the *Theaetetus* and the *Sophist*, another 'grid-mapping of the highest human activities' distinguishing knowledge from praxis (Castoriadis, 2002: 19). Castoriadis, like the Eleatic Stranger, is riveted to the *diaīresis*. Making little of the opening lines of the dialogue, he simply notes 'a short preamble' and then moves on to analyze the first definition of the statesman.

Castoriadis straightway expresses his outrage at Plato's use of the monarchical idiom — the *Statesman* (*politikos*) is subtitled 'On Kingship' (*peri basileias*) and 'the royal art' is *basilikē technē*. He calls these terms 'an enormous abuse of language', 'a monstrosity for Greece', and a deceit on Plato's part, since Plato knows full well that the Greeks took great pride in having overcome monarchical forms of government, as despotic and barbarian (Castoriadis, 2002: 119, 130). The Persians had kings; the Greeks had statesmen.

The search for the statesman culminates in a definition of the 'royal man' as a shepherd; but this definition is fragile, the divisions incomplete, and it leaves the statesman's right to govern vulnerable to challenge by other feeders and rearers. A further division shows him to be a caretaker of a specific herd of creatures. But many arts care for people; the true statesman must be separated or divided from these rivals to properly establish his unique fitness for rule. The stranger monologues at great length, a very tedious and boring *diaīresis* but for the comic absurdity of a species-part distinction that names human beings not rational animals nor conflicted multifaceted souls, but two-footed, wingless creatures of the class of gregarious and tame herd-stock (*Statesman*: 262a–268c).[4]

Then, the Stranger suddenly abandons *diaīresis* for *mythologos*, and enters into the 'first digression', the myth of the reign of Kronos (268d). Here two cosmic eras are depicted: a timeless age when Father Kronos shepherds the world toward perfection by constant attendance and right measure, and then the 'reverse universe' of counter-perfection, under the reign of the neglectful Zeus.

> At one time the god himself guides the all (*tō pan*) traversing its cycle in conjunction with it. But at another time, he lets go, when the periods have achieved the measure of the time appointed by him. Then [the cosmos] reverses spontaneously (*automaton*) back to the opposite direction, since it is alive and has a share in *phronēsis* thanks to the one who fitted it together in the beginning (269c4–d2).

The present era represents loss—of wholeness, divine guidance, and lawfulness—as individual things rush blindly toward natural destruction—age, disease, pain, and death—under the blank eye of a careless god.[5]

Castoriadis sees revolutionary metaphysics concealed in this mythical tale, Plato's growing sympathy for the actual over the ideal, which will crystallize later in the dialogue and become full-blown in the *Philebus*. The myth, interprets Castoriadis, witnesses Plato's abandonment of the ideal world of the forms (*eidoi*) as the sole realm of the 'real'. Hereafter, the realm of historical human affairs will be fully real, though corrupt and wanting political and philosophical doctoring. The image of retreating and careless gods undermines the significance of the ideal as model for human affairs. When the gods fail, Castoriadis' Plato is admitting an essential gap, 'a cleavage in Being', between the law (perfect gods, ideal

---

4   All Plato quotations come from Plato (1989).
5   The fallen age echoes Hesiod, *Works and Days* (1991: lines 170–200), and also echoes Plato's *Phaedrus* (246a ff), where individual soul breaks off from the Whole-Soul.

forms) and the lived reality of frail material and human things (Castoriadis, 2002: 30). This, for Castoriadis, is the first dawn of Plato's 'anti-utopianism' (31).

This dawn is quickly followed by another. The 'second sailing' for a fresh definition (launched at *Statesman*: 279b) sees the Stranger 'boringly hold[ing] forth' (he admits at 286b) for seven long Stephanos pages, to redefine the statesman as a kind of weaver. The royal weaver entwines the various activities or arts necessary to the life of the city: 'the primitive species, then ... the instruments, vessels, vehicles, shelter, diversions, and nourishments' (289a–b). Castoriadis finds here yet another concession to reality and another glimpse of Plato's new metaphysics: all the arts of the city are *necessary*, even those which provide mere amusements to the citizens. Castoriadis highlights this passage as a critical moment in Plato's corpus: 'the humanization of Plato' (2002: 42).

After three more 'incidental points', the Stranger embarks upon a second digression on the differing forms of regimes (*Statesman*: 291d), followed by a third digression that declares statesmanship to be a science. The peculiar talent of the statesman is the application of a 'real criterion' in judging constitutions, a 'scientific understanding' of governance (293c) that renders unnecessary the laws. The Stranger explains why the statesman is not beholden to the laws: 'Laws can never issue an injunction binding on all, which really embodies what is best for each; it cannot prescribe with perfect accuracy what is good and right for each member of the community at any one time' (294a–b).

The statesman, as a dedicated doctor to his materially-challenged citizen-patients, jettisons universal prescriptions, and personally 'attends the bedside' of every citizen at every moment, measuring each individual situation as it arises and indicating the best course of action for every challenge. Kronos may be absent, and Zeus may not care, but the true statesman steers the ship of state with the individualized care of the *Timaeus*' *demiurgos*, measuring at every moment.[6] The statesman knows what is best for each occasion because he, like Kronos, embodies the highest form of the *phronēsis* that all things share, the highest form of the virtue of *sophrosune* (prudence) as it pertains to the art of governance — the right handling of situations, the right measuring of appropriate responses.

Castoriadis feigns scandal at the statesman's bedside manners. He charges Plato with attempting to 'fix the things in the city into place, to stop the evolution of history, to stop self-institution, to suppress self-

---

6 In Hesiod's myth depicting the ages of mortals, too, Kronos' guardian daemons, resurrected from an earlier golden age, counsel and protect the later, imperfect humans (1991, *Works and Days*: lines 109–24).

institution', since the image implies absolute power invested in a single ruler, whose singular scientific expertise makes impossible his consultation with others. Castoriadis pushes the image further than Plato does, claiming that rule and indeed truth are vested not merely in the godlike *phronēsis* of the statesman, but in the knowledge and the will of this royal man, a will that is not to be reined in, even by city laws (2002: 5, 29, 123).

The prognosis seems dim for Plato, but Castoriadis will soon reveal this harsh reading of the dictatorial statesman as a set-up, meant to stage the ultimate redemption of the beloved Plato. Castoriadis makes two calculated interpretive moves to accomplish the redemption: first, the laws are reinterpreted as Plato's 'absolutes' so their abandonment represents a rejection of absolutes *per se* (16–7); and second, the impossible ideal of a bedside counsellor-ruler is reinterpreted as an admission of the impossibility of dictatorship, the more impossible, the more a city grows. Castoriadis cites Plato's 'lawless dictatorship' as evidence of his (Plato's) abandonment of absolutist politics, his departure from political elitism, and his surrender to historical reality. Castoriadis highlights a radically elitist, anti-democratic, even dictatorial Plato only to deliver us to a Plato who has overcome all these anti-democratic sins. Having admitted that utopias cannot work, a new 'anti-utopian' Plato yields to the social-historical and to the radically democratic.

The dialogue could well end after this definition has been fleshed out, but almost as an afterthought, the *diaīresis* begins anew to shift the focus of the statesman's weaving from the arts of the city to the virtues of citizens (*Statesman*: 308e–309e).

> Taking the human characteristics of energy and temperance, the royal man assembles and unites their two lives through concord and friendship and, thus producing the most excellent and most magnificent of all fabrics, envelops therein in each city, all the people, slaves and freemen, draws them together in its weft and, assuring the city, without lack or failing, all the happiness it can enjoy (283c–285c).

This 'incidental point' represents the 'principal compositional quirk' (*bizarrérie*) of the dialogue for Castoriadis. The Stranger tells how the virtues are to be blended:

> Whatsoever is sharper than the occasion warrants, or seems to be too quick or too hard, is called violent or mad, and whatever is too heavy or slow or gentle, is called cowardly and sluggish; and almost always we find that the restraint of one class of qualities and the courage of the opposite class, like two parties arrayed in hostility to each other, do not mix with each other in the actions that are concerned with such qualities (308b).

Expert mixing cures fundamental rifts in the city's integrity, without which 'the men who have these qualities in their souls are at variance with one another' (308c). For Castoriadis, the closing mixing analogy encapsulates Plato's final word on statesmanship. Ignoring the obvious allusion to compulsory eugenics in the virtue-mixing analogy, Castoriadis asserts this final imagery as Plato's condemnation of prior attempts at political theory 'in the *Republic*, as well as ... the *Laws*' (2002: 30).

For Castoriadis, Plato is in this dialogue trading in two of his most critical theories—his theory of virtue as knowledge of the forms (*eidoi*) is exchanged for a new view of virtue as a mixing art; and his idealistic ontology is abandoned for process ontology. The political implications of these theory-shifts mean a jettisoning of utopian politics with its ideal city, its ideal laws, and its ideal rulers, for a compromise with reality—an imperfect state with its imperfect laws, incompetent rulers, and faulty citizens, struggling in real historical situations to recreate themselves and their systems anew. The statesman's weaving and the two types of measure (at *Statesman*: 283c–284c) admit that the human historical world, a mixed reality of shifting identities and conflicting attributes, has little to do with the ideal. Human lives are better, happier, for those imperfections and eccentricities finding measure (*metrios*) in communities of just distribution. Castoriadis interprets: '[n]o regulation will ever be able to get a tight grip upon the perpetual alteration of social and historical reality. ... [S]uch a regulation ... kills the social-historical; it kills its subject and its object' (2002: 31). Plato is

> once and for all condemn[ing] the reign of the instituted and seek[ing] the correct relationship, the just relationship between the instituting and the instituted, ... a Constitution of society that would permit society itself to fulfill this role, which even the royal man, if ever he were to exist and to be accepted by all the citizens, would never be able to fulfill, that of the correct government, therefore of self-government at all echelons (Castoriadis, 2002: 31).

Plato, in Castoriadis' reading, has, by the close of the dialogue, become a process philosopher, a moral relativist, and a radical democrat.

III

How Quirky is Castoriadis' Reading of Plato?

Castoriadis sees the *Statesman* as a critical turning point in the Platonic corpus witnessing Plato's 'humanization' (2002: 42). He makes sense of, brings order to, this 'quirky' dialogue by making three assumptions: Plato posits theories; Plato places his theories in the mouths of chosen interlocutors, including the Eleatic Stranger in this dialogue; and the theories transform over time, thus granting an evolutionary reading of Platonic philosophy. Citing dramatic transformations in Platonic theory allows Castoriadis to resolve the new ideas of this dialogue with contradictory views proposed in other dialogues — before and indeed after it — resulting in the redemption of Plato as a reformed idealist *cum* enlightened democrat.

Castoriadis' democratization of Plato depends on an evolutionary sorting of theories across the Platonic corpus, but is he justified in this reading or is it a sophism — a deceitful misuse of the Platonic *logoi*? To account Castoriadis' reading as legitimate, we must begin by agreeing with Castoriadis' attribution of theories to Plato.

Is Plato a theoretician?

There are great difficulties with this attribution. Plato writes dialogues which stage living philosophy because, as he admits in the *Phaedrus* (258d, 259e ff, 278a) and again in the *Seventh Letter* (341b, 344c ff), he sees great dangers in written discourse. Dialogues are as close as Plato can come *in writing* to overcoming the troublesome limitations of writing — its tendency to harden and blur out dangerous truths to just anyone, and its failure to conform to the soul of the listener, and fill its peculiar needs in a living language that is meaningful *for that soul*. Any theory-view of the dialogues must first answer Plato's critique of written discourse *per se*. Moreover, if Plato is serious about presenting 'theories' to contradict the Socratic doctrine of humility, would he stage his initial treachery of Socrates' doctrine by launching the 'theories of soul's immortality' in the emotionally charged setting of the impending death of Socrates in the *Phaedo*? Furthermore, if Plato is presenting theories, why the mixing of literary style? Why close each logical proof and argument by falling into metaphor and myth, since the latter, elusive appeals to the imagination, could only undermine the authenticity of the former? If Plato is rigorously constructing philosophical theories, why does he repeatedly resort to myth, explanations that belong to a pre-philosophical era?

In fact, throughout the dialogues, Plato repeatedly challenges the ideas that come to be accounted his theories; he introduces them with disclaimers and apologies, and with gestures of shame and concealment (such as veiling Socrates' head), to undermine in advance the authenticity and reliability of the positions being explored. Socrates reports some as hearsay, others as secret doctrine, and others as opinions of the many (which are never to be trusted for their truth). Indeed, if we study the individual contexts and the introductory passages launching the 'theories', we soon notice that the explorations speak *to* a particular audience, more than they express the speaker's ideas, let alone Plato's.

Can Platonic theories be sorted in an evolving order?

Even if we grant the existence of Platonic theories, can we grant that they evolve?[7] Once we admit the notion of a theory, then we simply find ourselves faced with far too many of them! Plato seems to launch an idea, take it back, redeem it again, and then toss it for another, perhaps simpler, perhaps more complex. There is no clear logic to these 'sailings' that would grant a definitive chronology.

Take, for one clear example, Plato's explorations of the soul: at one time, a physical principle of life, at another, a charioteer and steeds, at another, a many-headed monster; once, an eerie shade in the underworld, then a mere principle of movement; in a single dialogue, a perishable attunement and then an un-attuned force; now beautiful, then ugly and burdened with moral barnacles; better in motion than at rest, now incapable of rest and always moving, at one time invariable and incomposite; then singular, self-serving and individualistically wayward, then again a fragment of the universal Whole-Soul (*psyche pantos*), caring and embracing all. The soul, after being explored in each of its various aspects, returns to an earlier simpler image; this is its 'real image' after all, we are told. The whole exploration follows no logic, and so remains utterly baffling.[8]

---

[7] Martha Nussbaum sees Plato evolve from a hardened idealist to a passionate, realistic lover of faulty human things, but she cites the moment of transition between the *Symposium* and the *Phaedrus*, explaining that Plato's newfound erotic love for Dion of Syracuse teaches him the 'fragility of goodness' and opens him to truths about beauty, love, and the human condition that could not be gleaned from rational contemplation of the forms (Nussbaum, 1986: 189–97). B.A.G. Fuller too supports an evolutionary view of Plato, yet his reading leads to an altogether opposite conclusion to Castoriadis': Fuller sees Plato moving from a youthful flexibility in mystical ontological speculation toward a hardened absolutism. Far from gaining a sudden appreciation for reality, Fuller thinks 'Plato's mysticism grows [increasingly] puritan [from his middle-aged writings such as the *Statesman*] and finally fanatic in the Laws' (Fuller, 1931: 281–2). Not all scholars accept the evolutionary reading, however. Edward Urwick sees Plato's politics as *consistently* 'perverse and unreasonable', 'hopelessly reactionary' and 'absurdly ideal' throughout the entire corpus. Urwick charges that Plato is 'forever harking back to a golden age where human beings lived, like veritable children, in complete submission to divinely wise guides' (1983: 43–4). Urwick, as many other scholars, does not understand Plato to ever abandon his utopist tendencies. Though Plato may, at one time, mull over society and its ills (*Republic*), at another explore the nature of best governance (*Statesman*), and at yet another carve out the contours of the second best state (*Laws*), Plato remains constant in his politics. According to Urwick: 'No other politics interests [Plato] in the least', 'his interest is not in the laws but in the [utopian] goal which is his vision' (45).

[8] Equivocation, modal fallacy, ontological mismatch, and special pleading are but a few of the many faults of the six 'proofs' of its immortality. T.M. Robinson notes: 'The remarkable thing is that the same Socrates who is so adamant about correctness of definition in ethical discourse in the so-called "Socratic dialogues" makes so little attempt to give a coherent, internally

Who speaks for Plato?

Even if we grant Plato as a theoretician and allow that his theories can be sorted chronologically, how can we be certain whose voice among the many interlocutors of the various dialogues speaks for him? Plato is a master of concealment, and, even in the *Apology* that stages Socrates' trial, a historical event at which we know Plato to have been present, Plato doggedly refuses to reveal himself and declare his philosophical position.

One could certainly make an argument that Plato speaks through Socrates, the paradigmatic philosopher, master of the tradition and of Plato's youthful philosophical experience, whose death provided the motivation for Plato to abandon political life, tragedy, and poetry, and join the quest for wisdom. But in the (dramatically) earliest dialogues, Socrates is depicted as holding no theories. His explorations of the crucial terms of philosophical import invariably consist in *reductio ad absurdum*, demonstrating the impossibility of certain human knowledge that might be declared *theoria*.

If we grant that Plato expresses theories by placing them in the mouths of chosen speakers, can we count the Eleatic Stranger as a worthy spokesperson for Plato, as Castoriadis automatically does? The Stranger is a student of Parmenides, the 'reverend and awful' Presocratic whom Socrates has already murdered in the (dramatically earlier) *Theaetetus* (at 152e). Furthermore, the Stranger does not strike one as the calibre of person that Plato would choose as his mouthpiece. Indeed the Stranger is negatively (if subtly) contrasted to Socrates in fundamental ways; Castoriadis would have seen this, had he more carefully considered the opening framework of the dialogue, always a crucial indicator of a dialogue's content and direction.

At the outset of the *Statesman*, Socrates thanks Theodorus for his introduction to the Stranger; the Stranger is not as gracious as Socrates, accepting the compliment without reciprocation. The Stranger does not invite Socrates to discussion, but settles for poor imitations of Socrates—the inexperienced Young Socrates and Theaetetus, the Socrates-look-alike. Socrates and Plato are leery of imitations. Moreover, the dialogue's opening framework witnesses Socrates admonishing Theodorus, a mathematician, for wrongful measurement, in equating the three proposed dialogue subjects: sophists, statesmen, and philosophers are not equal things, Socrates warns. The sophist is the least of these unequals, but, as soon as the

consistent definition of the soul in the *Phaedo*' (1970: 32). It is absurd to imagine that a thinker of the stature of Plato failed to notice the faulty logic of his own arguments, or is attempting to deceive us by slipping us logically faulty and mutually-contradictory 'theories'. Huntington Cairns assures us in his Introduction to the *Parmenides*: '[Honesty] is only what is to be expected from Plato, never out to defend his own views, always with one object alone, to know the truth' (1989: 920).

diaīresis begins, we see that the Stranger has more in common with the sophist than with either of the higher human kinds.

Indeed, the Stranger had already distinguished himself from philosophers and aligned himself with the deceitful sophists, when he admitted in the *Sophist* that he prefers monologue to dialogue. The Stranger cares little for the needs of his listeners; he is not playful and leisurely in his philosophy, as is Socrates, but serious and unrelenting, as is a sophist orator. The Stranger proves in the *Statesman* that he is neither philosophical nor statesmanlike, but of the lesser kind. Holding forth at unreasonable length and 'boringly' in his *diaīresis*, he evidences his lack of appropriate measure; he may be able to divide and separate, but he possesses nothing of the superior art of 'measuring things rightly' that characterizes the statesman and Socrates, who always tailors his discourse to fit its difficult concepts to the needs of his interlocutors.

There is insufficient evidence to allow that the Eleatic Stranger speaks for Plato. Strangers, Plato and all Greeks knew, are under the sign of the neglectful god Zeus, who is a careless guide. Zeus has great skill in the arts of war, is devious and shrewd in martial strategy, but he is a fickle ruler, an inconstant helmsman, and certainly no philosopher. Strangers, again as Plato and all Greeks knew, must be welcomed generously, bedded and fed, and helped on their travels, but they should not be trusted—they may turn out to be gods or they may turn out to be monsters. Plato is neither of these.

Plato shifts from image to image, and from logical 'proof' to mythical tale. Perhaps the sole Platonic position of which we may be certain is mirrored in this shiftiness, staged rather than argued, proven, or theorized, performed in the performative contradictions of the corpus. Plato's tireless explorations can be compared to living philosophical speech, living truth among good-natured friends that fits the needs of the listeners. Does Socrates' living speaking not mirror the god's and act out the task of the statesman of our dialogue, who sits at the bedside of every person and leads her toward the moral light?

We only very rarely catch glimpses of Plato, as he evades our intrusive will for his 'theories'. We see him in Socrates' method in the *reductio ad absurdum* of Socratic humility. We witness him in the performative aspect of his corpus, as he takes up each new image, each myth, each logical discourse, much as one might take up a beautiful piece of pottery, turn it about, admire its contours, test its strength, its fragility, its beauty, its flaws, and measure its ability to 'hold water'. In enacting exploratory method again and again to investigate matters of philosophical import,

Plato is simply practicing the human wisdom that Socrates has taught him is prudent and fitting a philosopher.

It seems safe to assume, then, that Plato never makes a serious attempt to posit theories. We can never be certain of his definitive position on any matter explored in the dialogues, with the possible exception of his position on positioning *per se*, his theory on the viability of theories. His multiple depictions of the nature of the soul, his multiple 'proofs' of immortality (misinterpreted from *logoi*), his cities *in eidoi* (cities in the form of ideas, wrongly interpreted as 'ideal cities'), a reverse universe, ships tossed at sea, monsters who patrol the deep, orderly parades of gods ascending the crest of the heavens, horses writhing in sweat and blood as they wrestle to mate with their beloved—each of these depictions represents an experiment in thought to charm the soul of the reader, to challenge our hardened truths, and to call us to our higher instincts and to the philosophical life.

IV

Apologia for Plato's Anti-Democratism

Is Plato a radical democrat or is he anti-democratic? What is the place of common people in his philosophy? We do know that the image of commoners he places in the mouth of the Eleatic Stranger is a crude one: ordinary people are herd animals, needing constant attendance by leaders of higher knowledge and skill, if they are to be kept from running amuck. To press the imagery of the ominous myth of the reverse universe, commoners comprise the class of human beings most bound by the material necessity that holds sway during the decadent present era under the reign of the careless Zeus.

We see, from the imagery of the *Republic*, that commoners are least receptive to the benefits of the formative arts—education, gymnastics, music, and philosophy. They are granted no leisure time for reflection in the 'simple city' (*Republic*: 2.372).[9] In the second city, they are excluded out of hand from the education that can be expected to better more responsive souls (*Republic*: books III–VII).

However, if Plato believes that commoners are a hopeless class, degraded on the scale of natural distinctions to the basest materiality of their drives, then why does he have Socrates admit, in great shame, that natural distinctions are a lie (*Republic*: 3.414b)? There are no diverse metals in the hearts of

---

9 Even in the simple city, the one most pleasing to Socrates, the worker class is admonished to mind their own business, keep to their specific labours, and refrain from wasting their time in the marketplace, waiting about and mixing with each other, no doubt a sure occasion for getting into trouble and hatching plots of revolution (*Republic*: 2.372).

men, Socrates admits with veiled head to the scandalized Glaucon. Plato sees no real justification for a state's hierarchical orderings, no justification for the distinctions that keep common people in their lowly places. Indeed, the 'truth' of the *Republic* that outweighs the 'noble lie' is that anyone of sufficient merit, anyone with the talent and motivation, can assume any rank in the hierarchy that he or she rightly deserves. Any task, even that of the statesman, is attainable by any person (male or female) who demonstrates the merit that sets her or him apart from the common many.

Plato is an elusive thinker. He insists that we make our own way toward truth. Insofar as Plato gives us any hint of his position on important matters, we may assume that he aligns himself with Socrates. Plato, like Socrates, is likely a rigorous meritocrat, neither passionately supportive nor vehemently obstructive of things mediocre — common values, petty concerns, or ignoble people. Common things are not his concern, since they are as incapable of any real harm as they are of any great good; great things, not small, are precarious (*Republic*: 497d). Plato admits the democratic state as the least harmful of the worst kinds of states, but that admission does not mean that Plato — and we — must settle for the mediocre. Those who are seeking to institute justice in their social worlds must concern themselves with higher things and greater goods, lifting ourselves from the common to the loftiest ideals.

Modern scholars will be loathe to admit their own illiberal tendencies. But students of history can understand Plato's demand for breaking from the mediocre herd of one's society to reach for higher ideals and more exacting rules of engagement. Ordinary people comprised the 'Liverpool 38' who, caught up in their mundane affairs of shopping, walking the streets, and riding the buses, witnessed two ten-year-olds abduct two-year-old Jamie Bulger from outside the butcher shop, walk him, bully him, and thrash him, the two-and-a-half-mile trek to the railway line where they beat him to death; no one intervened. Ordinary Rwandans, fired by the demonizing rhetoric of their leaders, slaughtered their Tutsi neighbours, till nearly a million corpses clogged the roads and the rivers of that paradisiacal post-colony. The general herd of ordinary Germans followed Hitler enthusiastically to the 'Final Solution', and not for the comprehensible reasons they claimed in the aftermath. Most recent scholarship (Aly, 2007) shows that ordinary Germans were neither bureaucratically banal in their evil, nor ignorant of the depth of Nazi barbarism, nor fearful of reprisals for non-participation. Ordinary people became enthusiastic Nazi supporters because they were the direct beneficiaries of Nazi looting of their European victims. Common people driven by their appetites were quite happy to support projects of murder, pillage, and genocide.

Plato recognizes what every corrupt leader knows, every military trainer, every war-mongering president, every genocidal regime: it takes a great mind to concoct great schemes of destruction, but those schemes can only be realized by conscripting masses of willing executioners—mindless, common, uneducated people who follow their appetites and their leaders as blindly as herd animals, and rarely ask moral questions.

Castoriadis is a great thinker, as he was an exemplary citizen-activist labouring for political and social justice. However, as a scholar of Platonic philosophy, he sadly misses the mark. His reading of Plato as a radical democrat, overcoming his severe elitist convictions as he reaches philosophical maturity, is insincere and unjustified by the text. It constitutes a sophism. But perhaps Castoriadis is less interested in accurately portraying the ancient thinker's political thoughts than in highlighting his own innovative ideas. Perhaps his 'quirky' reading of Plato's *Statesmen* is meant to shock and scandalize the reader for the sake of his (Castoriadis') higher purposes: to prod us toward our own most passionate political awakening as fully engaged, self-managing, self-motivating, self-instituting democratic citizens.

References

Aly, G. (2007), *Hitler's beneficiaries: plunder, racial war, and the Nazi welfare state*, trans. J. Chase (New York: Metropolitan Books).

Cairns, H. (1989), 'Introduction to *Parmenides*', in *The collected dialogues*, by Plato/eds. E. Hamilton and H. Cairns (Princeton: Princeton University Press).

Castoriadis, C. (2002), *On Plato's Statesman*, trans. D.A. Curtis (Stanford: Stanford University Press).

Fuller, B.A.G. (1931), *History of Greek philosophy* (New York: Henry Holt & Company).

Hesiod (1991), *The works and days; Theogony; The shield of Herakles*, trans. R. Lattimore (Ann Arbor: University of Michigan Press).

Nussbaum, M. (1986), *The fragility of goodness* (Cambridge: Cambridge University Press).

Plato (1989), *The collected dialogues*, eds. E. Hamilton and H. Cairns/trans. L. Cooper (Princeton: Princeton University Press).

Robinson, T.M. (1970), *Plato's psychology* (Toronto: University of Toronto Press).

Urwick, E. (1983), *The platonic quest* (Santa Barbara: Concord Grove Press).

Vidal-Naquet, P. (2002), 'Foreword: Castoriadis and the *Statesman*', in *On Plato's Statesman*, by C. Castoriadis/trans. D.A. Curtis (Stanford: Stanford University Press).

Andy Hamilton

J.S. Mill's Elitism
A Classical Liberal's Response to the Rise of Democracy

I

Introduction[1]

Elitism today is the residue of the liberal scepticism concerning democratic government. Classical liberals in the early decades of the nineteenth century had profound forebodings concerning the apparently inevitable advent of democracy. In response, they advocated elitism as a brake on the 'tyranny of the majority'. While other liberals were concerned with the danger of 'democratic despotism', John Stuart Mill diagnosed a culture of mediocrity engendered by democratic forms of government. Mill at first followed Samuel Taylor Coleridge and Auguste Comte in espousing *illiberal elitism*, the view that the intellectual and cultural elite should constitute an estate of society—a church or caste with formal powers. He subsequently rejected illiberal elitism on the grounds that it did not foster individual autonomy, but still maintained *liberal elitism*, according to which the intellectual elite must exert influence through recognition of their authority in their sphere. In *On Liberty* his position is further nuanced, so that it is questionable whether he really was an elitist at all. I advocate a position that constitutes a middle way between elitism and populism. Elitism should be contrasted with populism, and not with (i) egalitarianism, or (ii) individualism in the sense of Mill's Liberty Principle. I conclude by considering the relation between elitism and a meritocratic standpoint which affirms individual autonomy.

---

1   Thanks to: Jason Gaiger, Erich Kofmel, Dean Machin, Jonathan Riley, Geoffrey Scarre, Julia Skorupska, John Skorupski, Nick Southgate, Roger Squires, and the audiences at the J.S. Mill Bicentenary Conference in Yokohama, Japan, September 2006, and the Fourth Annual Conference 'Workshops in Political Theory' in Manchester, England, September 2007.

II

Mill and the Advance of Democracy

Democracy is 'the inexorable demand of these ages', Thomas Carlyle commented (2005: 213). 'It is too bad', wrote Chateaubriand, 'but that is the way it is; what can we do?' (in Stromberg, 1996: 31). J.S. Mill was almost correct in holding that democracy had arrived without any support from intellectuals—in Europe at least. The idea of settling important matters by majority vote was regarded as deplorable, and fear of democratic despotism was widespread. 'It will no longer be a despot that oppresses the individual, but the masses', Flaubert thought (in Stromberg, 1996: 31). Palmerston commented in 1862 to Lord John Russell, architect of the 1832 Reform Act, that history shows 'that Power in the Hands of the Masses throws the Scum of the Community to the Surface' (in Bentley, 1984: 158).

Liberals were prominent in sharing these concerns. Classical nineteenth-century liberals wished to undermine the ancient privileges of monarchy, church and aristocracy, in order to create equality for all under the law, and in that sense might be regarded as pro-democratic. But they asserted the values of individualism over both despotism and democracy, and in their concern with the limits of government, recognized a tension between democracy and liberty. So in the earlier part of the nineteenth century, our present concept of 'liberal democracy' would have seemed paradoxical or even contradictory. Macaulay, Whig historian and in some respects a liberal, commented in his speech in the House of Commons on the 1842 People's Charter 'that, in our country, universal suffrage is incompatible ... with everything for the sake of which forms of government exist; ... it is incompatible with property, and ... consequently incompatible with civilisation' (1889: 626).

This view was widely shared among liberals. Benjamin Constant, leading theorist of early nineteenth-century French liberalism, contrasted, in *De la liberté des anciens comparée à celle des moderns*, the demand that power should be limited, with the demand that it should be distributed: 'The ancients aimed at a distribution of power among all the citizens of a given state, and they referred to this as freedom. For the moderns, the goal is security in their private possessions. For them, liberty refers to the guarantees of these possessions afforded by their institutions' (1820: IV/253). Constant regards these aims as incompatible; where all participate directly in collective decisions, the individual ends up being subordinated to the authority of the whole—here he has Rousseau in his sights. Hence he concludes: 'We today are no longer able to enjoy the liberty of the ancients, which consisted in their continual and active participation in collective power. Our freedom, by contrast, must reside in the peaceful enjoyment of private independence' (IV/253). He saw unlimited popular sovereignty as an evil no matter in whose hands it is placed.

Liberalism is a modern standpoint while democracy is ancient (Bobbio, 2005: 25; see also Graham, 2002). In his succinct but magisterial *Liberalism and Democracy*, Norberto Bobbio argues that while classical liberals were suspicious of democracy, 'modern [formal] democracy' is a natural extension of liberalism. In the *procedural* sense of government by the people, democracy is linked to the formation of the liberal state; where it has the *substantial* sense of government for the people, its relation to the liberal state is much more problematic—in this sense, for instance, it could be manifested by a despotism that enforces equality among citizens (31–2).[2] Bobbio argues that Constant's counterposing of liberalism and democracy is less historically accurate than contrasting ancient organicism and modern individualism—for both liberalism and democracy 'have a common starting-point: the individual' (41).

For Jeremy Bentham and the Philosophic Radicals, including J.S. Mill, democracy was at most a means, not an end in itself. Mill's famous phrase '*the tyranny of the majority*' derives from Alexis de Tocqueville's *Democracy in America*, which has been described as 'the single most important authority in Victorian debates about democracy' (Jones, 2000: 66).[3] De Tocqueville, leading liberal of the 1815–48 era, made the contradiction between liberty and democracy the guiding theme of *Democracy in America*. He writes:

> Our contemporaries ... conceive a government which is unitary, protective, and all-powerful, but elected by the people. Centralisation is combined with the sovereignty of the people. ... They console themselves for being under schoolmasters by thinking that they have chosen them themselves. ... Under this system the citizens quit their state of dependence just long enough to choose their masters and then fall back into it (1968: II/899–900).

J.S. Mill is not so scathing about democracy, but still cautious. When a functioning democracy, the USA, appeared, he writes in *On Liberty*,

> [i]t was now perceived that such phrases as "self-government", and "the power of the people over themselves", do not express the true state of the case. ... The will of the people, moreover, practically means the will of the most numerous or the most active *part* of the people—the

---

2 As he points out, Rousseau is unusual in advocating both forms of democracy, in that his strongly egalitarian ideal is realizable only through the formation of the general will.
3 De Tocqueville refers also to the 'despotism of the majority'.

majority, or those who succeed in making themselves accepted as the majority (ch. 1, par. 4; his emphasis).[4]

While the tyranny of custom exists in all societies, he holds, the tyranny of the majority is engendered specifically by democratic forms of government. His *elitism* results from attempts to overcome it. The nineteenth century was the era of elitism, both liberal and illiberal.

According to Mill, popular cultural tyranny is maintained directly through the state, and indirectly by social forces. *On Liberty* is concerned with both manifestations — Mill is much less concerned with coercion by individuals:

> Protection ... against the tyranny of the magistrate is not enough: there needs protection also against the tyranny of the prevailing opinion and feeling; against the tendency of society to impose, by other means than civil penalties, its own ideas and practices as rules of conduct on those who dissent from them; to fetter the development, and, if possible, prevent the formation, of any individuality not in harmony with its ways, and compel all characters to fashion themselves upon the model of its own (ch. 1, par. 3).

Some authorities argue that Mill's consistent viewpoint throughout his political writings was not strictly democratic (Burns, 1968: 328).[5] Others believe that it was (Robson, 1968: 224; Bobbio, 2005: 57). The dispute of course turns on what one means by democracy — a complex and highly contested ideal, whose justifications are equally contested. These are not issues I enter into here, for my concern is with the philosophical manifestation of liberalism's fear of democracy. But one obvious distinction must be noted. Democracy is often taken to mean 'majority rule' or 'one person one vote', and in that sense Mill was not a democrat strictly speaking, since he believed in plural voting and other mechanisms to qualify majority power; he does not agree with many democrats that people are equal in the moral and intellectual qualities required for the exercise of political power. However, he clearly believed in representative government, whose justification in terms of the encouraging of autonomy overlaps with that of majoritarian democracy. One could say, with C.L. Ten, that he believes that democracy is ideally the best form of government; if the social conditions which make it feasible are present, which Mill denied they were yet, it is the best (1998: 375). Liberalism and pure democratic thought, far from being indissolubly linked, are in fact two-way independent — though it may also be recognized that since our notion of democracy is a liberal one, the conflict passes unnoticed. We are so familiar with the linking of liberalism and democracy in the

---

4 For ease of reference, given the multiplicity of editions, citations of Mill's *On Liberty* are by chapter and paragraph number.
5 Alan Ryan claims that we are used to regarding Mill as an 'aristocratic liberal', though he qualifies the image (Ryan, 2007: 158).

concept of 'liberal democracy' that we fail to note the former's implicit qualification of popular rule through a set of basic liberties.

It will be useful to chart the development of Mill's thought concerning the democratic ideal. After his nervous breakdown in 1826, Mill assimilated influences beyond the Philosophic Radicalism of his youth, and these led him to qualify the Radicals' commitment to democracy. He questioned their advocacy of elected representatives as bound delegates, and focused on the need for power to be exercised by the fittest persons. As he put it 1832 in an article in the *Examiner*: 'The sovereignty of the people is essentially a delegated sovereignty. Government must be performed by the [judicious] few, for the benefit of the many'. The alternative of direct democracy was 'mere mob-government' (1963–91: XXIII/417–8). This qualification remained a leitmotif of his political thought for the rest of his career.

In his review of de Tocqueville's *Democracy in America* in 1835, Mill describes the existence of a leisured class as a safeguard against the tyranny of mass opinion (1963–91: XVIII/85–6). Spurred by de Tocqueville, he looked increasingly to a power to rival that of the masses, rather than relying on people's ability to choose wise rulers. His essay on Coleridge marked his severance from orthodox Radical doctrines, and strongly supports Coleridge's idea of a 'clerisy', 'an endowed class, for the cultivation of learning, and for diffusing its results among the community' (Mill, 1963–91: X/150; see also Burns, 1968: 299). The high tide of conservatism in Mill's thought occurred around 1840 (Burns, 1968: 305). In his second review of de Tocqueville, he expresses sympathy with the latter's fears of a tyranny of the majority, and looks for a counterbalancing force to mass opinion in 'an agricultural class, a leisured class, and a learned class' (1963–91: XVIII/198). Thereafter his radicalism was reinvigorated as he fell more under the influence of Harriet Taylor; he no longer felt the need for a leisured class, but held rather that society at large should not be overworked (Burns, 1968: 313).

By the time of *Representative Government*, Mill was firm in his requirement of a skilled professional administration. He had a constant concern for the quality of representatives, and believed that Thomas Hare's scheme of proportional representation would ensure that an assembly contained 'the *élite* of the nation'. Mill did not 'look upon equal voting as among the things which are good in themselves'. It is

> less objectionable than inequality of privilege grounded on irrelevant or adventitious circumstances, but in principle wrong, because recognising a wrong standard, and exercising a bad influence on the voter's mind. It is ... hurtful, that the constitution of the country should

declare ignorance to be entitled to as much political power as knowledge (Mill, 1973: 288).

Proportional representation checks the tendency of representative democracy towards collective mediocrity. The voting strength of those with plural votes should not outweigh that of the rest of the community, so that the former will not be able to enact their own class legislation. To reiterate, Mill believed in representative government, but does not assume that people are equal in the moral and intellectual qualities required by the exercise of political power. That is, he is a liberal elitist.

III

Defining Elitism

Elitism, then, was the response by both liberals and non-liberals to the advent of democratic forms of government. *Liberal elitism*, it is argued by John Skorupski, is essential to the political thought of Mill and other classical liberals (Skorupski, 1999). Elitism becomes a recognizable standpoint only in an incipiently democratic age, when the prerogatives of caste or social elites come into question; the aristocratic radicalism of Carlyle or Nietzsche seems too extreme in its illiberalism and rejection of democracy even to be regarded as illiberal elitism. But how should elitism be defined? The Shorter OED offers 'advocacy of or reliance on the leadership or dominance of a select group' — in the language of elitism's present-day critics, a group that is self-perpetuating, exclusive and non-meritocratic. Elitism, as Skorupski characterizes it, is the denial of populism. This characterization allows elitism to bear the weight of philosophical analysis, whilst acknowledging many of its everyday connotations. However, most commentators have neglected it, instead contrasting elitism with egalitarianism — the requirement that a large share of resources should be devoted to the developed elite, as Wendy Donner puts it (1991). This is a mistake, I believe. It is true that elitists tend to reject egalitarian distribution, but elitism should be defined in opposition to populism rather than to egalitarianism. (Although the claim that elitism is opposed to autonomy has more justification, this, I will argue, is also largely incorrect.)

In order to obtain a characterization of elitism, therefore, we need to examine the elitism-populism polarity. The opposition between populists and elitists focuses on certain kinds of expertise. Populists have to allow that neuro-surgeons, physicists and professional sportsmen must possess genuine skill or expertise — no one objects to elitism in brain surgery, or in selection of the Olympic team. What populists deny is the elitist claim that — as Skorupski puts it — moral, cultural, and spiritual ends and values invite substantive and not merely instrumental deliberation, and that some individuals are more penetrating judges of these questions than others. On this view, elitism is both a moral and a political standpoint. The claim is that there are moral authorities—'experts' would have the wrong connotations—, and that these should have social influence in their sphere. In its liberal version, on Skorupski's view, elitism does not regard these judges as equipped with special vision of an esoteric Platonic domain; rather, we recognize them as, 'in a particular department of human responses, ... registering more sensitively, or in the light of better information or greater reflection, natural dispositions which we also share'. Skorupski holds that, according to liberal elitists, the 'natural influence' of such judges must not be impeded (1999: 210).

While classical liberalism held that one can deliberate about ends and values, modern liberalism has largely abandoned elitism, and bases equality of respect and ethical neutrality on the uncriticizability of ends.[6] Populist modern liberalism holds that individuals deserve equal respect just because their ends and values are unappraisable. For Skorupski, this 'modernist liberalism' is a pallid deviation from classical liberalism.

One should distinguish between *moderate or liberal elitism*, the position of nineteenth-century classical liberals, which affirms that the best judges 'are socially vital and must exert a due influence through the recognition of their authority in their sphere', and *strong or illiberal elitism*, the view that such an elite should constitute an estate of society—a church, vanguard party or caste—with formal powers (Skorupski, 1999: 195).[7] The latter was the view of Coleridge, Comte and socialists such as Claude-Henri de Saint-Simon, who, like his mentor Comte, proposed authoritarian government by engineers and economic experts. Ernest Renan, French essayist of the 1848–71 era, had this position in mind when he commented that 'the aristocracy of which I dream would be the incarnation of reason: a papacy of true infallibility. Power, in its hands, could not but be beneficial' (in Stromberg, 1996: 34). The contrast here is between an elite with influence and one with power, and it has considerable plausibility when applied to the evolution of Mill's position. His associationism, with its assumption

---

6   Mill did not have an instrumentalist conception of reason; he believed that autonomy or 'moral freedom' involved mastery of the passions by the rational self, and a capacity to recognize and act on rational principles and ends—an appropriation of the German ideal of self-development (see Skorupski, 1999: 205–9).

7   The Church of England's present status in moral matters makes it something like an estate, if an enfeebled one; a different example is the *Académie Française*. Although liberalism and democracy do not coincide conceptually, and one could imagine an argument that strong elitism, though undemocratic, was not illiberal; however, illiberal and anti-democratic elitism, and also liberal and democratic elitism, are practically coextensive.

that everyone has intellectual potential, always qualified his elitism, but he moved away from and then back to liberalism.

After abandoning his Radical heritage, Mill as we have seen followed Coleridge and Comte in espousing illiberal elitism, and supported the former's idea of a clerisy. By 1840, when Mill's thought was at its most conservative, he sympathized in his review of de Tocqueville's *Democracy in America* with the latter's fears of majority tyranny, and looked to counterbalance mass opinion with 'an agricultural class, a leisured class, and a learned class' (1963–91: XVIII/198; see also Burns, 1968: 305). Subsequently, he rejected strong elitism for failing to foster individual autonomy, and maintained moderate elitism. The educated class with leisure to engage in free enquiry is no longer to be formally constituted as a clerisy or Comtean *élite*.[8] However, despite Mill's elitism, I will argue that *On Liberty* offers a glimpse of an alternative position. After his Coleridgean period, Mill no longer believed that the One or Few should have the power to force their views on others, though in safeguarding the freedom of each to draw up their plan of life, the exemplary gifted few must have the freedom to 'point the way'. Mill's liberalism is anti-authoritarian but not anti-elitist. As Skorupski comments: 'True liberalism is not populism and the real difference between them is one of the most important lessons Mill has to teach' (Skorupski, 1989: 354; see also Skorupski, 1999).

In the twentieth century, illiberal elitism assumed a corporatist and even totalitarian form. In *Notes Towards the Definition of Culture*, T.S. Eliot defines high culture as the preserve of 'superior individuals', and wants to replace the existing class system by what he describes — or mis-describes — as a meritocracy headed by a cultural elite:

> [T]he superior individuals must be formed into suitable groups, endowed with appropriate powers …. Those groups … will direct the public life of the nation; the individuals composing them will be spoken of as "leaders." There will be groups concerned with art, … science, and … philosophy, as well as groups consisting of men of action: and these groups are what we call *élites* (Eliot, 1962: 36).

Efforts to make high culture accessible to all, through the democratization of the education system, lead to falling standards, Eliot argues; artistic excellence implies a limited, privileged audience.[9]

Note how Eliot, as a modern proponent of elitism, focuses on culture and the arts. It is *cultural elitism* which has become the primary target of

---

8 Different interpretations of the transitions in Mill's thought are discussed in Ryan (2007: 157–9).
9 F.R. Leavis, Christopher Fry and Clive Bell also held elitist views, though without Eliot's fascist sympathies.

populists.[10] To describe opera as an elitist art form is to say, as current sloganeering has it, that it is 'obscure, not relevant to ordinary people, socially exclusive'. Other kinds of elitism now considered objectionable include the remains—or more than this—of *social elitism* in English public schools and ancient universities, and American Ivy League universities. *Administrative elitism*, closest to Mill's aspirations, has never really been a target of populists. One version espouses technocratic government, which attempts to treat moral and cultural questions as social scientific ones. Douglas Jay's pronouncement that 'in the case of nutrition and health, just as in the case of education, the gentleman in Whitehall really does know better what is good for people than the people know themselves' (1937: 317), shows how administrative elitism merges with paternalism. Mill would accept Jay's claim, but—unlike T.H. Green perhaps—deny its interventionist implication; as we will see, he aims to strike a balance between elitism and paternalism. The ideal of a humane mandarin bureaucracy, which began to be realized in Mill's time by the Northcote-Trevelyan reforms of the civil service, is elitist in placing a brake on democratically-elected government: 'the informal "mixed constitution" of mandarin democracy averted the formation of the mass society that liberal thinkers dreaded' (Lind, 2005: 37).[11]

Is liberal elitism still defensible? I will suggest that there is now a realizable alternative to both elitist and populist liberalisms—that is, meritocratic liberalism. (Liberalism has always been meritocratic in aspiration, of course.) Thus I wish to advocate a meritocratic middle way between elitism and populism, while conceding that much of what seems objectionable in elitism results from tone and presentation rather than substance, and that the contrast between elitism and meritocracy remains elusive. This position involves arguing against the possibility of a *meritocratic elitism*, of which more shortly.

---

10   It is interesting that Mill's 'higher pleasures' are usually regarded as cultural—and Mill himself contrasted pushpin and poetry. John Gray convincingly argues that the higher pleasures are those that require the exercise of autonomy, but it is not possible to explore this difficult issue here (1996: especially 73–86).

11   Mill was sceptical about civil service reform, and the possibility of talented recruits for the civil service; he had contempt for the stasis of Chinese society, which had been run by mandarins for over two thousand years.

IV

Culture and Elitism

The main target of contemporary populists, to reiterate, is *cultural elitism*, allegedly embodied in the major opera houses, ancient universities, and public service broadcasting, especially BBC Radio 3. Ivy League universities and British public schools are socially elitist and anti-meritocratic. Just as political elitism appears only in an incipiently democratic age, so cultural elitism appears only in an era of mass culture. Populists target high culture, and claims to objectivity in aesthetic judgement which underlie the existence of a canon. For them, the art world of curators, connoisseurs and critics possesses only the illusion of expertise, attempting to legislate on what are in fact purely subjective matters of taste and opinion. Elitism, in contrast, is committed to high culture and objectivity in aesthetic judgement — which are not, in the strict sense, elitist in themselves, I have argued — , but is also characterized by its dismissal of popular culture and of what I term *the democracy of taste*, the claim that even the neophyte's responses have a status in critical discourse (Hamilton, 2008). These dismissals are misconceived, I believe. So while there is considerable truth in elitism, my rejection of it does not result from pusillanimous reluctance to engage with political correctness — which while correctly diagnosing inadequacies in elitism, criticizes them from the standpoint of crass philistine subjectivism.

Our question of cultural elitism could not have arisen for Mill — so-called elite culture did not yet have a rival in the mass culture propagated by the culture industry. There was then no ideological counterweight to (high) culture. Mill's elitism in part arises from fears for individual freedom, but he also regarded the social tyranny of the majority as constituting a general threat to cultural ideals. Like his arguments for freedom of expression in *On Liberty*, therefore, his elitism embodies collective values as much as, or more than, individualist ones.[12] Mill shared with Matthew Arnold a passionate concern about the cultural impact of democracy. As Edward Alexander puts it, Mill and Arnold became representative figures in the Victorian period through 'their recognition that the great problem of modern life is the preservation of the ancient humanistic ideal of culture in democratic society' (1965: 12).

For Mill, the danger is a democratically-imposed stagnant conformism, for Arnold it is anarchy, that is, insufficient state intervention. The latter's *Culture and Anarchy* insisted on 'the urgent necessity, in the reign of democratic ideas,

---

12 On these arguments for freedom of expression, see Skorupski (1989: 369–84).

of maintaining or of building up the culture of the spirit as a counter-weight to the brutality and violence which is [democratic ideas'] natural bent' (in Knights, 1978: 120).[13] Mill's essay *Coleridge*, which as we saw marked his partial regression to illiberal values, expressed similar sentiments on the internal threats to liberal culture:

> the relaxation of individual energy and courage; the loss of proud and self-relying independence; the slavery of so large a portion of mankind to artificial wants; ... absence of any marked individuality, in their characters; ... the demoralizing effect of great inequalities in wealth and social rank (Mill, 1963–91: X/134).

Mill and Arnold lamented the lack of an intellectual community in Victorian England, treating Ancient Greece as their cultural and political ideal, and it is not surprising that the debate over elitism often turns into the question of the status of intellectuals—'elite' means either 'intellectual elite' or 'social elite', or maybe 'cultural elite'—or the university (see Warnock, 1989; Collini, 2006; Furedi, 2006). The university now performs many of the functions of the leisured class assumed by Mill, though it is also true that everyone in western liberal societies now has leisure.

The 'mass' feared since the Greek origins of democracy, for instance by Burke and Carlyle in their responses to the French Revolution, had been the mob. This was how most Victorians saw it, for instance Dickens in *Barnaby Rudge* and *A Tale of Two Cities*. De Tocqueville presented a different picture of a mass that arose not from violent revolution but from American representative government—a passive body that nonetheless induces conformity in freer spirits, and a 'new physiognomy of servitude' (Tocqueville, 1968: vol. 2, sec. 1, ch. 2). Mill takes up this account, anticipated in some of his own earlier work, with alacrity.[14] Finally, there is a third sense of 'mass', a genuine 'low culture' expressed through art at least since the medieval era, though we should be careful in attributing historical unity to it:

> [T]he artistic low culture ... had long overlapped with the dominant high culture: in the comic portraits that stole into the borders of illuminated manuscripts, the misericords hidden under choir stalls, the gargoyles leering from dark corners and high columns, the chapbook illustrations and broadsheet woodcuts; ... tough, realistic studies of men and women making shoes, stirring pots, ploughing fields, dancing and playing music, coexisted with fantasy and symbol, a combination that flowered in the art of Bosch or Breughel (Uglow, 2002: 58–9).

---

13 The concept of the clerisy is also discussed in Collini (2006: 76–9, 320–1). If Mill writes like a self-appointed Royal Commission, Arnold writes like a self-appointed leader writer for the *Daily Telegraph*, and is almost unreadable today.
14 On these two senses of mass, see for instance Levin (2004), and also Ryan (2007: 160).

This low culture is not our current mass culture; only when the population has leisure can it generate a truly popular or mass art. In the nineteenth century the great majority of the population had little chance of appreciating the classics. However, it is this final sense of 'mass' — connected in some ways with de Tocqueville's sense, and stressing ideas of cultural stagnation which he shared with Adorno — which has become the target of twentieth-century elitists.[15] A different sense of 'mass' means a different but related motive for elitism.

V

Later Liberal Thinkers on Culture and the Elite

It is definitive of elitism in any form that 'high' cultural goals such as museums, the arts and sciences, higher education, public service broadcasting, libraries and the reading of literature deserve support, though elitist and other liberals may not agree that this support is best given by the state. Populists reject these cultural goals as ends, treating them at best merely instrumentally, for instance as vehicles of economic growth; neutralist liberals such as Rawls (1971), in contrast, maintain that insofar as such support promotes ethical ideas, the state should not be involved. Although neutralism and populism interestingly share epistemological assumptions, my concern is not with the (possibly mischaracterized) debate between neutralism and perfectionism, but with that between elitism and populism. I believe that there is a middle way between elitism and populism which supports high culture, and which rejects the narrow, static conception of it assumed by contemporary liberals.

While the question of Culture is inescapable to many Continental philosophical traditions, contemporary liberal theory neglects it. It interprets cultural elitism in attenuated and indirect terms, as a claim about distributive justice, in particular resource-allocation to elites, and ignores the possibility of culture as a general good. Focusing on resource-allocation expresses a static conception of cultural value encouraged by classical utilitarianism, and at odds with Mill's richer, German Idealist-influenced stress on the progressive development of human autonomy. It also, as noted earlier, pulls elitism into a misleading opposition with egalitarianism. This static conception is both instrumentalist and philistine, that is, it regards the aesthetic as inessential to human well-being. Transcending this conception enables one to locate a middle way between elitism and populism.

---

15 Adorno's cultural elitism is discussed in Hamilton (2007: ch. 5).

To reiterate, elitism is characterized in opposition to populism, not egalitarianism; it is not a doctrine about distributive justice. However, Rawls' neutralist or sceptical liberalism, which says that government should not promote specific spiritual, moral or cultural goods, even if aesthetic experience, for instance, is part of human well-being, takes inegalitarian resource allocation as the hallmark of elitism (1971); so does Hurka's account (1993: 164). The result is an unduly time-bound, static perspective. The classics are not, as these writers assume, 'the preferences of the elite'; they are the common heritage of humankind, and no partiality is implied by state support for them. This claim clearly needs further defence, but that is not my project here; I am assuming the unacceptability of populism which rejects the concept of the classics.[16]

Donner also contrasts elitism with egalitarianism, discerning that dichotomy in Mill's work; she locates an opposition between elitism and individualism, too. As an egalitarian, she holds, Mill would not devote a large share of resources to the developed elite, while as an individualist he would not—as she puts it—impose elite values on ordinary individuals. 'His own mode of laying out his existence is best', and all have a right to liberty of self-development:

> Mill's liberty principle commits him to allow a sphere of personal freedom to those who have not [through education] developed themselves, and so he cannot be regarded as an elitist in the self-regarding domain. ... Mill may justly be denominated an elitist in the public sphere if he holds that the choices of the developed can be judged more worthy of societal pursuit [= liberal elitism]. ... An extreme form [of the latter elitism] is that in which those who are not yet developed are not allowed to participate in public choices [= illiberal elitism] (Donner, 1991: 159; my parenthetical additions).

We have seen that elitism is mischaracterized as the opposite of egalitarianism. Is it also a mischaracterization to oppose elitism and autonomy, or should we follow Donner in also criticizing the position as paternalist and authoritarian?

VI

Authority and Autonomy

'Liberal elitism' does not seek to 'impose' elite values on the non-elite, in apparent contravention of Mill's Liberty Principle; it is not a contradiction in terms. However, there is something in what Donner says. We can begin to examine the question by looking at how Mill himself characterizes

---

[16] This issue is discussed further in the introduction of Hamilton (2007).

authority relations. His first instructors 'had always identified deference to authority with mental slavery and the repression of individual thought', he wrote (1961: 188; see also Friedman, 1968: 385ff). But he soon came to fear that a mass society exhibited too little as well as too much authority; social pressure is a simulacrum of authority, while real authority figures are lacking. In *Auguste Comte and Positivism*, Mill concedes to Comte that it is 'the necessary condition of mankind to receive most of their opinions on the authority of those who have specially studied the matters to which they relate'. But 'in order that this salutary ascendancy over opinion should be exercised by the most eminent thinkers, it is not necessary that they should be associated and organised' (1963–91: X/313–4).

Note the indubitably elitist reference to 'receive their opinions' and 'salutary ascendancy'—though here Mill's comments can be construed as including scientific knowledge, and not just moral and cultural matters. In *The Spirit of the Age*, Mill writes more judiciously, though perhaps more generally: every man 'should follow his reason as far as his reason will carry him, and cultivate the faculty as highly as possible. But reason itself will teach most men that they must, in the last resort, fall back upon the authority of still more cultivated minds, as the ultimate sanction of the convictions of their reason itself' (1963–91: XXII/244).

On Liberty, in contrast, specifies a more active contribution from the uninitiated. Mill famously writes: 'No government by a democracy or numerous aristocracy ... ever did or could rise above mediocrity except in so far as the sovereign many have let themselves be guided ... by the counsels and influence of a more highly gifted and instructed One or Few'. He argues that 'when the opinions of masses of merely average men are everywhere become or becoming the dominant power', a corrective is needed in 'the more and more pronounced individuality of those who stand on the higher eminences of thought'. Benign social deviants—who will include a sprinkling of visionaries and geniuses along with harmless eccentrics—must be allowed to show through 'experiments in living' the alternatives to custom.[17] Mill then adds the claim of *individual autonomy*: 'If a person possesses any tolerable amount of common sense and experience, his own mode of laying out his existence is the best, not because it is the best in itself, but because it is his own mode' (ch. III).

If, as elitism asserts, some people are more penetrating judges of cultural and moral questions than others, then it is still the case that each individual

---

17 As Ryan argues, Mill does not consider whether these 'experiments' realize convergent and divergent conceptions of the general good—each person at least learns what is the best life for them, but not necessarily the best life for humans. The picture seems to be of a variety of routes leading in different and non-competing directions (2007: 156–7).

must ultimately decide these questions for themselves. This seems to be one implication of the 'individual autonomy' claim. As Mill recognized, what is required is not 'the blind submission of dunces to men of knowledge, but the intelligent deference of those who know much, to those who know still more' (1963-91: X/313-4). The undermining of deference since the Victorian era has been liberating, and reinforces the possibility of un-self-abasing respect for intellectual authority. The ideal of liberal education and the university is that a teacher inspires autonomous agents, not slavish adherents. This ideal underlies Mill's defence of freedom of expression, which is based on a model of honest dialogue in a world of imperfectly rational and moral human beings. He realizes that not everyone can participate equally in dialogue; but on this question also, *On Liberty* qualifies the conception of authority found in the *The Spirit of the Age* and *Auguste Comte and Positivism*.

Is the preceding, rather more egalitarian, picture of authority an elitist one? To return to Skorupski's characterization: elitism holds that some individuals are more penetrating judges of moral, cultural, and spiritual questions, and should be socially influential in their sphere. My response is that this characterization is necessary but not sufficient for elitism, which interprets these claims as requiring a unitary elite, self-perpetuating in the sense of non-meritocratic, and rejects popular culture and the democracy of taste. Thus one should perhaps question Benn and Peters' claim that '[e]very society, however democratic, has its elite' (1959: 158-9). Although Skorupski's characterization of elitism is not anti-meritocratic, the popular conception of it is, and in this respect should not be ignored.

Meritocracy is a system of social organization where appointments are made on the basis of ability rather than wealth, family connections or class. Its critics regard it merely as a new legitimation for social elites. When Michael Young first used the term in *The Rise of the Meritocracy* (1958), it was as a pejorative, referring to a dystopia where social position is determined by 'IQ plus effort'—a divided society in which 'deserving' winners hold down 'undeserving' losers. A recent critic, Roy Hattersley, holds that 'meritocracy only offers shifting patterns of inequality' (in Kellner, 2001: 25). Their objection simply seems to be that meritocracy is unattainable—that any hierarchy will create an entrenched and self-perpetuating elite, not effectively open to all the talents—, rather than that it is objectionable. These critics rightly criticize the rigid stratification and low social mobility increasingly prevalent in western societies, especially the US and Britain—but these are factors which undermine meritocracy. Without meritocracy, how would scientists, surgeons, generals, engineers, teachers, town planners, bankers, broadcasters, artists and athletes be selected? The alternative is the insanity of Mao's Cultural Revolution or Pol Pot's 'Year Zero'.

What would a meritocratic alternative to elitism, and to cultural elitism in particular, involve? It asserts that authorities constitute an open and not an entrenched elite, and affirms the more balanced notion of authority required for that openness. Mill was writing in a pre-meritocratic age, when western culture was largely the preserve of a class or classes with a virtual monopoly on leisure. Today, almost everyone in western liberal societies has sufficient leisure to become an aesthete in a minimal but essential sense, that is, they can regard art and the aesthetic as ends in themselves. Meritocracy recognizes, and requires, that those who are capable of appreciating high culture—even though they may be a minority—originate in any section of the population. 'The elite' is not 'self-perpetuating'; its composition is in flux, it is not unitary. Mill's elitism clearly requires that the few are well-qualified; but before universal education, it was impossible for qualified positions to be filled from all social classes.

Why not accept, as Skorupski seems to, that there can be a meritocratic form of elitism, in which elites let newcomers join their ranks on merit? Claims have been made that the British Establishment is such an elite. Robert Skidelsky says that it is

> not a closed order or corporation but an elastic governing class with an instinctive sense of self-preservation, and therefore an exceptional capacity for self-renewal ... expressed ... in the meritocratic selection of its elite, and the authority and honour given to exceptional ability. In England ... rebels ... were absorbed by the established order and used to strengthen its defences [against revolution] (2004: 834).

The claim is questionable. There was nothing meritocratic about the landed aristocratic element of the Establishment, while the civil service had old-school-tie traditions; rebels such as Wilde, Shaw, Russell, Strachey, Churchill and Aldous Huxley were tolerated at best.

More important, meritocracy is not so easily defined as first appears. 'Appointing on merit' combines the notion of 'most deserves the job' with 'will be best at doing it', and assumes that the latter is a conclusive reason for the former. 'On the basis of ability' presumably means 'ability to do the job'. Academic success, especially when the result of much effort, is usually regarded as a better predictor of job success than parentage, type of school or social charm. But traditionalists must have thought Etonians more capable of performing the duties of a civil servant or diplomat than state school applicants. The root of the issue is that elites usually have partisan views about what constitutes relevant merit. When the British Medical Association dismisses homeopathy, it uses a phrase like 'without merit'. Professional or labour elites such as guilds and unions have combined to define merit and value, excluding people and practices that do not conform; thus elites construct the conditions of their own meritocracy. The challenge, then, is to define a robust concept of meritocracy that properly expresses its self-proclaimed fairness; perhaps—and this has Hegelian and Marxist overtones—one where the elite is self-consciously self-destructive.

The options facing us are therefore:

(1) elitism is acceptable when it is made meritocratic;
(2) elitism is unacceptable because it cannot be made meritocratic;
(3) 'meritocratic elitism' is unacceptable because meritocracy is essentially elitist.

The debate over cultural elitism is a particular form of this debate. The 'agenda' of artistic elites is reflected in their unwarranted dismissal of popular culture, while the question of the democracy of taste and the neophyte's right to contribute suggest that in the arena of culture the concept of meritocracy requires further development than I have attempted so far. In this article I have explained how liberal elitism arises from scepticism about democracy, and examined it in relation to populism and meritocracy. Further treatment of these cultural issues must remain material for another occasion.

References

Alexander, E. (1965), *Matthew Arnold and John Stuart Mill* (London: Routledge and Kegan Paul).
Benn, S.I., and R.S. Peters (1959), *Social principles and the democratic state* (London: George Allen and Unwin).
Bentley, M. (1984), *Politics without democracy: 1815–1914* (London: Fontana).
Bobbio, N. (2005), *Liberalism and democracy*, trans. M. Ryle and K. Soper (London: Verso).
Burns, J.H. (1968), 'J.S. Mill and democracy, 1829–61', in *Mill: a collection of critical essays*, ed. J.B. Schneewind (London: Macmillan).
Carlyle, T. (2005), *Past and present* (Berkeley: University of California Press).
Collini, S. (2006), *Absent minds: intellectuals in Britain* (Oxford: Oxford University Press).
Constant, B. (1820), *Collection complète des ouvrages* (Paris: Béchet Libraire).
Donner, W. (1991), *The liberal self: John Stuart Mill's moral and political philosophy* (Ithaca: Cornell University Press).
Eliot, T.S. (1962), *Notes towards the definition of culture* (London: Faber and Faber).
Friedman, R.B. (1968), 'An introduction to Mill's theory of authority', in *Mill: a collection of critical essays*, ed. J.B. Schneewind (London: Macmillan).
Furedi, F. (2006), *Where have all the intellectuals gone? Confronting 21st century philistinism* (London: Continuum).

Graham, G. (2002), *The case against the democratic state: an essay in cultural criticism* (Exeter and Charlottesville: Imprint Academic).

Gray, J. (1996), *Mill on liberty: a defence* (2nd ed.; London: Routledge).

Hamilton, A. (2007), *Aesthetics and music* (London: Continuum).

Hamilton, A. (2008), 'Criticism and connoisseurship', in *Critical exchange: European art criticism of the eighteenth and nineteenth centuries*, ed. C. Adlam (Amsterdam: Rodopi).

Hurka, T. (1993), *Perfectionism* (Oxford: Oxford University Press).

Jay, D. (1937), *The socialist case* (London: Faber and Faber).

Jones, H.S. (2000), *Victorian political thought* (Basingstoke: Macmillan).

Kellner, P. (2001), 'Yes, we still need meritocracy', *New Statesman*, 130 (4545): 25–9.

Knights, B. (1978), *The idea of the clerisy in the nineteenth century* (Cambridge: Cambridge University Press).

Levin, M. (2004), *J.S. Mill on civilization and barbarism* (London and New York: Routledge).

Lind, M. (2005), 'In defence of mandarins', *Prospect*, October: 34–7.

Macaulay, T. (1889), *The miscellaneous writings and speeches of Lord Macaulay* (London: Longmans, Green, and Co.).

Mill, J.S. (1961), *The early draft of John Stuart Mill's autobiography*, ed. J. Stillinger (Urbana: University of Illinois Press).

Mill, J.S. (1963–91), *Collected works of John Stuart Mill*, ed. J.M. Robson (33 vols.; Toronto: University of Toronto Press).

Mill, J.S. (1973), *On liberty and Considerations on representative government* (London: Everyman).

Rawls, J. (1971), *A theory of justice* (Cambridge, MA: Harvard University Press).

Robson, J.M. (1968), *The improvement of mankind: the social and political thought of John Stuart Mill* (London: Routledge).

Ryan, A. (2007), 'Bureaucracy, democracy, liberty: some unanswered questions in Mill's politics', in *J.S. Mill's political thought: a bicentennial reassessment*, eds. N. Urbinati and A. Zakaras (Cambridge: Cambridge University Press).

Skidelsky, R. (2004), *John Maynard Keynes 1883–1946: economist, philosopher, statesman* (London: Pan).

Skorupski, J. (1989), *John Stuart Mill* (London: Routledge).

Skorupski, J. (1999), *Ethical explorations* (Oxford: Oxford University Press).

Stromberg, R.N. (1996), *Democracy: a short analytical history* (Armonk: M.E. Sharpe).

Ten, C.L. (1998), 'Democracy, socialism and the working class', in *The Cambridge companion to Mill*, ed. J. Skorupski (Cambridge: Cambridge University Press).

Tocqueville, A. de (1968), *Democracy in America*, eds. J.P. Mayer and M. Lerner/trans. G. Lawrence (2 vols.; London: Fontana).

Uglow, J. (2002), *Hogarth: a life and a world* (New York: Farrar, Straus and Giroux).

Warnock, M. (1989), *Universities: knowing our minds* (London: Chatto & Windus).

Young, M. (1958), *The rise of the meritocracy 1870–2033: an essay on education and equality* (London: Thames and Hudson).

Tuula Vaarakallio

The Rhetoric of False Appearances and True Essences
Anti-Democratic Thought in France at the Turn of the Twentieth Century

I

Introduction[1]

Democracy is bad and democracy is death, declared the French anti-democrats at the turn of the twentieth century. Their anti-democratic and anti-parliamentary thinking was often based on essentialism and the rejection of political pluralism — paradoxically, both on the right and the left sides of the political spectrum. This article examines how the hostility towards democracy and the parliamentary system of government manifested itself in French nationalism and revolutionary syndicalism and highlights similarities in the rhetoric of these two factions.

France has a long tradition of anti-parliamentarism — at least as long as that of French parliamentarism. The critique of the representative form of government and democracy dates back as far as the revolutionary era, a time when counter-revolutionary ideas prevailed and the aristocratic elite was mourning the loss of its privileges. The Revolution did not create any consensus whatsoever regarding the principles of the appropriate constitutional form. Until the establishment of the Third Republic (1875), France was a state which had to endure a remarkable level of constitutional instability, marked by the high number of different political regimes in power — from parliamentary monarchy to the Bonapartist empires.

---

1   This paper was first presented at the Fourth Annual Conference 'Workshops in Political Theory' in Manchester, England, September 2007.

Although the questioning and critique of the political regime remained strong in the Third Republic, the principle of democracy was broadly accepted. It had been concretized as early as 1848 with the introduction of manhood suffrage, and the freedoms of expression, assembly and the press were later granted by law (Roussellier, 2000: 247–8). Not all the critical factions in the country shared this republican spirit though, and at the turn of the twentieth century a number of them struggled against both the parliamentary regime and democratic principles in general.

In the following, I shall focus primarily on two different anti-democratic discourses, one on the extreme right and the other on the extreme left of the political spectrum. These two political-rhetorical examples are the nationalism of Charles Maurras and the revolutionary syndicalism of Hubert Lagardelle and others.

II

Maurras: Democracy is Death

Charles Maurras (1868–1952), a French nationalist, neo-royalist theorist and the figurehead of the *Action Française* movement, crystallized his anti-democratic thinking in his famous dictum: 'Democracy is evil, democracy is death' (see 1925: 121).[2] His words echo the old counter-revolutionary view of democracy and emphasize that his doctrine belongs to the school of counter-revolutionary traditionalism.

Maurras fervently struggled against the republic and democracy. His aim was to eliminate all democratic, parliamentary and republican institutions from politics, as well as to separate the political state from the social life of the nation. To that end, he propagated the theory of integral nationalism, which was the union of patriotism and hereditary monarchism, seen to serve to ensure and re-establish the ancient greatness of the France of the past. The republic, according to him, was the rule of the foreigner and only monarchy could put an end to it.

Integral nationalism was 'integral' in the sense that the nationalist objectives were attainable only trough its logic. Integral nationalism was ultimately achievable solely through rule by monarchy. It was bolstered by Maurras' conception of *politique naturelle*, which, in turn, was based on inescapable biological inequality and its subsequent natural hierarchies. To put it briefly, the individual is necessarily subordinated to social collectivities, such as the family, society or state, which, like the democratic

---

2   If not indicated otherwise, English translations are by me.

government, are doomed to fail if based on the 'myth of equality' or 'abstract liberty' (Maurras, 1937).

Contempt for the masses

Maurras did not conceal his contempt for the masses when he wrote in 1912 that 'the masses have feelings, but they have no memory. To depend on the initiative of their judgement and their votes is the greatest folly that can be committed under the guise of rationalism and philosophy'. Maurras' denial of the sovereignty of the people and parliamentarism emerged from this contempt. For Maurras, 'government by numbers inevitably meant the hidden government of the worst' (in Osgood, 1970: 60; see Maurras, 1931–34: II/76, III/202). The very idea of democracy is bad, since it prefers the worst over the best and quantity over quality (1936: 17). Here, the opposition between quantity, in other words government by numbers, and quality, or monarchism, is clearly highlighted. The adjectives used to describe what in this specific context is qualitative monarchism were 'hereditary', 'personal', 'national' and 'responsible', whereas government by numbers was regarded as 'anonymous' and 'irresponsible'.

The basis for Maurras' anti-democratic attitude can be found in his *politique naturelle*, centring on the concept of natural inequality. Maurras viewed the natural inequality between individuals as the foundation of human society, and the idea of democracy as profoundly false — it is 'at odds with nature'. He thus opposed authority and inequality to 'the dreamy hypotheses of liberals and democrats' (see 1936: 17–9). These 'dreamy hypothesis' refer most notably to the abstract ideas of the French Revolution, liberty, egalitarianism and individualism, which form, for Maurras, the basis of the *pays légal* (legal nation) and essentially exist in an ongoing conflict with nature (*la nature des choses*). According to Maurras, the principles of liberalism expressed in Rousseau's *Social Contract* or in the *Declaration of the Rights of Man and Citizen* are based on the 'false' assumption of liberty and the false assumption of equality, i.e. on the notion that human beings are born free and equal (12–3).

The parliamentary republic which claims to base itself on the 'national will' expressed through elections rests upon very random and unsafe foundations. This results directly from the incompetence of the voters and the fact that the elected government is inherently unstable and uncertain about its own future (54). Moreover, the state becomes 'a slave of the parliamentary parties, of electoral deals', and 'at the very moment when it is most necessary to stand firm, the system compels the foundations to be shaken' (1970: 225), as Maurras adds in his 1899 writing *Dictateur et roi* (*Dictator and King*; 1925: 446–63). The inherent weaknesses of parliamentary democracy lie in its lack of competent and continuous direction and any kind of unity in terms of its views, the exact opposite of what was to be expected from an anti-parliamentary monarchy due to the latter's responsible and personal style of governance.

Hence, the advantage of having a hereditary king as opposed to a representative democracy was located in the fact that political power in the personal-royalist regime would be in the hands of a so-called expert, whereas in a representative democracy it would remain in the hands of 'invariably ignorant and limited, often impoverished and corrupt' rulers (1970: 221). Maurras wrote that 'however independent, however honest, however intelligent the elector may be, he can never be competent to decide the majority of the questions put to him. This disability makes him either violent and blind or hesitant and fickle, or all simultaneously' (225). Representatives are thus elected haphazardly (i.e. the voter gives 'blank cheques' to anonymous candidates whose political intentions he only knows from election posters), and the elected may not necessarily be competent. Even in cases in which the electorate should choose wise men, they will inevitably become corrupted due to the inherent logic of parliamentary rule.

While Maurras did not rely on the people as the sovereign power to be capable of making decisions on any and all *political* issues, he was certain that at the provincial and local levels the people were capable of making decisions regarding their own *administrative* concerns. Thus, he made a clear distinction between the political and the administrative spheres. In his vision, the future monarchist France would have been based on *centralized political power*, that is, it would have had a sovereign king who ruled absolute, and a *decentralized local administration*, that would have been organized autonomously by each representative entity. Such entities he saw as constituted by various genuine, small and natural local, professional, moral and religious republics, that were to be examples of self-governing through free association. Maurras being willing to accept the representative system at the local level, parliamentarism could 'take refuge in these inferior states as long as it did not infringe upon the central power'. Political questions, though, which is to say, matters involving the 'general interest such as diplomacy, the armed forces, national police, high justice', could be settled only by a sovereign, independent power (in Osgood, 1970: 63; see 1931–34: II/6). In other words, politics should be left to the expert, to the absolute king, whereas administrative matters can be left in the hands of virtually anybody.

Against political struggles

Maurras viewed the parliament as a forum of divided opinions and interests, that is, as a forum in which *the* national interest, the common good, is subordinated to the private interests of the deputies (members of parliament). He perceived the national interest, first and foremost, as the will to resolve political problems with the best interest of France in mind. But in a state with numerous parties, it is the contradictory and short-sighted interests of individuals that prevail. Parliamentary rule, for him, is a regime that is naturally inclined towards corruption, electoral intrigue and political horse trading (see 1937: 220). The 'tyrannical diversity' of parliamentarism cannot be reconciled with the national interest, rendering it impossible for anyone to represent the national interest in a parliamentary government. This lack of unity was, according to Maurras, one of the most profound weaknesses of the parliamentary republic. Therefore, in order to both maintain the national heritage and traditions and act on behalf of the common good, the feasible solution was monarchism. An independent (*absolute* in Latin, as Maurras notes) sovereign would best represent (in the literal sense of the word) and even incarnate the national interest.

Parliamentarism was interpreted by Maurras as an arena of negative political struggle between rival private interests (1936: 59–60), while monarchism was bolstered by the notion of the personal power of the king, standing for a more personal kind of politics. Parliamentarians were seen to hide behind their legislative work in that the acts of politicians and their ramifications are not connected to them as individuals (32). In demanding the establishment of a more 'personified' politics, Maurras was criticizing the party machine (which, however, was quite vague in the Third Republic) and other political groups, and, more importantly, calling for a higher level of morality and responsibility amongst individual politicians in carrying out their legislative work (see 1936: 31).

Maurras was searching for a kind of political harmony which could be achieved through the establishment of a personal, hereditary and traditional monarchy. According to his conception, useless and harmful political and electoral struggles could be avoided by centralizing political power and placing it in the hands of the king, or, to put it more precisely, in the hands of one royal family. He wrote that '[i]n order to spare ourselves fruitless and dangerous electoral contests, to forestall the periodic recurrence of political agitation, and finally to ensure peace ... it is agreed that power must be entrusted to a family', and he considered the best choice to be 'the race of Capet', 'the oldest royal line in Europe' (Maurras, 1970: 236). Maurras thus contrasted 'peaceful' royal hereditary power to democracy, which he saw as a 'warlike goddess' (*déesse guerrière*) that could only lead to endless conflict.

As the sovereign, the king is above futile political intrigue and discussion. He is able to act and think more prudently and wisely and orientate himself towards the distant future because he is not dependent on electoral terms and the pressures they produce, as is the case with presidents elected by popular vote. Moreover, the existence of a royal family guarantees that 'the head of state will not idly gamble away the future of his dynasty', as the future of the king's family is directly linked to the future of the nation and vice versa (see Maurras, 1936: 52). Finally, there would be no question as to who was governing France. In other words, in a hereditary monarchy, the 'two political maladies', namely 'the administration ruled by all, the state ruled by none', and 'the administration master of all, the state with no master at all', could be avoided (Maurras, 1970: 234).

Maurras also criticized the republican model of his time for being 'the government of discussion for the sake of discussion' (see 1936: 52). He was particularly astonished at the sheer number of useless and lengthy debates between incompetent parliamentarians and adamant in arguing that there cannot be such a thing as government by discussion (see 1937: 184; 1931–34: I/367). If we were to follow Maurras, no parliamentary discussion would be needed, because 'the good and national dictator', the king, would act and make decisions much more efficiently than any deliberating forum. The technically competent elite would act swiftly when dealing with matters of the state (see 1937: 183–4). What follows is that by supporting hereditary monarchism, Maurras appears to minimize the sphere of politics, i.e. the sphere of political opportunities, conflicts and overall deliberation. His distinction of political governance and practical deeds from 'theoretical' debate seems to suggest that debate plays no role at all in the former since politics is reduced to the practical government and deeds of one person. Maurras' *monarche* leaves no room for political manoeuvres other than those made by the king himself.

Maurras is known for having coined the slogan *la politique d'abord* (politics first!). This famous slogan has been interpreted in many ways, particularly with regard to his neo-royalism. Maurras' integral nationalism is based, at least to some extent, on a conception that actually minimizes politics. The core of the slogan is associated though with Maurras' conception of *raison d'État*, which starts from the idea that the national interest und subsequent policies always extend beyond morality, religion and justice. Maurras puts politics before providence (see 1931–34: I/459). The *raison d'État* was 'in the nature of things' and as such the public interest should always be placed before individuals or parties (see 1931–34: I/461). The king used his authority 'for purely national objectives' (1970: 220) and, thus, royal personal power would ensure that the *raison d'État* did not become transformed into a *raison de parti*, i.e. that it would not remain at the mercy of the continuously 'changing interests of persons and offices' (see 1936: 50).

The French interest thus formed a comprehensive starting point in Maurras' integral nationalism, and dictated the way in which all issues — whether the form of government, the Dreyfus Affair or some other topic — should be considered. Short, Maurras' politics was based on national relativism (see Thibaudet, 1920: 135) and the minimization of political struggle.

The regime of the foreigner

One further aspect of Maurras' repudiation of democratic parliamentarism is the thesis that describes parliamentarism as a 'foreign regime'. Maurras was convinced that France was full of 'eternal divisions', that is, geographic, cultural and racial divisions that have their historical roots in the distant past and cannot, therefore, be bridged by any kind of democratic system (see, for example, 1921: 203-5; 1937: 288-92). In addition to the fact that Maurras regarded democracy as 'a political disease' and 'a universal lie' (see 1937: 288), he argued that parliamentarism was not suited to France because of its foreign origins and inherent English and German features (see Thibaudet, 1920: 230-4). In Maurras' view, both France's cultural diversity and geographical breadth contributed to the preference for fast and continuous decisions to be made by a personal power (1936: 47). More importantly, however, Maurras pointed out that not only was republican parliamentarism a foreign regime as such, but the elective republic and its free political competition also provided the opportunity for domination of France by 'foreigners'.

Maurras was convinced that France was being governed by anti-national groups (*les dynasties d'étrangers*), namely the Four Confederated Estates (*les quatre états confédérés*), which were the Freemasons, the Protestants, the Jews and the *métèques*.[3] From Maurras' standpoint, this conspiracy perpetrated by the internal enemy and the false ideas related to the Reformation, Enlightenment philosophy (particularly Rousseau) and the 'anti-French' Revolution of 1789, served as evidence of France's decadence.

---

3 By *métèques*, Maurras was referring to foreigners who had been 'nationalized' too hastily, that is those who did not have deep family roots in France and should therefore be regarded as foreigners regardless of the fact that they may enjoy French citizenship. Behind the Maurrasian concept of *métèque* is, of course, the model of the Athenian polis, from which foreign residents were excluded too (see Maurras, 1931-34: III/41-50).

Maurras' outline of the anti-national forces and the plot they were assumed to be hatching against France also serves to illustrate the way in which he conceived of the *pays légal*: it was not only the questionable regime as such that he condemned, but he considered the potential danger that false liberalism and the false ideas connected to parliamentary republicanism might cause as equally destructive. It was a crucial advantage of hereditary monarchism that it provided the certainty that the personified power would not fall into the hands of foreigners. Maurras reasoned that only once major decisions were made 'with respect to France', and within that frame of reference only, France would be returned to the French (see 1931–34: II/10–1; Osgood, 1970: 60–4; Winock 1994: 127).

Finally, it is important to clarify the distinction Maurras made between the *pays réel* (real nation) and the *pays légal*. For Maurras, the *pays légal* was the false appearance of political institutions, whereas the *pays réel* signified the 'real and true France', both at the level of political institutions (absolute monarchism) and at the broader national and even biological-cultural levels (the traditional France comprised of 'truly French' groups and 'races', etc.). In Maurras' view, the *pays légal* also represented a false elite (Jews, Freemasons, foreigners, Protestants), which conspired against the *pays réel*, politically and otherwise. In this plot, the false 'nations' within the nation allegedly hold the political power, and the republican form of government is seen as the result of the ideas, philosophies and theories (Revolution, Reform, Rights of Man) connected, in one way or another, to these false 'nations' or estates and their representatives.

III

Syndicalism: Against 'Democratism'

Like Maurras, the revolutionary syndicalists are also known for their intense anti-democratic and anti-parliamentary views. The faction of revolutionary syndicalists emerged when the socialists entered the French parliament in 1893. It was then that the more radical syndicalist group separated itself from parliamentary socialism in an attempt to offer an alternative to electoral democracy. At the same time, some militants who belonged to more violent anarchist groups also joined the revolutionary syndicalists—from which the term 'anarcho-syndicalists' results (Dubief, 1969; Rosanvallon, 1998: 287).

Later, revolutionary syndicalism became a distinct branch of socialism that differed from both parliamentary and anarchist socialism. The syndicalist thinker Hubert Lagardelle (1874–1958) argued this point by saying that viewing the class struggle as analogous to socialism implied that syndicalism was inherently socialist, since there was no class struggle beyond syndicalism (1908: 3). According to Lagardelle, French (revolutionary) syndicalism arose from 'the reaction of the proletariat against democracy' (see 1908: 36). Syndicalism, as he notes, is an attack against 'the *popular form* of bourgeois dominance'. The principal enemy may then be reduced to the neologism of 'democratism', which was frequently used by the syndicalists.

The starting point of syndicalist socialism was 'an inversion of terms of traditional socialism' (see Lagardelle, 1911: 81). This means that instead of taking on the more traditional role of a political party and aiming at gradual reforms, 'the centre of gravity' for revolutionary syndicalists was the autonomous syndication of the working class, which was distinct from the 'creations of the bourgeoisie', in other words from political parties and the entire 'regime of parties' (see Lagardelle, 1911: 82–3). Thus, it was only natural that the syndicalists preferred to take the 'revolutionary' as opposed to the 'democratic' road along the path to social transformation (Lagardelle, 1902a: 625).

Their means of direct action in revolutionary combat were strikes, sabotage and general strikes. Sabotage might take the form of a minor uprising against the *patron* conducted at members' place of work, and they regarded the general strike as the ultimate non-parliamentary weapon in their goal of creating a socialist revolution (see, for example, Griffuelhes and Niel, 1909; Lagardelle, 1905).

Disillusionment with politics

The ideological core of revolutionary syndicalist thought was based on the concept of 'double political disappointment', according to Pierre Rosanvallon's interpretation (see 1998: 287–8). First, despite the high hopes of the republicans and socialists, universal male suffrage failed to close the gap between the classes. Second, they were disappointed with the prevailing republican regime, which had failed to improve the social circumstances of the working class.

This scepticism towards electoral democracy was combined with the idea of working class separatism (*séparatisme ouvrier*), which was influenced by the tradition of Pierre-Joseph Proudhon as well as the Manifeste des Soixante (*Manifesto of the Sixty*), a manifesto signed by a group of sixty Parisian workers in 1864. In this view, republican democracy was criticized for confusing the classes, denying the inescapable social differences between them, and instead enthroning an abstract voter in the centre of politics (see Rosanvallon, 1998: 287–8). The concept of the separation of the working class from the other classes aimed to illustrate the inherent weaknesses of the civic universalism of the Revolution and democratic theory, that is, the idea that society is an abstract entity consisting of individual citizens who are all equal in the eyes of the law. According to the *Manifeste des Soixante*, the gap between the working class and the bourgeoisie was widening. For them, universal male suffrage and the equality of citizens were abstractions which had nothing to do with their everyday lives and did nothing to solve the problems of the working class. The manifesto called for the separation of working class representation and the nomination of labour candidates. Thus, the separation thesis signified the political emancipation and social identification of the working class and meant that, 'in this case, separation became a new condition of equality; representation was no longer a source of confusion but a distinction' (see Rosanvallon, 1998: 96).

The separation thesis was then radicalized by the revolutionary syndicalists. They echoed the former separatists by arguing, for example, that 'the illusory work of the union of classes is carried on by democracy' (see Lagardelle, 1908: 5). Lagardelle saw syndicalist socialism as differing quite radically from the 'vulgar democrats'. According to him, the working class should be a distinct class, with a distinct programme, organized in autonomous economic institutions (1902b: 678–9). He lamented that the economic reality of the working class passed completely unnoticed by the democrats and that democracy strove only to achieve spiritual and not economic ends (1902c: 891–2). Lagardelle said that:

> Democracy considers the citizen, the "political" man, as a separate entity from the social category to which he belongs. It tries to guarantee everybody equal rights, legal rights, liberty etc. ... [Democracy] disregards the differentiations created by the material conditions between men and groups: it stands beyond the classes and class conflicts (see 1902c: 891).

That is why, surprisingly, syndicalists in general and Lagardelle in particular vigorously condemned one of the principles of democracy, the equality of rights. In the name of equality, men and classes are considered as having the same interests. Differences are reduced and antagonisms destroyed, although the 'economic reality is nothing if not struggle between opposing interests' (see Lagardelle, 1902c: 892). The syndicalists saw political equality as a veil that obscures true social and economic injustice. The republican and bourgeois conception of equality was far removed from the socialist ideal of equality as expression of social justice and equal economic premises. That such a dichotomy between conceptions of equality can be found in far-left anti-democratic thinking is also argued by Marc Angenot (2004: 7–9). One is false and represents the prevailing society against which citizens should revolt; the other is perfect and true and seen as attainable in the future through the struggle against the bourgeois state.

Political democracy, according to Lagardelle, is a false (*fictive*) form of government, because it views people as mere abstractions, in other words, it sees citizens as forming a political body that is the basis of the general will (1902d: 1013). Lagardelle juxtaposed the 'abstract man' and the 'real man', which is not an abstract term but one that is quite concretely defined. Emphasizing that 'the political and proletarian milieus have nothing in common', he argued that the 'economic organization of the proletariat knew only "real men", workers who gather together for the defence of their material and moral interests' (see 1902d: 1014).

In line with Angenot, Lagardelle also makes a distinction between abstract equality (*égalité abstraite*) and real equality (*égalité réelle*). He claims that 'real equality' is dominant in the 'democracy of the working class', which is the unity of groups organized by the proletariat. Real equality is based on the differences that exist between workers, as there is a great deal of variation in their abilities, Lagardelle notes (see 1902d: 1015). Thus in the workers' democracy, the proletariat, the 'real men', organize themselves into syndicates in which the differences between workers are recognized. Because of this inevitable variation of skills and abilities, the most qualified and 'conscious' are selected to join various occupational groups. These groups eventually form the competent workers' government, which then represents the entire proletariat (Lagardelle, 1902d: 1014-6). The point is that the workers' democracy operates in the 'realm' of production, which, according to Lagardelle, is 'difficult and therefore cannot be conducted by the procedures of political government' (see 1902d: 1015).

Homogeneous interests

We can identify another distinction between two concepts here, namely that of political democracy (*la démocratie politique*) and workers' democracy (*la démocratie ouvrière*). These concepts are used to describe the spheres in which political and syndicalist actions take place: one is based on the condemned representative parliamentarism and the other is dedicated to the autonomous economic organization of the working class.

Similarly, the proletariat, including the syndicates and the 'wise government' above them, are opposed to the people, the unconscious masses. The rule of the majority and universal suffrage are to be abandoned, since the masses are considered too ignorant to make decisions on their own behalf. According to Lagardelle, the sphere of politics is too large and complex for the masses to master. Regardless of whether we refer to representative democracy or direct democracy by means of referenda, both require at least a certain degree of enlightenment among the population. As Lagardelle notes, this is an unattainable goal, as it is impossible to educate the masses to the degree required for them to exert political control, which is an essential aspect of political democracy (1902d: 1013–4).

What is interesting about Lagardelle's writings on democracy is that he acknowledges the inherently paradoxical nature of the working class' revolt against 'the ideal government of the people by the people' (see 1902d: 1013–4). This paradox becomes even more obvious when considered in light of the aforementioned 'disappointment' argument. That is to say that the syndicalists attacked democratic forms of government for not materializing to their liking; in practice, democracy failed to live up to their conception of it. Lagardelle wrote that the syndicalists were not against democracy in principle, but rather against how it was carried out in France at the time: 'We renounce the abuses of a principle and not the principle'. According to him, the democratic model—with its cynical political machinery to which nothing is sacred—could not be the model for the French state. But 'what is true for an old democracy is not true for a burgeoning democracy', he noted, referring here specifically to Russia. He claimed that democracy in France was in a deep crisis, as it was seen as sustaining bourgeois domination and leading to decadent political practices, scandals, corruption and powerlessness of the parliament, as had been the case throughout the course of the Third Republic (see 1911: 83–5).

Perhaps Lagardelle's view can be related to the tacit endeavour to question the definition of democracy and the concept of equality, and to call for a rhetorical redescription of them (see Skinner, 1996: ch. 4). This, in turn, might have resulted in the replacement of the republican and bourgeois definitions of democracy and equality with new syndicalist interpretations. Alphonse Merrheim, an activist of the Metal Workers' Union, reminds us, however, that syndicalism is inherently opposed to parliamentarism. He wrote in the theoretical review of syndicalists, *Le Mouvement Socialiste* (which was headed by Lagardelle), that 'it is not the voters, the *passives*, that count, but the *actives*. The number does not make the law, but the will. Quality takes precedence over quantity'. Here, Merrheim emphasized that syndicalist action is the action of the minorities: 'The sighted persons guide the others' (see 1910: 245). The members of the active syndicalist minority and their government are carefully selected. The entire organization of the working class is based on a strong hierarchy that takes shape 'naturally', which means that the selection process and hierarchy themselves are 'profoundly democratic', as Lagardelle argues, adding that 'the workers' democracy is as fixed and organic as the political democracy is uncertain and chaotic' (see 1902d: 1015-6).

In relation to this, let us turn to Rosanvallon's analysis. First, following Rosanvallon (see 1998: ch. VI), it must be noted that each occupational group is regarded as an organic entity that cannot be broken down. In other words, the syndicate is the conscious formation of an occupational or professional group which represents the class to which individuals belong and not the individuals themselves. This is the case despite the fact that the differences between individual 'real men' seem to be recognized over the course of the process of selection to various groups. Second, the relationships between different syndicalist organizations do not follow the rules of political representation, for example, those of the voter and the deputy. Instead, as Rosanvallon argues, the representativeness of syndicalism originates in identification — it is the expression of a social essence or social fact, not a political construction (see 1998: 300). This is to say that the representativeness of the syndicate does not need to be proven or measured by an electoral procedure. The syndicate is representative as such. It is founded on common, homogeneous interests and 'on the natural community of sentiments'. Therefore, as Rosanvallon concludes, one may interpret the syndicalist form of 'representation' as a reversion to an *essentialist* conception of representation (see 1998: 301, 309).

The homogeneity of interests is thus the defining characteristic of the syndicalist organization. Because the syndicate is comprised exclusively of workers with common interests, there is no need for discussion, at least not in the sense of examining questions from different points of view in the presence of adversaries (see, for example, Palonen, 2004; 2006: ch. 7; Lagardelle, 1902d: 1016). Unlike in parliamentary discussions, the weighing of alternatives is not necessary in syndicalist organizations, as they are inherently homogeneous in terms of their interests and have no need to negotiate with their enemies. This point is expressed explicitly, for example, by Émile Pouget, who, quoting Karl Liebknecht, argues that negotiation with one's adversaries always leads to the sacrifice of one's principles: 'The principles are indivisible. We either hold on to them completely or we sacrifice them completely. *Qui parle avec ses ennemis parlemente, qui parlemente pactise ...*' (see Pouget, 1976: 171).

With regard to this notion, Rosanvallon points out that parliamentarism and the organization of workers are inherently contradictory because they belong to two contradictory realities. Parliamentarism is an arena of the deliberation of different political parties which represent heterogeneous and even conflicting interests. The syndicate, for its part, expresses homogenous interests and is thereby always in radical and antagonistic conflict with others (see 1998: 292).

IV

Conclusion: False Appearances versus True Essences

When examining the rhetoric of these two political extremes, the nationalist and the syndicalist sides, one can clearly detect characteristic dichotomies within them. Certain antithetical pairs form the framework upon which their argumentations are based. In nationalist rhetoric, Maurras makes manifest a categorical opposition between parliamentary democracy and hereditary monarchism, that is between the *pays légal* and *pays réel*. In syndicalist rhetoric, à la Lagardelle, electoral democracy is opposed to autonomous organization and the actions of the working class. This is to say that there is a clear distinction in both discourses between something that is supposed to be false as such and something that is absolutely true in essence. In my view, the most important aspect of this distinction is that it appears to be unconditional.

This opposition between appearance and reality brings us to the dissociation of ideas in the form of philosophical pairs discussed by Chaïm Perelman (see Perelman, 1982: ch. 11; Perelman and Olbrechts-Tyteca, 1958: §90). In his 'new rhetoric', Perelman analyzes an argumentative technique denominated as philosophical pairs. This argumentative method uses antithetical philosophical pairs in any given rhetorical genre, i.e. the ultimate Kantian dissociation into the categories of phenomenal reality (reality as it appears) and noumenal reality (the reality of things in themselves), which corresponds to the pair of appearance/reality. According to Perelman, this kind of reasoning by dissociation 'can be applied to any idea, as soon as one makes use of the adjectives "apparent" or "illusory" on the one hand, and "real" or "true" on the other' (1982: 134). The 'pair-factor' is also evident when adjectives are used determinately; the expression 'apparent peace' highlights the absence of 'true peace', which demonstrates that 'one adjective is a reflex of the other', Perelman argues (see 1982: 134). As such, the other part of the philosophical pair need not be expressed explicitly in order to reconstruct the pair and highlight the opposing concept.

My principal aim is not to tackle the philosophical essence of or values behind the terms (see Perelman, 1982: 131), but to draw an analogy between the philosophical pair of (false) appearance/(true) reality and the other pairs frequently used in the discourse examined here, which thereby correspond to the argumentative strategy. I intend to underline that the dichotomy between allegedly false appearance and genuine reality seems to be a characterizing aspect of the rhetoric examined here, and that, therefore, the concept of antithetical pairs discussed by Perelman is, in this context, very elucidating.

The rule of majority versus the rule of minority

One can identify numerous antithetical pairs in the nationalist and syndicalist discourses examined here. Both nationalists and syndicalists rejected the notion of the people as a source of political legitimacy. Both sides expressed contempt for the masses, thereby opposing the rule of majority (people, masses) to the rule of minority (king or syndicate). As well as the use by both of the qualifiers of competence and incompetence/ ignorance.

Maurras drew a clear distinction between the incompetence of the masses (electorate) and the competence of the hereditary king. According to him, parliamentary and democratic politics should be replaced by personal power, i.e. with the wise political manoeuvres of the king. Royalism thus ensures that the political decision making remains firmly in the hands of an expert, the king, who possesses the natural competence to reign, contrary to the incompetent representatives of the people, the parliamentarians. Lagardelle, for his part, found the masses not only too ignorant to rule but also too unaware (unconscious) to make the right decisions. As such, the syndicalists would not have wanted to give the unconscious and passive majority political power by means of universal suffrage. Instead, they intended to bestow power on active and conscious members of the working class.

Regarding the focus on competent and conscious minorities, Rosanvallon emphasizes that, rather paradoxically, revolutionary syndicalism followed the reactionary and 'pro-elitist' anti-democratic thinking outlined by, for example, François Guizot and Ernest Renan. According to Rosanvallon, revolutionary syndicalism employed *le viel ideal capacitaire* (the idea that defines one's political rights according to one's personal 'capacities') in a new context. Thus, one may occasionally encounter a kind of conservative anti-individualism in revolutionary syndicalism similar to that in traditionalist nationalism (1998: 301–2).

Against politics?

Also, both Maurras' nationalism and revolutionary syndicalism aimed at drawing a distinction between the political state and society, thus creating an antithetical dichotomy between political and social life. According to Maurrasian thought, political power should be placed primarily in the hands of one sovereign, while civil society was to deal with minor issues, which were defined as non-political or administrative. The sovereign king would have saved France from ongoing decline, the indications of which were, among other things, its unstable governments and squabbling parliamentary regime. Representative democracy and the parliamentary system of government were rejected because they were associated with pluralism, controversy and unpredictable deliberation, all of which are epithets diametrically opposed to nationalist ideology. The syndicalists used the concepts of political democracy and workers' democracy to refer to the dichotomy of the political and the social. These concepts defined the spheres of political action (interpreted as 'false') and economically determined activities within the syndicates (which were highly recommended). The syndicalists thus wanted to reduce the sphere of politics, the role of the state and the parties 'to their natural positions', as Lagardelle once pointed out (see 1911: 86). The syndicalists saw themselves as operating outside the sphere of politics, or at least on its periphery. In other words, if one follows the terminology of Marcel Merle (1962), they were pursuing a sort of doctrinal antipolitism with their complete contempt for political action.

Politicians are viewed with suspicion for a number of reasons: they represent falsified ideologies, they are corrupt or become so when surrounded by existing political practices, and they are self-serving and tend to think only of the next elections and their own interests. These were common allegations in both the nationalist and syndicalist camps. Both were extremely suspicious of parliamentary politics and the political parties in the parliament. In the case of the syndicalists, this was due in part to the fact that they did not consider political deliberation between different groups and interests important, as the syndicate represents homogeneous interests and is thus inherently in radical and antagonistic conflict with other groups. Parliamentary politics was seen as disillusioning the workers to the extent that they would lose their own political identity. The syndicalists wanted to express their will directly through autonomous syndicates as opposed to corrupt intermediaries such as parliamentarians and politicians. In relation to this idea, Nicolas Roussellier argues that in the age of nationalism and socialism, deliberation (which is necessarily related to parliamentarism and representative democracy) was viewed with a great deal of scepticism. The 'spectacle of deliberation' was rejected because it reveals the artificial divisions of the nation (nationalism) and quite hypocritically obscures the divisions of society (socialism, syndicalism; 1997: 20).

Both extremes denied the equality of citizens, although for different reasons. For nationalists like Maurras, natural reality and traditional order dictated the existence of unavoidable hierarchies, 'necessary inequalities', as Maurras himself put it, among individuals and citizens. For the syndicalists, equality as a principle of democracy was to be rejected in the name of class struggle. Equality (abstract equality, that is) was conceived of as a bourgeois notion with which the ruling class was able to conceal the existing differences between the classes and attempt to damage the authentic identity of the working class. It was only in the workers' democracy that real equality could thus become manifest. While the nationalists based their rejection of equality on biology, the syndicalists based theirs on class interests and class struggle. The concepts opposed to equality differed in nationalist and syndicalist rhetoric, but the distinction is still clear.

Both discourses also included the unconditional rejection of 'abstract' ideas and the call for 'real' ones. This may be related to the fact that many varieties of nationalist and socialist anti-democratic thought denied the abstract conception of the 'individual' and emphasized the social context and collective identity instead, as Joseph Femia notes (2001: 40). These collectivist beliefs led the nationalist and syndicalist sides to rest on their fixed ideologies. Their respective 'philosophy of life' acquired the status of natural laws that defy questioning. There is no need to question anything.

Finally, we can conclude that not only was anti-democratic thinking shared by both extremes of the political spectrum in France at the turn of the twentieth century, but their rhetoric was often quite similar. Although they were not always identical in substance, they did share certain common argumentative strategies, such as the use of antithetical pairs as indicated above. There were also a number of theoretical influences, such as positivism, that affected both extremes equally. And it is worth mentioning that a number of activists quite easily switched from one side to the other. Hubert Lagardelle himself is a good example, as he moved first from the far left to Maurras' camp and then, ultimately, served as Minister of Labour in the Vichy regime.

References

Angenot, M. (2004), *La démocratie, c'est le mal* (Saint-Nicolas: Les Presses de l'Université Laval).
Dubief, H. (1969), *Le syndicalisme révolutionnaire* (Paris: Armand Colin).
Femia, J.V. (2001), *Against the masses: varieties of anti-democratic thought since the French Revolution* (Oxford: Oxford University Press).
Griffuelhes, V., and L. Niel (1909), *Les objectifs de nos luttes de classes* (Paris: La Publication Sociale).
Lagardelle, H. (1902a), 'Socialisme ou démocratie', *Le Mouvement Socialiste*, April 5: 625–32.

Lagardelle, H. (1902b), 'Socialisme ou démocratie', *Le Mouvement Socialiste*, April 12: 673–87.

Lagardelle, H. (1902c), 'Socialisme ou démocratie', *Le Mouvement Socialiste*, May 10: 889–97.

Lagardelle, H. (1902d), 'Socialisme ou démocratie', *Le Mouvement Socialiste*, May 30: 1009–16.

Lagardelle, H. (1905), *La grève générale et le socialisme* (Paris: Edouard Cornély et Compagnie).

Lagardelle, H. (1908), 'Avant-propos,' in *Syndicalisme et socialisme*, ed. H. Lagardelle (Paris: Librairie des Sciences Politiques et Sociales).

Lagardelle, H. (1911), 'La critique syndicaliste de la démocratie', *Le Mouvement Socialiste*, no. 228.

Maurras, C. (1921), *La démocratie religieuse* (Paris: Nouvelle Librairie Nationale).

Maurras, C. (1925), *Enquête sur la monarchie* (Paris: Arthème Fayard).

Maurras, C. (1931–34), *Dictionnaire politique et critique* (5 vols.; Paris: A la Cité des Livres).

Maurras, C. (1936), *Nos raisons contre la république, pour la monarchie* (Paris: Edition de l'Action Française).

Maurras, C. (1937), *Mes idées politiques* (Paris: Arthème Fayard).

Maurras, C. (1970), 'Dictator and king,' in *The French right from de Maistre to Maurras*, ed. J.S. McClelland/trans. J. Fears (London: Jonathan Cape).

Merle, M. (1962), 'Inventaire des apolitismes en France', in *La dépolitisation: mythe ou réalité?*, ed. G. Vedel (Paris: Armand Colin).

Merrheim, A. (1910), 'Le parlementarisation du syndicalisme', *Le Mouvement Socialiste*, April: 241–7.

Osgood, S.M. (1970), *French royalism since 1870* (The Hague: Martinus Nijhoff).

Palonen, K. (2004), 'Max Weber, parliamentarism and the rhetorical culture of politics', *Max Weber Studies*, 4 (2): 271–90.

Palonen, K. (2006), *The struggle with time: a conceptual history of 'politics' as an activity* (Hamburg: LIT Verlag).

Perelman, C. (1982), *The realm of rhetoric* (Notre Dame and London: University of Notre Dame Press).

Perelman, C., and L. Olbrechts-Tyteca (1958), *Traité de l'argumentation: la nouvelle rhétorique* (Paris: Presses Universitaires de France).

Pouget, É. (1976), *Le père peinard* (Paris: Galilée).

Rosanvallon, P. (1998), *Le peuple introuvable* (Paris: Gallimard).

Roussellier, N. (1997), *Le parlement de l'éloquence* (Paris: Presses de la Fondation Nationale des Sciences Politiques).

Roussellier, N. (2000), 'Deux formes de la représentation politique: le citoyen et l'individu', in *La démocratie en France, vol. 1: idéologies*, ed. M. Sadoun (Paris: Gallimard).

Skinner, Q. (1996), *Reason and rhetoric in the philosophy of Hobbes* (Cambridge: Cambridge University Press).

Thibaudet, A. (1920), *Les idées de Charles Maurras: trente ans de vie française* (vol. 1; Paris: Éditions de la Nouvelle Revue Française).

Winock, M. (1994), 'L'Action Française', in *Histoire de l'extrême droite en France*, ed. M. Winock (Paris: Seuil).

Alexandre J.M.E. Christoyannopoulos

Tolstoy's Anarchist Denunciation of State Violence and Deception

I

Introduction[1]

Leo Tolstoy (1828-1910) believed that, democratic or not, the state is a violent and deceitful institution and that in a truly Christian society the state would be obsolete. Indeed, he was particularly suspicious of democratic states because of the aura of legitimacy which they claim for themselves. Even though today he is better known for his fictional work, a century ago he was just as famous for the radical political views he developed in the last three decades of his life. Elsewhere, I offer an extended review of the literature on Tolstoy's Christian anarchism and a discussion of his critique of war, patriotism and universal conscription (Christoyannopoulos, 2008a).[2] My main aim here is to demonstrate that Tolstoy considered all states, whether democratic or not, to be prone to violence and deception. Tolstoy's anarchism is a strictly non-violent, pacifist form of anarchism inspired by Jesus' teaching and example, and deeply critical of the sort of violence that the term 'anarchism' has often been associated with. In that Tolstoy continues to be the most famous voice among Christian anarchist

---

1   The author wishes to thank Stefan Rossbach, Nassos Christoyannopoulos, Sharif Gemie, Ruth Kinna, Erich Kofmel, and the three anonymous referees for their helpful comments on earlier drafts of this paper, an extended version of which was published in *Anarchist Studies* (Christoyannopoulos, 2008a).

2   For other helpful introductions to Tolstoy's anarchist thought, see for instance Guseinov (1999); Hopton (2000); Marshall (1993); Stephens (1990); Woodcock (1975).

thinkers, his analysis provides a good introduction to the Christian anarchist position on this topic.

Several of the arguments against the state that Tolstoy articulates in numerous books and pamphlets are here reorganized thematically. These themes constitute the headings of the two main sections of the paper. The first of these two sections focuses on Tolstoy's condemnation of state violence, by exploring his views on law, economic exploitation and the effect of the structure of the state on its members. The second then explores two examples of the state's mechanisms of deception: the hypocrisy of its leaders and the ingrained evasion of responsibilities. The paper concludes with a short section that hints at the contemporary relevance of Tolstoy's writings on the state.

Tolstoy often contrasts the modern state with an ideal Christian society to illustrate the incompatibility of Jesus' principles, which he admired, with the state, which he loathed. His understanding of Christianity was deeply rationalistic: for him, Jesus was simply 'the highest representative of [humanity's] wisdom' (2001: 507) — what he taught was actually confirmed by reason, and superstitions like the Resurrection were all fantastic stories added later by elites whose interest was to distort the essential teachings of Christianity (1902; 1934 [*Church and State; A Reply to the Synod's Edict of Excommunication, and to Letters Received by Me Concerning It*]). A critical discussion of this understanding of Christianity, however interesting, is too big a subject for this paper. The contention to note here is that for Tolstoy the essence of Jesus' rational teaching is to be found in the Sermon on the Mount, where Jesus supersedes Old Testament law with his new commandments not to be angry, not to judge, not to swear oaths, to love one's enemy, and in particular not to resist evil but to turn the other cheek (Tolstoy, 1902). Even when nominally 'Christian', Tolstoy argues, the state breaks all these guidelines. The comparison with Jesus' standards is often made in the same breath as the more 'empirical' description of the state. Together, they combine to form a moving condemnation of the modern state. Some of the power of Tolstoy's writing rests precisely in the contrast between the reality of officially Christian statehood and the Christian ideal. So although the specific aim of this paper is to present Tolstoy's critique of the state without considering his alternative, references to Jesus and Christianity have been kept to preserve all its intensity.

II

State Violence

The main lesson Tolstoy learnt from his rediscovery of Christianity at an advanced age was that violence is never justifiable, because it always causes more violence further down the line (Kennan, 1887; Tolstoy, 1987 [*The Law of Love and the Law of Violence*]). It is therefore not surprising that his criticisms of the state focus on various aspects of state violence.

Law

In *The Slavery of Our Times*, Tolstoy declares that 'the essence of slavery lies ... in the fact that legislation exists—that there are people who have power to decree laws profitable for themselves' (1948: 108). The one characteristic of all laws is that their enforcement is based on the threat of punishment: if one man does not fulfil them, 'those who have made these laws will send armed men, and the armed men will beat, deprive of freedom, or even kill, the man who does not obey the law' (110).[3] Violence or the threat of it is critical to the enforcement of law, and for Tolstoy self-evidently a sign of enslavement: 'being compelled to do what other people wish, against your own will, is slavery' (120). As long as violence is used to compel people to obey a law against their will, there will be slavery.

The problem, Tolstoy argues, lies in the combination of law with social pluralism. Every state action is considered good by some and pernicious by others—in other words, there are always disagreements about state action. As long as there are some people who disagree with any given state action, with any given law, all state activity eventually requires violence to be enforced (n.d.: 148). Thus all state activity logically results in slavery. The very existence of the state is inescapably bound to violence and slavery.

Tolstoy furthermore rejects the idea that laws reflect the will of the whole people since, he says, those who wish to break these laws are always more numerous than those who wish to obey them (1948: 109–10).[4] More to the point, if laws expressed the will of the people, violence would not be necessary to enforce them. In fact, Tolstoy insists,

---

3   At this point, it is worth admitting that Tolstoy's language is clearly male-centric: he always speaks of 'men', never—or very rarely—of 'women'. Given the stated aim here of frequently quoting Tolstoy's own words to convey his poignant voice, this unfortunate bias cannot but be regretfully reflected in this paper.

4   This argument is, admittedly, rather questionable; but Tolstoy's point is that since laws are made by the affluent minority against the interests of the poor majority, a majority of people are bound to disagree with such unfair legislation—such laws certainly do not represent their will.

> everyone knows that not in despotic countries only, but also in the countries nominally most free—England, America, France, and others—the laws are made not by the will of all, but by the will of those who have power, and therefore always and everywhere are such as are profitable to those who have power: be they many, or few, or only one man (111).

Tolstoy thus rejects the standard case for preferring representative democracy to authoritarianism. In an anonymous epigraph to one of Tolstoy's chapters, the tone of which suggests it was actually written by himself, one can read:

> When among one hundred men, one rules over ninety-nine, it is unjust, it is a despotism; when ten rule over ninety, it is equally unjust, it is an oligarchy; but when fifty-one rule over forty-nine (and this is only theoretical, for in reality it is always ten or eleven of these fifty-one), it is entirely just, it is freedom! Could there be anything funnier, in its manifest absurdity, than such reasoning? And yet it is this very reasoning that serves as the basis for all reformers of the political structure (1987: 165).

According to Tolstoy, the idea that the rule of the majority is somehow an embodiment of 'justice', of 'freedom', is utterly ridiculous. Democratic or not, '[l]aws are rules, made by people who govern by means of organised violence for non-compliance with which the non-complier is subjected to blows, to loss of liberty, or even to being murdered' (1948: 112). Laws are written by those in power, in line with their own interests; and since they require violence to be enforced, they amount *de facto* to slavery.

Tolstoy also addresses the argument that people need to be guided, that they need to be taught how to live in a way that ensures the well-being of the entire community. Fine in principle, he says, but what proof is there that those legislators 'are wiser than those on whom they inflict violence?'. Actually, he continues, '[t]he fact that they allow themselves to use violence towards human beings, indicates that they are not more, but less wise than those who submit to them' (118). A violent guide is neither wise nor rational. As another anonymous epigraph to one of his chapters reads: 'Why does man have reason if he can only be influenced by violence?' (1987: 161). For Tolstoy, reason and violence are mutually exclusive:

> One of two things: either people are rational beings or they are irrational beings. If they are irrational beings, then they are all irrational, and then everything among them is decided by violence, and there is no reason why certain people should, and others should not, have a *right* to use violence. In that case, governmental violence has no justification. But if men are rational beings, then their relations should be based on reason, and not on the violence of those who happen to have seized power. In that case, again, governmental violence has no justification (1948: 119; Tolstoy's emphasis).

For Tolstoy, no government can rationally justify the use of violence to educate the population. Social order is maintained either by reason or by violence.

In the last years of his life, while Tsarist Russia was in increasing political turmoil, Tolstoy wrote a pamphlet (*I Cannot Be Silent*) in which he insisted that both the government and the revolutionaries were equally immoral in their use of violence to justify their aims (1937). But, he noted, revolutionaries only acted as the government taught them to. They were 'educated' by a violent state under enslaving laws, so their violent conduct was like that of a misbehaved child mimicking unruly parents. Yet just as the child's behaviour is understandable, Tolstoy argued, the revolutionary policy was at least coherent: unlike the government, revolutionaries did not pretend to be Christians but repudiated all religion; unlike the government, their actions were consistent with their proclaimed philosophy (1937: 404–9).

In short, Tolstoy considered all laws to amount to violence and thus slavery, be they passed by democratic or by despotic governments. By their very nature, these laws cannot educate — they can only exhaust reason. And their purpose is none other than the economic exploitation of the populace.

Economic slavery

As Terry Hopton remarks, for Tolstoy exploitation is a product of the economic system just as violence is a product of the state system; but economic exploitation *is* in fact violence, only a form of violence that is 'more subtle and more pervasive' precisely because it is less obvious than yet equally restraining as direct physical violence (Hopton, 2000: 39). Tolstoy argues that the state uses its legitimized monopoly of violence against its own poorer citizens in order to maintain the wealth of the privileged. Throughout his writings, he describes several instances of such economic exploitation that he himself witnessed, and then uses these cases as starting points for his ensuing reflections on the ills of state power (for instance, n.d.: 1–10; 1948: 67–72; 2001: 307–407).

Tolstoy argued that all states were exploitative no matter how they were constituted: authoritarian Russia was using more visible methods than liberal regimes, but that was the only difference. In fact, his critique could easily be adapted by those who, today, see capitalism as slavery disguised as benevolent investment. The following cynical statement, for example, has hardly lost any of its potency in the twenty-first century:

> If the slave-owner of our time has not slave John, whom he can send to the cess-pool to clear out his excrements, he has five shillings of which hundreds of Johns are in such need that the slave-owner of our times

may choose anyone out of hundreds of Johns and be a benefactor to him by giving him the preference, and allowing him, rather than another, to climb down into the cess-pool (1948: 95).

Although modern slavery is not as explicit and visible as it was in pre-emancipation America, it is slavery nonetheless. In fact, economic slavery is even worse than the slavery described in history books, because it is veiled under the illusion of free choice, and is considered natural, even beneficial. The slave owner of today is not the wealthy colonist anymore, but the benevolent business owner, the shareholder. Indeed, the poorer members of any (local or, today, global) community face little choice: 'for a bare subsistence, people, considering themselves freemen, [think] it necessary to give themselves up to work such as, in the days of serfdom, not one slave owner, however cruel, would have sent his slaves to' (71). Just to get bread on their table, poor employees are obliged to put up with humiliating working conditions. The economic model championed by the enlightened state and protected by its laws ensures that 'one way or the other, the labourer is always in slavery to those who control the taxes, the land, and the articles necessary to satisfy his requirements' (100). Today's labourer is no better than yesterday's slave, and the state system ensures that things remain that way.

Why, other than to protect the wealthy, would laws (hence violence) need to be invoked, for instance, to defend the private ownership of land? Only large swathes of misused land, of stolen property, need to be protected by aggressive legislation. For Tolstoy, '[t]hings really produced by a man's own labour, and that he needs, are always protected by custom, by public opinion, by feelings of justice and reciprocity, and they do not need to be protected by violence'; but '[t]ens of thousands of acres of forest lands belonging to one proprietor, while thousands of people close by have no fuel, need protection by violence' (117). Laws on private property only protect those who should not own what they have appropriated for themselves. Laws protect the wealthy.

Throughout history, new excuses have constantly been sought to justify the uneven distribution of the burden of labour across society. Thus '[i]n olden times, men who utilized the labor of others asserted, first, that they belonged to a different race; and secondly, that they had from God a peculiar mission,—caring for the welfare of others; in other words, to govern and teach them' (n.d.: 143). The justification was biological and theological. But over time, this justification gradually lost its ground. So, Tolstoy submits, new excuses had to be devised, and this time 'science' provided the explanation (141-7).

This new justification for the 'idleness of all so-called educated people' (and the concomitant slavery inflicted upon the rest of the population), according to Tolstoy, runs like this: 'We men who have freed ourselves from the common human duty of taking part in the struggle for existence, are furthering progress, and so we are of great use to all human society, of such use that it counterbalances all the harm we do to the people by consuming their labor' (145). In other words, this apparently uneven division of labour is the best possible distribution to ensure the progress of society as a whole. Society is like a natural organism, with different members performing different functions, so the current distribution of labour is the most natural to reach — it is the natural equilibrium of a healthy, organic society (153–71).

Of course, for Tolstoy, this 'scientific' justification for an unjust economic system is, quite simply, another cunning lie concocted by those who benefit from it. For a start, this theory is not drawn from 'the natural properties of human societies', but merely from a 'particular case' (76). That a society must reach such uneven division of labour is not a universal truth, but only what happens under specific circumstances. And the defining feature of these circumstances is the presence of a privileged minority in charge of a powerful state that defines the rules by which the majority is to live, and that uses force to ensure compliance with these rules.

Under these conditions no division of labour can be described as 'natural'. If the division of tasks happens by itself, guided by reason and conscience, then this division of labour is a right one; but as soon as any form of coercion distorts the workforce's choices, then the result is 'usurpation of other men's labor', which is far from natural or just (173). Tolstoy accepts that there has always been a division of labour, but it is what guides it that defines whether or not it is acceptable. If guided by reason and conscience, by the free and rational choice of workers, then the division is just; but if distorted by violence, then it cannot be right (176–80).

And it is no good to declare that this division of labour allows science to flourish or humanity to progress because new technology multiplies the poor workers' plight at least as much as it allegedly relieves it: 'Though a workingman, instead of walking, can use the railway, it is this very railway which has caused his forest to be burned, and has carried away his bread from under his very nose, and put him into a condition which is next door to slavery to the railway proprietor' (183–4). The new knowledge and technologies made available by science are much more accessible to the wealthy few than to the enslaved workforce, which means that it is the privileged slave owners, rather than the slaves, that stand to gain the most from 'scientific progress'.

So those who invoke sociological laws to justify their comfortable position in the current economic system are just fortunate liars. They may say '[i]t is not we who have done all this; it has been done of itself; as children say when they break any thing, that it broke itself. ... But that is not true' (133). One need only watch the lifestyle of these people and realize that they are not innocent. They like to think that their prosperous lifestyle has no connection with the economic and political violence perpetrated by the state,

> [t]hey like to believe that their privileges exist of themselves, and result from voluntary agreement among people, and that the violence enacted also exists of itself, and results from some general, higher juridical, political, or economic laws. They try not to see that they enjoy their advantages as a result of the very thing which forces the peasants who have tended the wood and are of great need of the timber to yield it up to a wealthy landowner, who took no part in tending it during its growth and is in no need of it — that is, the knowledge that if they do no give it up they will be flogged or killed (2001: 315–6).

But it is not so. Even if they try to hide from the truth and do their best to forget it, these wealthy few and the state system they grandiloquently defend are responsible for the economic exploitation of the masses (315–8).

A violent machine with violent elites

In sum, because it instigates wars against its neighbours, because it imposes laws upon its people, and because it exploits its workforce, the state is a vicious, brutal and pernicious machine. The state kills, steals and enslaves. Hence

> [a]ll that well-being of the people which we see in so-called well-governed States, ruled by violence, is but an appearance, a fiction. Everything that would disturb the external appearance of well-being, all the hungry people, the sick, the revoltingly vicious, all are hidden away where they cannot be seen (Tolstoy, 1948: 113–4).

Even if it tries its best to appear holy, the state structure is a malicious system that transgresses all that Jesus' rational teaching stands for.

The state, therefore, is an organization that 'resembles a cone of which all the parts are completely in the power of those people, or that one person, who happens to be at the apex', an apex which 'is seized by those who are more cunning, audacious, and unscrupulous than the rest' (2001: 516). So even in a 'democracy', one must not be deluded into thinking that the rulers are honest 'representatives of the aggregate of citizens', because all they are is 'a set of men who do violence to others' (162). Democratic or not, the leaders of a state can only be bullies: 'To seize power and retain it, it is necessary to love power', but love of power comes with 'pride, cunning, and cruelty' (164). Because of the very structure of the state, to reach its apex, one needs characteristics that come with immorality and viciousness.

In any case, assuming that good persons could reach this apex, they would quickly be corrupted since the state's mechanisms require the transgression of the most basic principle of morality:

> All men in power assert that their authority is necessary to keep bad men from doing violence to the good, thus assuming that they themselves are the good who protect others from the bad. But ruling means using force, and using force means doing what the man subjected to violence does not wish done, and to which the perpetrator would certainly object if the violence were applied to himself. Therefore to rule means to do to others what we would not have done to ourselves — that is, doing wrong (265).

Hence only the wicked can ever be rulers. No good person can ever head a state. In other words, by the very nature of the state, '[t]he evil always domineer over the good and inflict violence on them' (267; emphasis removed).

The state's existence is being justified on the grounds that it prevents violence and injustice, yet it brings about violence and injustice itself. Tolstoy borrows a comparison made by Eugen Schmitt: '[G]overnments, justifying their existence on the ground that they ensure a certain kind of safety to their subjects, are like the Calabrian robber-chief who collected a regular tax from all who wished to travel in safety along the highways' (Tolstoy, 1948: 124-5). The state sells itself to its subjects by proposing to keep them safe, yet the only real threat to their security comes from the state itself — and sure enough, if the subjects do not pay and obey, various laws ensure that their safety is indeed at risk. Moreover, the system is very cunning: once established, the state (like the Calabrian robber chief) can easily maintain itself, as taxes are collected by troops which are maintained by means of these very taxes (n.d.: 106).

The state justifies its existence to curb internal dissent and violence, but in the process grants itself a monopoly of violence that, in this case, is unchecked by any moderator — so it freely uses and misuses its supremacy, and thereby behaves exactly like the villain it is supposed to eradicate, only on a much broader scale (2001: 186-7). But coercion can only work while the other is weaker; one day the weak will grow strong and retaliate by using the same brutal techniques that had kept them in check (Kennan, 1887; Tolstoy, 2001: 269). In other words, state violence breeds more violence, and the ensuing vicious cycle brings society further and further away from Jesus' teaching.

In sum, for Tolstoy, a state cannot but be violent and must therefore be un-Christian and irrational. Christian states do not escape this verdict: all the states that have allegedly adopted Christianity have forced both their own peoples as well as neighbouring ones to act against their will (1987: 158–60). Because of its very structure and because those who lead it cannot be anything but immoral and self-interested, the state is necessarily violent and domineering.

III

Organized Deception

Over and above its inherent violence, Tolstoy fiercely denounces another key characteristic of the state: its structure of deception.[5] This section examines Tolstoy's understanding of deception and the ways in which it becomes manifest in the state.

Hypocrisy of state authorities

Since for Tolstoy the cause of state violence lies in the very existence of the state, war, for instance, cannot be eradicated by peace conferences and alliances — for the scourge of war to disappear, the state itself must disappear. To pretend that international treaties and alliances can eradicate war, Tolstoy says, is sheer hypocrisy.

Who would enforce such treaties anyway (1937: 222–7; 2001: 160)? Other states using their armies? How would that be different from war? Peace treaties are based on cooperation between existing states, but, according to Tolstoy, it is the very existence of these states that causes wars in the first place (Brock, 1972: 460). Besides, these treaties are never honestly lived up to: soon enough, state leaders always find a way to argue that this or that war does not actually contravene this or that international treaty (Tolstoy, 1937: 226–7). They sign treaties with the stated aim of ensuring peace, but months later argue that this or that new danger faced by their people is an exception to the treaty and must be dealt with using the tools of war (2001: 512–5).

As to bilateral alliances to allegedly guarantee peace, they are blatantly alliances for war. Tolstoy devoted a whole essay to the 1893 celebrations for the then recent Franco-Russian alliance, warning that although state leaders pretended that this alliance was a peaceful one, it was in fact a clear declaration of warlike intentions against Germany. Why else would millions

---

5 Thus the two main lines of criticism articulated by Tolstoy — of state violence and deception — reflect the two forms of anarchist criticism of government highlighted by Kinna (2005: 46).

continue to be spent on the military, and why else would the military advantage of this alliance be stressed by the press (2001: 442–5, 512–5)? These alliances are agreed precisely because of their military advantage; they are clearly geared towards future wars.

But the hypocrisy of state authorities and associated elites does not apply only to the international sphere. Whether on war or on more domestic concerns such as economic slavery, they only propose amendments to current arrangements that do not deprive them of their privileges (1948: 91; 2001: 237). They defend the feebleness of the changes they introduce with the need to preserve 'culture' or 'civilisation' (1948: 91–4; 2001: 398). The current state and its economic system, they say, is what brought about 'culture', so we must guard against introducing too radical a change lest it destroy this unique cultural heritage. But a culture that is the product of violence rather than reason and which results in oppression is not one that Tolstoy is prepared to preserve and defend.

Affluent elites will also invoke 'iron laws', such as the natural division of labour mentioned above, to claim that things *cannot* be changed substantially anyway. Some will rely on the theological justification, inspired by official Christianity, which states that people have different destinies; others will point to the Hegelian idea that the state is a historical necessity; others still will put forward the scientific view whereby society is like a biological organism — but they will all hide behind some false theory to explain why they do not realize the only change that would really improve the condition of the people: the abolition of the state and the honest implementation of Jesus' rational teaching (n.d.: 206–23).

None of these 'iron laws', Tolstoy argues, are immutable. Instead, the current conditions of society 'merely result from human laws concerning taxes, land, and above all, ... concerning property'. Thus 'it is not some sociological "iron" law, but ordinary man-made law, that produces slavery' (1948: 101). Man-made laws are written precisely to enslave the people, and the claim that their plight cannot be radically improved is just another hypocritical statement by the elites to defend the status quo.

Clearly, then, the authorities do not live by the Christian values that they profess. Christianity proclaims the equality of men, yet these elites are busy justifying the unequal system that they happen to benefit from (n.d.: 141–7). Moreover, their hypocrisy 'corrupts, embitters, and brutalizes people' because it 'wipes out in men's consciousness the difference between good and evil and thereby debars them from avoiding evil and seeking good, depriving them of the very essence of true human life and therefore blocking the path to all improvement' (2001: 378).

The irresponsible lifestyle daringly enacted by the upper class in the name of Christianity corrupts the consciousness of those that look up to it. 'Instead of changing their way of life' and becoming shining beacons of Jesus' sensible teaching, these elites 'try by all means to stifle and deaden consciousness' (181). The pinnacle of their hypocrisy is finally reached when, having thus brutalized people, they 'then produce these same people ... to prove that it is impossible to deal with people except by brutal violence!' (287). This completes the self-fulfilling logic of the elites' hypocrisy.

Evasion of responsibility

As already mentioned, economic and political elites shrug their shoulders at the exploitation of the masses, as if there was no other choice. They actually believe their own lies about this being the result of unalterable laws (Tolstoy, 1948: 72–7). Tolstoy in fact suggests that 'people of the well-to-do classes, believe this because they *must* believe it' (85; emphasis added). That is, either they must realize that their whole way of life is based on robbery and murder, and that they are 'very dishonourable men; or they must believe that all that takes place, takes place for the general advantage, in accord with unalterable laws of economic science' (85–6). Consciously or unconsciously, they shut their eyes to their true responsibility and blame external iron laws; they must believe that they are not at fault, because otherwise, surely, they would stop.

Furthermore, the state system is so arranged that it becomes easy to think that somebody else is responsible for state violence. Hopton explains how each individual unit shifts responsibility either higher up or lower down the system (2000: 37). Tolstoy's own words deserve to be reproduced here:

> At the bottom of the social ladder soldiers with rifles, revolvers, and swords, torture and murder men and by those means compel them to become soldiers. And these soldiers are fully convinced that the responsibility for their deed is taken from them by the officers who order those actions. At the top of the ladder the Tsars, presidents, and ministers, decree these tortures and murders and conscriptions. And they are fully convinced that since they are either placed in authority by God, or the society they rule over demands such decrees from them, they cannot be held responsible. Between these extremes are the intermediate folk who superintend the acts of violence and the murders and the conscriptions of the soldiers. And these, too, are fully convinced that they are relieved of all responsibility, partly because of orders received by them from their superiors, and partly because such orders are expected from them by those on the lower steps of the ladder (2001: 351).

At each rung of the ladder, men think they are merely fulfilling their 'duty', they are just doing the job they were appointed to do (320, 352–8). Some are bound by oaths of allegiance, others are just honouring their professional function—but they are certainly not answerable for the cruel deeds committed by the state as a whole.

As a result, the moral responsibility that men are built to feel is diluted in the system. Tolstoy explains:

> Not a single judge will consent to strangle with a rope the man whom he has condemned to death in his court. No one of higher rank will consent to snatch a peasant from his weeping family and shut him up in prison. ... These things are due to that complicated machinery of Society and the State, which makes it its first business to destroy the feeling of responsibility for such deeds, so that no man shall feel them to be as unnatural as they are. Some make laws, others apply them. Others again train men and educate them in the habit of discipline, in the habit, that is to say, of senseless and irresponsible obedience. Again others, and these are the best trained of all, practise every kind of violence, even to the slaying of men, without the slightest knowledge of the why and wherefore. We need only clear our mind for an instant from the network of human institutions in which we are thus entangled, to feel how adverse it is to our true nature (1902: 46–7).

This subdivision of tasks is the only explanation for why men collectively commit such barbarous acts. They lose sight of the fact that their own contribution is at least partly morally responsible, along with the contribution of all the other individual units in the complex machinery, for the violence they inflict upon others (2001: 349).

Thus all the units of the state system are hypnotized into feeling they have special duties (358). They forget that they are just men, equal to other men, and instead

> represent themselves to others as being ... some special conventional beings: noblemen, merchants, governors, judges, officers, Tsars, ministers, or soldiers, not subject to ordinary human duties but to aristocratic, commercial, governatorial, judicial, military, royal, or ministerial, obligations (354).

They are intoxicated by their social function and overlook their most basic moral responsibilities as human beings.

Even the ruling classes hypnotize themselves to some extent (360). Still, consciously or unconsciously, they are the ones who perpetuate the system: Tolstoy believes that the subdivision of tasks that alleviates any feeling of responsibility for a public execution 'is carefully arranged and planned by learned and enlightened people of the upper class' (1937: 396). To some extent, state authorities are hypnotized just like everybody else; but as the men lucky enough to get an education, as the men formally in charge of the state machinery, they also ensure that the various tasks of any act of state violence remain cleverly subdivided so as to alleviate anybody's potential feeling of responsibility. And of course, when the church (with its alleged moral aura) then comes in and approves of public executions, people are led to believe that it is not such an immoral or evil thing after all (399–402).[6]

So the complex machinery of the state, supported as it is by the church, ensures that nobody takes moral responsibility for the immoral acts committed in the name of the state (or Jesus). People blame immutable laws for the social ills they do nothing to improve; and they shift responsibility for acts of state violence either above themselves, to those who formally ordered them, or below, to those who asked for these orders to be sent, or to those who will actually commit the dirty work for them. The result is moral depravity on a collective scale. Hence Tolstoy's quotation from Kant: 'We live in an age of discipline, ... but it is still far from being a moral age' (in Tolstoy, 1987: 211). Morality is sacrificed for discipline; it is diluted in the state machinery.

IV

The Contemporary Relevance of Tolstoy's Critique

What, then, does Tolstoy's thought tell us? His recurring theme is that, democratic or not, the state is a prison that humanity must break out of, but this can only happen if the violence and deception that it is guilty of is exposed. Tolstoy was not comfortable with being called an anarchist because the violence that was then routinely associated with the term was contrary to the non-violence that formed the basis of his own condemnation of the state. Yet this condemnation and his hopes for a stateless society make him an important figure in the broad and eclectic pantheon of anarchist thinkers (Hopton, 2000). Besides, he found it curious that people 'are afraid of anarchists' bombs, and are not afraid of this terrible organization which is always threatening them with the greatest calamities' (Tolstoy, 2001: 517) — they fear exceptional and sporadic bombs but not permanent oppression by the state.

Even though he was active a hundred years ago, Tolstoy's accusations of state violence continue to be (almost self-evidently) relevant today.[7]

---

6 Tolstoy's extensive criticisms of the church constitute too big a topic for this chapter — suffice to note here that he was just as critical of the church as of the state, and that in fact he considered them accomplices in each other's depravity.

7 Equally relevant today is his call for humanity to forego once and for all the use of violent means to try to achieve however laudable ends (a view that obviously defines Tolstoy's position in the

Laws still lead to violence in the sense that Tolstoy described. Economic exploitation has now spread to a global scale — which if anything makes the hiding away of what disturbs any external appearance of harmony even easier. And power is still said to corrupt even the initially most promising political leaders.

As to the state's structure of deception, again, little seems to have changed. The United Nations was created to eradicate war, and yet great powers still seek, hypocritically, either to use its mechanisms to legitimize their next war or to bypass these mechanisms altogether. Domestically, too, leaders shy away from truly radical reform by claiming that private property or the division of labour are fundamental tenets of any sound political economy. Units within the state system continue to evade responsibility for state violence: police officers using the full force of the law on demonstrators will say they followed orders, the legislators who passed the initial law will say they were just representing the views of their constituency, and those in between will similarly argue they are just fulfilling their duty.

Therefore, even if Tolstoy passed away long ago, his critique of the state as violent and deceptive continues to resonate in the twenty-first century, despite several waves of democratization. Indeed, his criticisms are just as pertinent to democratic states as to more obviously dictatorial ones. This paper has sought to analyze Tolstoy's anarchist critique thematically to introduce him to new readers and to invite further readings of his work. If his assessment of the state is even partly right, then his call to humanity to shake itself out of its self-inflicted hypnosis and live in love and forgiveness — which he saw as the only possible solution to all this violence and deception — might be considered anew.

References

Brock, P. (1972), *Pacifism in Europe to 1914* (Princeton: Princeton University Press).

Christoyannopoulos, A.J.M.E. (2008a), 'Leo Tolstoy on the state: a detailed picture of Tolstoy's denunciation of state violence and deception', *Anarchist Studies*, 16 (1): 20-47.

Christoyannopoulos, A.J.M.E. (2008b), 'Turning the other cheek to terrorism: reflections on the contemporary significance of Leo Tolstoy's exegesis of the Sermon on the Mount', *Politics and Religion*, 1 (1): 27-54.

Guseinov, A.A. (1999), 'Faith, God, and nonviolence in the teachings of Lev Tolstoy', *Russian Studies in Philosophy*, 38 (2): 89-103.

Hopton, T. (2000), 'Tolstoy, God and anarchism', *Anarchist Studies*, 8 (1): 27-52.

Kennan, G. (1887), 'A visit to count Tolstoi', *The Century Magazine*, 34 (2): 252-65.

---

everlasting debate among anarchists over the use of violence). This particular call and its relevance to the 'war on terrorism' is discussed elsewhere (Christoyannopoulos, 2008b).

Kinna, R. (2005), *Anarchism: a beginner's guide* (Oxford: Oneworld).

Marshall, P. (1993), *Demanding the impossible: a history of anarchism* (London: Fontana Press).

Stephens, D. (1990), 'The non-violent anarchism of Leo Tolstoy', in *Government is violence: essays on anarchism and pacifism*, ed. D. Stephens (London: Phoenix).

Tolstoï, L.N. (n.d.), *What to do?*, trans. I.F. Hapgood (London: Walter Scott).

Tolstoy, L. (1902), *What I believe*, trans. F. Mayo (London: C.W. Daniel).

Tolstoy, L. (1934), *On life and essays on religion*, trans. A. Maude (London: Oxford University Press).

Tolstoy, L. (1937), *Recollections and essays*, trans. A. Maude (London: Oxford University Press).

Tolstoy, L. (1948), *Essays from Tula*, trans. E. Lampert (London: Sheppard).

Tolstoy, L. (1987), *A confession and other religious writings*, trans. J. Kentish (London: Penguin).

Tolstoy, L. (2001), *The kingdom of God and peace essays*, trans. A. Maude (New Delhi: Rupa).

Woodcock, G. (1975), *Anarchism: a history of libertarian ideas and movements* (Harmondsworth: Penguin).

Thomas Crombez

'The Sovereign Disappears in the Voting Booth'
Carl Schmitt and Martin Heidegger on Sovereignty and (Perhaps) Governmentality

I

Introduction[1]

There is no text that stands in greater contrast to the exalted and intoxicating declarations of support by German philosophers to the National Socialist revolution during the early 1930s than Bertolt Brecht's play of 1941, *Der aufhaltsame Aufstieg des Arturo Ui* (*The Resistible Rise of Arturo Ui*). Still, Brecht's blunt portrayal of the leading Nazi personalities as gangsters and 'super clowns' makes it possible to point out a distinctive loophole in the philosophers' eulogies. It concerns their use of the concept of sovereignty, exemplified by the Führer and the unified will of the German people. When the ghost of Ernesto Roma (Ernst Röhm) appears to his murderer, Arturo Ui (Adolf Hitler), he tells him that, while he may 'trample the city with a hundred feet', he should be careful to 'trample not the feet' (Brecht, 2002: 92 [scene 14]). As it had become clear after the 'Night of the Long Knives', or so-called Röhm Putsch (June 30 to July 2, 1934), the National Socialist regime conceived of itself as fully self-sufficient, able to deploy its supporters at will but also to withdraw and even exterminate them. Absolute sovereignty is not a giant with feet of clay, but a giant that claims to stand without feet.

---

[1] An earlier version of this paper was published in *Pli: The Warwick Journal of Philosophy* (Crombez, 2006).

The aim of this paper is to show how sovereignty and its self-referential paradox are at work not only in National Socialist politics, but also in the philosophizing of some of its major proponents. The concept of sovereignty is strongly embedded in the early modern context that gives rise to it (e.g. in Machiavelli, Jean Bodin, or Thomas Hobbes). During this period, according to Quentin Skinner, the modern idea of the state emerges. It is an abstract form of public power, 'separate from both the ruler and the ruled' (1978: II/353). However, the great increase in centralized power could still be perceived as flowing towards a single personified instance of rulership, the monarch. Christopher Pye and Louis Montrose have therefore drawn attention to the peculiarity of sovereignty to the early modern epoch: 'At this historical juncture, the body politic inhered in the body of the prince' (Montrose, 1986: 307; Pye, 1990: 3). Later thinkers such as Jean-Jacques Rousseau or John Austin had great difficulties changing the concept into the (inherently problematic) notion of 'popular sovereignty'. It is striking that, faced with the development of Fascism, a number of philosophers tried to retrieve the early modern notion of sovereignty. Although this paper will deal chiefly with German philosophers supporting the National Socialist government, or at least feeling strongly related to the Nazi revolution of 1933, it should be pointed out that Georges Bataille, for example, first developed his notions of sovereignty and sovereign man in the 1933 essay *La structure psychologique du fascisme* (*The Psychological Structure of Fascism*).

In order to reveal and analyze sovereignty, Michel Foucault's distinction between the logic of sovereignty and the logic of governmentality will be used. His definition of sovereignty is strongly present in Carl Schmitt's writings, but also makes a surprising apparition in Martin Heidegger's texts of the early 1930s, where we may distinguish three figures of sovereignty. They will serve as evidence when checking if Slavoj Žižek's notion of ultra-politics, which is so relevant to Schmitt's conception of sovereignty and 'politics' in general, also applies to Heidegger's perspective. Once it is established that the radicalization of the logic of sovereignty is typical for Schmitt, Heidegger, and other philosophers and ideologues of the same epoch, it will be suggested that this radicalization might stem from a failure to recognize the workings of governmentality.

II

The Logic of Sovereignty under National Socialism

In his speech to the Reichstag on July 13, 1934, Hitler himself elaborately illustrated how the self-referential paradox of sovereignty suffused the mechanics of the National Socialist revolution. The murderous campaign against the alleged Röhm Putsch is defended on the grounds of a budding conspiracy by the SA's top echelon, supported by two generals of the Reichswehr, that was to result in a new *coup d'État*. Hitler carefully has to distinguish these renegade 'revolutionaries', his former brothers in arms, from the true National Socialist 'revolutionaries' who have seized power just one and a half years before. His rhetorical strategy is based on the Fallen Angel narrative. Röhm and his co-conspirators 'have become Revolutionaries who worship Revolution as Revolution and wish to see in it a permanent condition'. They are restless, violent fanatics who do not understand that the revolutionary state of emergency is valid no longer, and hence 'have lost all inner relation to the human order of society' (in Fest, 1970: ch. 2.6).

By turning Röhm into some kind of Lucifer, the Chancellor implicitly paints a picture of himself as a divine angel of retribution. As was already clear to his contemporaries, this meant a radical departure from modern political thought, since the executive power was made to coincide seamlessly with the judicial power: 'In this hour, I was responsible for the fate of the German nation, and therefore I became the supreme judge of the German people!' (in Fest, 1970: ch. 2.6).[2] What was left unsaid, however, is that this concept of leadership unifying all state powers implied a reactivation of the feudal notion of sovereignty, which was not to be fully developed until the early modern period, with Bodin's *Les six livres de la République* (*Six Books of the Commonwealth*) in 1576 and Hobbes' *Leviathan* in 1651. Foucault, in his 1976 lectures at the Collège de France entitled *Il faut défendre la société* (*Society Must Be Defended*), defined sovereignty as relating to territory (2003). Its chief objective, as elaborated in 1978 in *La 'Gouvernmentalité'*, is how to maintain and expand this territory, in relation to which it occupies a position that may be marked as singular, external and transcendent (1994: III/638–9). It is a power that is not primarily interested in the land itself or the people inhabiting it. This other kind of power, which Foucault terms 'governmental', develops only during the early modern period. The logic of governmentality is concerned with the governance of the bodies of those who inhabit the territory. Foucault identified this as the rise of biopolitics.

---

2   'In dieser Stunde war ich verantwortlich für das Schicksal der deutschen Nation und damit des deutschen Volkes oberster Gerichtsherr!' (Domarus, 1973: I/421)

To clarify the difference between the workings of sovereignty and governmentality, consider the case of an epidemic.[3] The appropriate reaction for a ruler under the logic of sovereignty (for example, the medieval remedy against the plague) is to determine which individuals are diseased and which ones are healthy, and then to expel the diseased. Under the logic of governmentality, on the other hand, the diseased are not excluded by the governing instance, but included. During the modern period, the medieval remedy was gradually abandoned. An inflicted city was instead partitioned into districts that were placed under the authority of certain supervisors, who became responsible for the control of every person living in a district. Disease was no longer expelled, but controlled and contained. At first, governmentality takes on the form of disciplinary logic (surveillance and control), but later on its scope vastly widened. During the eighteenth and nineteenth centuries, it is no longer just particular bodies that are checked, but a series of statistic variables describing all bodies and what they produce: mortality and natality, disease rates, fertility, productivity, etc. If bodies may be said to be disciplined during the first stage of governmentality's development, it is the aim of its second stage to regulate the variables defining a population (Foucault, 2003: 246–7). Both stages together produce a thorough 'normalization' of the social body.

During the last lecture of the 1976 course, Foucault gave a rough sketch of how totalitarian regimes could be described in terms of sovereignty and governmentality. Nazi society 'has generalized biopower in an absolute sense, but [it] has also generalized the sovereign right to kill'. Nazism makes the logics of both sovereignty and governmentality coincide. However, Foucault only focused on the 'thanatopolitics' of both the Final Solution and Hitler's last order for the destruction of the German people's living conditions. He described the appearance of 'an absolutely racist State, an absolutely murderous State, and an absolutely suicidal State' (2003: 260). He does not apply his distinction to the genesis of the Nazi state from the 1933 revolution onwards, nor to its peculiar organizational structure, its definition of leadership, or its ideology.

Is it possible to describe Hitler as a sovereign agent? Although from 1933 onwards he is consequently referred to as the German people's supreme and most able leader, this does not make him a particular 'sovereign' figure. As has been argued by thinkers such as Claude Lefort and Alvin Gouldner, the typically monarchic notion of rulership disappeared gradually from the democratic revolutions of the eighteenth century

---

3   Foucault gave this example in his lectures entitled *Les anormaux* (1999: 41 ff), and subsequently in *Surveillir et punir: naissance de la prison* (1975: ch. 3).

onwards (Lefort, 1988; Gouldner, 1950).[4] It was not replaced. Democracy indeed led to the emergence of leadership, but this was a wholly new and different concept. Hitler, as a modern leader, is not at all like the external and transcendent monarchs. On the contrary, he embodies the German nation. He lived their experiences (the trench warfare of 1914–18, the uncertainties of the post-war crisis), he shares their hopes and desires, and he is the upholder of their culture. He is certainly not an absolutely heterogeneous figure vis-à-vis the German nation, but, on the contrary, its ideal citizen, a *primus inter pares*.

Although sovereignty is definitely not reanimated by Hitler's Chancellorship, it is impossible to ignore how the concept is partially reactivated. Some important aspects of Nazi Germany's organization and propaganda may only be properly understood within the framework of sovereignty made absolute. When Hitler declares judiciary power to coincide with executive power, he is providing a textbook example of what Foucault designated as the circularity of sovereignty (Foucault, 1994: III/645–6). In the sixteenth century, jurists and philosophers had argued that the sovereign aimed for the common good. Therefore, the common good is equated with obedience to his laws. The philosophical elaboration of sovereignty boils down to a hidden tautology. The very word 'sovereignty' expresses being superior to others (from Middle French *suverain*, deriving from Latin *super*). There is little intellectual achievement in defining the superiority of one as the inferiority of the others. The only gain is that one has identified the particular form that domination by a sovereign instance takes. Sovereignty conceives governance as giving law, from an external position, to the inhabitants of its territory. Governmentality, on the other hand, governs by means of (mainly internalized) norms. In the conventional doctrines, the circularity of sovereignty may be said to appear under the form of its logical illimitability. Both Bodin and Hobbes had insisted that the sovereign's power be absolute and indivisible, because otherwise his decisions could always be contested. Hence, the sovereign power would not be sovereign at all. By declaring sovereignty to be absolute, however, Bodin and Hobbes had constructed a form of power that could no longer be legitimized, since in that case, it would again depend on something external to itself. Both did try to find a remedy to sovereignty's illimitability, as will be discussed in the third part of this essay.

Applying Foucault's distinction between governmentality and sovereignty to the Nazi state, we may provisionally conclude that it intensified both political technologies and their rhetorical registers, at the same time.

---

4   For an overview of leadership studies, see Trachman (2000).

The regime recognized normalization as a central tool and goal of governance. It pursued the governmental aim of population control up to the extremes of eugenics and murderous thanatopolitics. It redefined the democratic leader as being totally immanent to the people he commanded, and merely bringing to perfection its innate abilities. Simultaneously, however, it appealed strongly to the logic of sovereignty. Nazi propaganda stressed the German territory or soil, and the restoration of the Reich to its 'original' size. The 'governmental Führer', or the first among equals of the German people, coexisted with a 'sovereign Führer' who called upon his singular nature to attribute all legislative, executive and judiciary power to himself.

What expression do the paradigms of sovereignty and governmentality find in the philosophical writing that emanated from, or was at least strongly related to, the National Socialist revolution? Although the field of philosophy and, wider still, the social sciences under Nazism is large and differentiated, just two of its major players will be studied here, in order to gauge what results may be expected from an exhaustive assessment.

III

Carl Schmitt

The crucial paradox of Schmitt's work is the attempt to legitimize an authority that is defined as illegitimizable. He clearly seems to have been aware of this paradox and to have cultivated it, by means of a lucid style that relentlessly repeats and mutually redefines the same terms (state of emergency, sovereignty, decision, and the primacy of the 'political', i.e. of existential conflict based on a true distinction between friend and foe). In order to construct this paradox, we should follow Schmitt's train of thought, starting from his critique on liberalism and parliamentary democracy.

Schmitt criticized the liberal postulate of law as a deducible system of norms that spans the totality of human experience. In liberalism, according to Schmitt, the law has no final ground, except for the state and the constitution, which are themselves part of the law. The universality of law is a false presumption, because the idea of law is in need of an authority to implement it. The alleged 'groundlessness' of the liberal tradition was a central argument to many conservative intellectuals of the 1920s and 30s. Schmitt's problem was one of authorization. He believed to have found the false circularity in legal positivism, by pointing out that law cannot be its own authority. We should not heed the call of legal positivists such as Hans Kelsen when they demand an impersonal and checkable instance of sovereignty (such as the state, or the League of Nations on an even higher level). On the contrary, it must be fully acknowledged that the sovereign instance enforcing the law must have a face.

Sovereignty was defined as a function of the state of emergency in *Politische Theologie* (*Political Theology*), 1922. The emergency is totally heterogeneous as compared to the normal situation. The 'homogeneous medium' that all norms require in order to be applicable, can only be installed by a fully self-sufficient, sovereign agent (Schmitt, 1934b: 19–20). In Schmitt's definition of the modern state, the executive power comes first. It guarantees a zone of 'peace, security and order' that is the very condition for the legislative und judicial powers to come into existence at all (28–9; see also 1940: 148). According to Foucault, this would be a typically sovereignist definition. It is based on the notion of legitimacy, or a 'law of laws' that makes law possible.[5]

Schmitt, in order to escape the self-referential paradox he discerned in liberalism, namely the groundlessness of law, conceived an authority that implied an even more naïve version of the self-referential paradox. In his 1934 essay *Der Führer schützt das Recht* (*The Führer Protects the Law*), Schmitt endeavoured to legitimize the repression of the Röhm Putsch. No civil court of law can react quickly enough to grave political danger. Only the Party or the SA is up to this task and in such matters 'totally stands alone'. In the German original, the self-referential nature of this claim is fully acknowledged and even intensified: 'Hier steht sie ganz auf sich selbst' (1940: 202). It is only when his own authority as a National Socialist intellectual was undermined by *Das Schwarze Korps*, a periodical related to the SS, that he must have realized how the entirely 'free-standing' instance of sovereignty that he had erected did not have any need for his legitimations, either. By 1937, he would be stripped of all of his offices, except for his chair at the University of Berlin.

Sovereignty functions in a circular way. The legitimacy that it may endow its laws with ultimately flows from no other source than itself. This legitimacy is theoretically non-existent, because if it existed theoretically, this would imply sovereignty to be in need of theory. The perfectly self-referential nature of sovereignty is best illustrated by another attempt of Schmitt to describe the sovereign political unity: 'a community that struggles and maintains itself' ('eine kämpfende und sich durchsetzende Gesamtheit von Menschen'). Any true 'political' community succeeds in 'preserving its own being' or 'persisting in its own being' ('das eigene Sein

---

5   '[T]he theory of sovereignty ... attempts to show, how a power can be constituted, not exactly in accordance with the law, but in accordance with a certain basic legitimacy that is more basic than any law and that allows laws to function as such' (Foucault, 2003: 44).

zu wahren, *in suo esse perseverare*': 1934a: 8–10).[6] In the end, all of his attempts at defining sovereignty boil down to obvious and rudimentary self-assertion. Schmitt criticizes liberalism for doing away with the sovereign, i.e. the 'unitary people', in favour of formal democracy's 'addition sum of secret and private individual wills, meaning in truth the uncontrollable desires and resentments of the masses'. As a result, 'the sovereign disappears in the voting booth' ('der Souverän verschwindet in der Wahlzelle'). But the bottom line of his sovereignism cannot be anything else than nationalism pure and simple. Schmitt must stake all he has left on 'the heroic attempt to persist in and maintain the dignity of the state and the national unity against the plurality of economic interests' (see 1940: 110–1). There is little difference between this position and the way in which Hitler employs the term 'national self-assertion' ('nationale Selbstbehauptung') in *Mein Kampf* (1925–26: I/pars. 233, 358; II/par. 714). As Hans Sluga has shown, the 'discourse of nationhood' in general, and of German primordialness in particular, was widespread during the First World War and the Weimar Republic, and found numerous expressions in philosophical writing, too. Mainstream philosophical conservatives, such as Felix Krueger, revelled just like Schmitt in tautological definitions: 'This nation ... wants to find itself, so that it becomes what it has always been in essence' (in Sluga, 1993: 121–2, 157).

The illusion of the homogeneous medium wherein norms can take effect, and which is guaranteed by the heterogeneous sovereign agency, is then dispelled as a properly 'ultra-political' illusion (Žižek, 1999: 241). Schmitt, focusing on the distinction between (internal) friend and (external) foe, deliberately smoothed out all conflicts traversing the 'friendly' social body. His disdain for the liberal 'primacy of internal politics' amounts to a disavowal of these politics as not being political at all, because they cannot be motivated by an 'existential conflict' grounded in a true distinction between friend and foe. The 'truth' of this distinction is, again in an insubstantial manner, inferred to be a function of the sheer intensity of the conflict to which it leads, or, alternatively, a function of the force with which a people asserts 'the essence of its political existence' ('das Wesen seiner politischen Existenz': 1934a: 14, 21, 32). At the end of Schmitt's writings of the 1920s and 30s, one is left with an empty battlefield full of national 'essences', struggling against each other in order to — assert their national essences.

On a last note, however, it should be indicated that Schmitt, in spite of his strong sovereignist tendency, did have an intuition that sovereignty

---

6   If not indicated otherwise, English translations of Schmitt and Heidegger are by me.

was no longer the only paradigm needed for social and political theory. In his report of January 1933 on the *Weiterentwicklung des totalen Staats in Deutschland* (*Further Development of the Total State in Germany*), there is an incisive sketch to be found of the 'liberal total state'. The Weimar Republic has become a complex welfare state that must provide for all of the diverse and contradictory desires of its many citizens. It is a total state, but merely in a weak and quantitative sense. The unity of the people's will is fragmented and can only be restored through a state that is total in a strong and qualitative sense, as it is developing at this very moment in Germany. Schmitt's piece succeeds simultaneously in acknowledging the modern state's intricate (governmental) grip on human life, blaming the liberal tradition for its contradictions, and projecting into the future an image of a 'true' total or governmental state resolving those problems.

> [T]oday we have in Germany ... merely a plurality of total parties ... that look after people from the cradle to the grave, from the nursery class through the gymnastic club and the bowling club, up to the interment and cremation society. They provide their followers on behalf of the party with the right world view, the right state form, the right economic system, and the right kind of sociability. They totally politicize the entire life of the people and they parcel out the political unity of the German people (see Schmitt, 1940: 187).

The critical flaw of this article is that earlier, when the National Socialist revolution was acclaimed for the strong total state it was going to establish, the very same expression of a 'politicization of the entire life of the people' was used, not in a derogatory, but in a laudatory sense.

On yet another occasion there is evidence of Schmitt's insight into governmental realities, that is once more drowned out by his fundamentally sovereignist outlook. In *Der Begriff des Politischen* (*The Concept of the Political*), 1927, he shows a great concern for normalcy, which is quite exceptional within a traditional sovereignist discourse. However, normalcy is only understood as the empty space wherein norms may function, a space the integrity of which is guaranteed by the heterogeneous, sovereign guardian. 'Normalcy' is merely another link in Schmitt's tautological chain. He does not get much further in elucidating the nature of modern normalcy than the quite pointless deduction that 'the achievement of a normal state consists chiefly in ... establishing the normal situation ... because every norm presupposes a *normal* situation, and no norm can apply to a situation that is wholly abnormal in relation to it' (see 1934a: 28–9). Despite Schmitt's flashes of insight into the workings of governmentality, it is the ultra-political logic of radicalized sovereignism that shapes his work. Surely, governmentality and sovereignty rub against each other at times, but it is the peculiarly archaic notions of the latter paradigm that prevail. In *Der Begriff des Politischen,* Schmitt still conceives modern states in a territorial sense. Furthermore, they are sovereign states because in some way they succeed in installing an (impersonal or personified) instance of sovereignty that is heterogeneously guaranteeing the homogeneous medium of law. Last but not least, a sovereign state may only be called sovereign when it has the power of life and death over its subjects (*jus vitae ac necis;* 28). On this decisive point, an unflawed awareness of governmentality would have acknowledged the shift, in modern political history, from the sovereign power 'to take life or to let live' towards the governmental power 'to "make" live and "let" die' (Foucault, 2003: 241). (Only at the end of the Second World War would it become clear to what extent the Nazi state had been evolving into an extremely potent 'sovereignist-governmental' conglomerate that exercised the double power to take life and make live).

IV

Martin Heidegger

Schmitt had been working on the concept of absolute sovereignty for years before he applied it to the National Socialist party and its leader. Heidegger's publications and lectures, on the contrary, had mainly dealt with phenomenology, metaphysics, and the history of philosophy, in particular the Presocratics and Plato. Before his treatment of sovereignty ('Herrschaft') in the section 'The Leap' of his *Beiträge zur Philosophie* (*Contributions to Philosophy,* written during the late 1930s when he had already resigned from the rectorship at the University of Freiburg), the concept is seldom encountered in his writings (Brogan, 2002: 245–6). However, sovereignty and its self-referential paradox, which is so conspicuous in Schmitt, do appear in Heidegger's work from the early 30s, albeit under three different guises.

Before we overview these three figures of sovereignty, it must be remarked that this is not an attempt to 'reveal' the 'proto-fascist' or 'crypto-fascist' tendencies of Heidegger's thought during the interbellum period. The most recent and thorough, but unfortunately also quite tasteless exercise in this domain is Emmanuel Faye's *Heidegger: L'introduction du nazisme dans la philosophie* (2005; *Heidegger: The Introduction of Nazism into Philosophy*). Its weighty 567 pages confirm Sluga's assessment that 'moral judgment on historical facts and persons is an exceedingly cheap commodity' (1993: 5; see also Žižek, 2003). Heidegger's post-war justifications (or the lack thereof) may very well be criticized, but still it should be granted that his engagement in Nazi 'politics' was a contingent event in the history of philosophy.

1. Heidegger's support for National Socialism was always overarched by a broader concern for western civilization, and for a renewal of the ontological questioning that began the history of philosophy and science. This did not prevent him from voicing his support for Hitler in a fashion directly reminiscent of Schmitt's panegyric definitions. The appeal to German students of November 3, 1933, for example, concluded that '[t]he Führer himself and alone *is* the present and future German reality and its law' (in Safranski, 1998: 232; 'Der Führer selbst und allein *ist* die heutige und künftige deutsche Wirklichkeit und ihr Gesetz': Heidegger, 1975–: XVI/184). This conflation of reality and law (Sein and Sollen) into a single incarnation was nothing less than a leap ahead into the entanglements of the ontic dimension.

Heidegger's 'political' and philosophical enthusiasm seems to have carried him back to a point where his interrogation of the openness of being had not yet begun. Being as such, more particularly the being of a whole people, was read as coinciding with one leader and his policy. As Lefort has demonstrated, this is the pre-eminent totalitarian illusion. A seamless union of state (or Party) and civil society is believed to be possible, smoothing out all internal conflicts (1986: 273–91). This insight is repeated by Žižek through his notion of ultra-politics. Heidegger hazily recognized the Nazi regime to be simultaneously governmental ('the Führer ... is the present and future German reality') and sovereignist ('and its law'). However, his attempt to legitimize it gave precedence to the framework of sovereignty, making all of 'German reality' converge in one sovereign figure. The discourse of law and its singular, external source, be it an embodied sovereign or popular sovereignty, constitutes the conventional logic of political philosophy. As such, it must have come quite natural to him, even taking into account that he had not paid much attention to political theory during his philosophical career. The result, however, was an obvious paradox. The law given by the Führer is always-already fully realized by himself. The governmental Führer, namely, the ideal citizen who embodies normalcy, always-already knows what law his counterpart, the sovereignist Führer, is going to declare in order to establish that normalcy. Heidegger, in his turn, got caught up in the circularity of sovereignty.

2. Not only the Führer, but the German people too is a figure of sovereignty. That became particularly clear in Heidegger's rectoral address of May 27, 1933, on *Die Selbstbehauptung der deutschen Universität* (*The Self-Assertion of the German University*). This figure of thought already stood in a much closer and more subtle relationship to his reflections and

lectures from 1930 onwards. But the vocabulary of the speech was in tune with contemporary National Socialist rhetoric, straining the central issue of ontological questioning up to a degree that paradox was unavoidable. When Heidegger concluded with a call to self-assertion, not only of the university, but of the people as such—'We do will ourselves' (1985: 480; 'Wir willen uns selbst': 1975–: XVI/117) —, the paradoxical conflation of reality and law rose again.

The specific ambition of the rectoral address was to reinterpret the established concept of 'self-assertion'. The first familiar meaning, that of national self-assertion, was only treated within the scope of the university's self-assertion. But this second and, in academic circles, much debated understanding of self-assertion, namely, if and how the university should defend itself against National Socialist 'politicization', was also ingeniously sidestepped by Heidegger. Already in the fifth paragraph, the 'self-governance' of the German university ('Selbstverwaltung') was boldly redefined as 'self-examination' (1985: 471; 'Selbstbesinnung': 1975–: XVI/108). This is a prime example of what has been termed Heidegger's attempt to 'steal the language' of the National Socialist revolution, in an effort to revolutionize the revolution from the inside. Karl Jaspers is reputed to have said that Heidegger's thoughts of a philosophical *coup d'État* went so far as to dream of 'leading the Führer' ('den Führer zu führen'; see Edler, 1990; Allemann, 1969; Minder, 1966; Nicholson, 1987: 174, 185; Pöggeler, 1985). The philosophical coup backfired. Not the Nazi revolution was made philosophical, but Heidegger's revolution nazified.[7]

Self-examination seemed to be the best way to reorientate the university's self-assertion, and that of the German people, towards the process of ontological questioning that Heidegger saw as the 'mass philosophical' mission of the highest importance. His appeal was primarily addressed to the university teachers and students, but its purport clearly ranged beyond the auditorium. He demanded that German teachers and students should be the first to place themselves again 'under the power of the *beginning* of our spiritual-historical being' ('unter die Macht des *Anfangs* unseres geistig-geschichtlichen Daseins'). This beginning is the 'setting out' ('Aufbruch') of Greek philosophy, where man for the first time engaged

---

7   His rectoral address tried to recycle a number of terms that had become part and parcel of Nazi language: 'Gefolgschaft' (a following, but also the specifical Nazi designation for personnel), 'deutsche Studentenschaft' (a seemingly abstract label for all German students, that had become the name for the Nazi students' association), 'Aufbruch' (setting out, start, but more specifically the 1933 revolution), 'Kampf', 'Entscheidung', etc. He did not succeed in re-signifying Nazi discourse, but instead his discourse blended in with the rhetorical and performative context of his utterances. On 'Studentenschaft', see Faye (2005: 92–6); on 'Aufbruch', see Edler (1990); on the rhetorical and performative context, see Sluga (1993: 8).

in the ontological difference. He 'stands up to the *totality of what is*, which he questions and conceives as the being that it is' (1985: 471; 'steht ... auf gegen das *Seiende im Ganzen* und befragt und begreift es als das Seiende, das es ist': 1975–: XVI/108–9). At this particular moment, the Greeks became aware that it is possible for 'that which is' ('das Seiende') to be only within the openness of Being.

Again, the commitment to the ontological question was conceived, just as in the inaugural lecture on *Was ist Metaphysik?* (*What is Metaphysics?*), 1929, and in other texts, as an experience that is not without its dangers, and subsequently not without heroism. It implies the 'completely unguarded exposure to the hidden and uncertain, i.e. the questionable' (1985: 474; 'völlig unbedeckten Ausgesetztsein in das Verborgene und Ungewisse, d.i. Fragwürdige': 1975–: XIV/111). The crucial fault of Heidegger's lecture was that it made a direct connection from this self-examination to the dynamics of the human will. When the university examines itself, this was taken to imply that it delimits its essence, and subsequently wills its essence, in this way asserting itself. Heidegger quickly achieved success when he personally tried to 'bring his philosophy into line' with the National Socialist revolution. It merely required a reinterpretation, albeit forced, of the ontological questioning process of western civilization within the rhetorical framework of national strength, self-assertion, will, people, and state. 'The will to the essence of the German university is the will to science as will to the historical mission of the German people as a people that knows itself in its state' (1985: 471; 'Der Wille zum Wesen der deutschen Universität ist der Wille zur Wissenschaft als Wille zum geschichtlichen geistigen Auftrag des deutschen Volkes als eines in seinem Staat sich selbst wissenden Volkes': 1975–: XVI/108). Just as in the case of Schmitt, it should be noted how thoroughly unoriginal Heidegger's philosophical effort was in a country rife with talk of nationhood.

Knowledge of the German university's essence is construed as the will to its essence. During his rectorship, at the Demonstration of German Science for Adolf Hitler on November 11, 1933, in Leipzig, Heidegger expounded on his dynamics of the (human) will applied to institutions and nations. Just as all being must answer to the 'primal demand ... that it should sustain and save its own essence' ('jener Urforderung alles Daseins, daß es sein eigenes Wesen erhalte und rette': XVI/188), so too the German nation must 'retain and save its own essence' (in Safranski, 1998: 265–6). Even in the summer of 1934, when he had already resigned from the rectorship because of the increasingly precise Nazi demands, he answered the question 'who "we" are' during his lectures on *Logik als die*

Frage nach dem Wesen der Sprache (*Logic as the Questioning of the Essence of Language*) by way of a hardline decisionist approach. 'We' are the people solely by our being here, at this very moment in history, in this very classroom attending Heidegger's lecture. This is no accidental fact. It is only so because of our conscious decisions: 'Thus, we exist through a series of decisions' ('Wir sind also durch eine Folge von Entscheidungen': 1975–: XXXVIII/57). Transferred from 'the small and narrow we of the moment of the lecture' to the people, our existence as a people is just as little accidental. We may *fail* at being a people. As a result, 'decision belongs to the people's nature' ('Das Volk hat Entscheidungscharakter': XXXVIII/70). Heidegger, in his turn, lost himself in the electrifying twists of tautology: 'we do will the will of a state that does not will itself to be anything else but a people's will to rule over itself and the form such rule takes' ('wollen wir den Willen eines Staates, der selbst nichts anderes sein will als der Herrschaftswille und die Herrschaftsform eines Volkes über sich selbst': XXXVIII: 57).

The escape into decisionism[8] and the adoration of the will did not make the fundamental problem of Heidegger's attempt at 'Gleichschaltung', or 'bringing himself into line', disappear. As was well known from both *Sein und Zeit* (*Being and Time*), 1927, and *Was ist Metaphysik?*, the experience of the ontological difference was only to be reached through certain 'moods' that, as Heidegger described them, were highly individual in nature. They found expression in such terms as angst, boredom, 'completely unguarded exposure', 'forsakenness' ('Verlassenheit': XVI/111), and 'self-oblivion' ('Selbstverlorenheit und Selbstvergessenheit': XXXVIII/49). How was this register of experiences to be merged with the language of people and state? In order to overcome this difficulty, Heidegger introduced a highly dissonant connection. It was at this precise point that his reinterpretation of self-assertion backfired.

While he was talking about self-examination and ontological questioning, every listener could relate to Heidegger's discourse as an individual. At specific points during the speech, however, this individual understanding was jerked into the sphere of a collective understanding. The process of 'questioning' was then suddenly turned from a personal experience into a national dynamic. This happened most explicitly when Heidegger described how 'science's' questioning would expose it, once again, 'to the fertility and the blessing bestowed by all the world-shaping powers of human-historical being, such as: nature, history, language; people, custom, state; poetry, thought, faith; disease, madness, death; law, economy, technology' (1985: 474;

---

8   On the origins of 'decisionism' in Schmitt, see Schmitt (1912; 1934b) and Hirst (1987).

'der Fruchtbarkeit und dem Segen aller weltbildenden Mächte des menschlich-geschichtlichen Daseins, als da sind: Natur, Geschichte, Sprache; Volk, Sitte, Staat; Dichten, Denken, Glauben; Krankheit, Wahnsinn, Tod; Recht, Wirtschaft, Technik': 1975–: XVI/111).

Heidegger's appeal to 'higher powers' distorted his existentialist perspective. It also realigned him with a specific aspect of the traditional sovereignist discourse. In the foundation texts of sovereignty, both Bodin and Hobbes thought it necessary simultaneously to declare that the sovereign's power be absolute and indivisible and to install a kind of emergency brake into their theories. In Bodin, it is the 'laws of God, and nature, and the human laws common to all nations' that curb the sovereign's power (which does not, however, detract from its absoluteness: 1577: 95; see also Ford, 1998). Sovereignty, it seems, may only be conceived as absolute as long as it remains within the horizon of certain 'higher powers' that are presumed to supersede even absoluteness. However, the theorists of sovereignty find it impossible, or unnecessary, to describe how exactly these 'powers' govern human reality and its sovereign agent(s). They are merely stationed at the limits of sovereignist theory as its transcendent guarantors.

By placing the German people's will-to-itself under the patronage of the 'world-shaping powers of human-historical being', Heidegger underlined its sovereign nature. The will of such a sovereign people coincides exactly with the law it gives to itself. After all, who may speak up to the workings of 'world-shaping powers'? In *Die Selbstbehauptung der deutschen Universität*, too, Heidegger gets entangled in the circularity of sovereignty. He would continue to do so for a long time. Even in his work of the late 1930s on Nietzsche, which he later presented as a tacit criticism of National Socialism's unbridled will to power, we can find a sovereignist statement such as: 'the community as an order of being is grounded in itself and does not receive its standards from another order' (in Sluga, 1993: 172).

3. A third sovereign figure of thought is fully native to Heidegger's reading of the allegory of the cave in Plato's *Republic*. From the 1930 essay *Vom Wesen der Wahrheit* (*On the Essence of Truth*) onward, he conceived a 'truth happening' ('Wahrheitsgeschehen'), developed throughout his lectures of the early 1930s and culminating in the publication of *Platons Lehre von der Wahrheit* (*Plato's Doctrine of Truth*) in 1942 (Safranski, 1998: 214–24). This figure was not directly linked to contemporary political vocabulary, 'brought into line' with his own philosophy. Still, it was structurally in tune with the Nazi revolution, since it provided the outline of a philosopher-leader who was, in radical sovereignist fashion, incommensurable with those he led.

In a letter to Karl Jaspers of December 20, 1931, Heidegger described the task of the philosopher as being a 'knowing leader and guardian' in the 'true public dimension' (in Safranski, 1998: 216; translation modified). In the lectures on Plato, held during the winter of 1931–32, the expression was elaborated:

> [T]he actual guardians of the being-together of people in the unity of the *polis* must be philosophizing people. It is not as if professors of philosophy should become Chancellors of the Reich, but philosophers should be *phulakes*, guardians. The rule and the order of governance of the state must be permeated by philosophizing people, who, out of the deepest and widest knowing that questions freely, determine measures and rules, and open up paths of decision.[9]

The philosopher-leader was based on the liberated prisoner from what Heidegger distinguished as the fourth and last stadium of Plato's allegory. For the sake of brevity, we will not examine the totality of the 'truth happening' as it is explained through the allegory of the cave. According to Rüdiger Safranski, Heidegger was not primarily interested in the real high point of the simile, when the liberated prisoner beholds the ideas (1998: 221). Most of his attention was focused on the process of liberation leading up to it, and on the experiences of the liberated prisoner once he returns to the cave to become a liberator himself. He faces a dangerous mission. Accustomed to the visions on the walls of the cave, those who are still imprisoned will probably not believe his story and might even try to attack and kill him. Heidegger stressed Plato's characterization of the event as violent. Just as being liberated was a long and painful process, the liberator will have to 'violently grab' the imprisoned and 'tear them loose' (1975–: XXXIV/85).

Heidegger had isolated the philosopher-leader from the context of the allegory and its interpretation by Plato. It was no longer the privileged relationship of the philosopher to the highest idea, namely the Good (*agathon*), that constituted the premise of his activities (governing the city-state, or else retreating into contemplation). Any such notion of absolute truth, disconnected from time, had been rejected. The idea of a 'truth happening' had introduced history as the starting point of any subsequent philosophical ethics. Hence, 'being free, being a liberator means participating in history' (in Safranski, 1998: 221; 'Freisein, Befreier-sein ist

---

9 '[D]ie eigentlichen Wächter des Miteinanderseins der Menschen in der Einheit der *polis* müssen philosophierende Menschen sein. Nicht sollen Philosophieprofessoren Reichskanzler werden, sondern Philosophen *phulakes*, Wächter. Die Herrschaft und Herrschaftsordnung des Staates soll durchwaltet sein von philosophierenden Menschen, die aus dem tiefsten und weitesten, frei fragenden Wissen Maß und Regel setzen, Bahnen der Entscheidung erschließen' (Heidegger, 1975–: XXXIV/100).

Mithandeln in der Geschichte': Heidegger, 1975–: XXXIV/85). Then his violence, too, had to be reconsidered. Not brutal force, but rather an enlightened form of 'tactfulness' is necessary to withstand the ridicule his attempt at liberation will provoke, and to select the one or two people that may be led out of the cave. Moreover, the liberator's violence is not arbitrary, but rather 'tactfulness of the highest, namely spiritual rigour, to which, before, the liberator has committed himself' ('der Takt der höchsten, nämlich geistigen Strenge, der er, der Befreier, sich selbst zuvor verpflichtet hat': XXXIV/81–2, 85).

It is the light of the ideas, more specifically the 'illuminated vision' ('Lichtblick') he has now acquired, that the liberator has committed himself to. He is on 'a sure footing on the ground of human-historical existence' ('einen sicheren Stand im Grund des menschlich-geschichtlichen Daseins': XXXIV/82). At this point it becomes clear how the rectoral address was firmly grounded in the whole of Heidegger's work during the 1930s. Man must be on sure footing not only to liberate others, but first and foremost to 'question himself', which is also a violent act. Just as in his rectoral address, 'self-questioning' is taken to mean decisionist self-assertion.

> The question is only posed, when man is positioned to decide on himself, i.e. under the powers that support and determine him, and deciding on his relationship to these powers. ... We take the question "what is man?" to mean, *who* we are, insofar as we *are*. We are only that, which we have the strength to expect of ourselves.[10]

Again we have reached the sovereignist province of the 'higher powers' that take man, defined as a self-asserting being, under their wing. It is a matter of discussion how much protection Heidegger accorded them to provide. After all, the unconcealedness (truth, *aletheia*) of being, to which the liberated prisoner is exposed, constituted 'the danger zone of philosophy' ('die Gefahrenzone der Philosophie'), an expression that rejoined the vocabulary of exposure and forsakenness (XXXIV/77). The crux of the matter, however, is that a mechanism resurfaced that was characteristic for the logic of sovereignty.

In the same way as the monarch's laws are strictly speaking incomprehensible to his subjects, because he transcends them, the philosopher-leader is incommensurable to those he is committed to liberate. 'Philosophy has its own law; its assessments are different' ('Die Philosophie hat ihr

---

10 'Die Frage ist nur dort gestellt, wo der Mensch zur Entscheidung über sich selbst, d.h. unter die ihn tragenden und bestimmenden Mächte und in die Entscheidung über den Bezug zu diesen gestellt wird .... Die Frage "was ist der Mensch?" verstehen wir als die, *wer* wir sind, sofern wir *sind*. Wir sind nur das, was wir uns zuzumuten die Kraft haben' (Heidegger, 1975–: XXXIV/76).

eigenes Gesetz; ihre Schätzungen sind andere': XXXIV/15). The 'higher powers' that the philosopher has obliged himself to no longer constitute an imperishable outer reality such as in Plato, but still he relates to history in a fundamentally different way than his contemporaries, grasping it as 'truth happening'. To the normal situation of the prisoners in the cave, his 'violence' must seem unreasonable and heterogeneous. To legitimize himself would be inappropriate and impossible, except by forcefully leading them up to the light.

V

Conclusion

Overviewing the three figures of sovereignty that run through Heidegger's thinking of the 1930s, we may conclude that he echoes the strong nationalism, decisionism, and sovereignism of Schmitt. Although Schmitt may have been aware of the workings of governmentality, his doctrine was strictly sovereignist. Equating legitimacy with force, he got caught up in what he himself had dubbed, as early as 1919, *Politische Romantik* (*Political Romanticism*: 1986). Paul Tillich described it as the adoration of sovereignty wanting to deduce 'political' legitimacy from nothing but intensity or will, that is to say, 'to create the mother from the son and to summon the father from nothingness' (in Safranski, 1998: 175). The self-referential paradox of absolute sovereignty ensnares Heidegger, too. In constrained accordance with his philosophy of authenticity, his writings of the 1930s developed a nationalist decisionism that could be grounded in nothing but its own self-assertion.

The main difference between the accounts of Schmitt and Heidegger is that the latter's writings show only the faintest awareness of governmentality. There is an intriguing report on 'machination' ('Machenschaft') to be found in the *Beiträge zur Philosophie* (1975–: LXV: part 2, §61). By the same token, both his inaugural lecture of 1929 and the rectoral address contained a stringent critique of science's specialization and its orientation toward professional training, which may well be read as symptoms of the normalizing power that pervades modern science according to Foucault (Heidegger, 1975–: XVI/108, 113–5, 372–3; see Foucault, 2003: 24–5).

As in Schmitt's case, we may conclude that Heidegger's work is ultrapolitical because of its exclusively nationalist decisionism. In his justifications of 1945 and later, he would point explicitly to his critique of modern science in order to indicate how he had vainly tried to combat the intensifying 'politicization' of the university (1975–: XVI/16, 373–8; 1985: 483–8). He failed to realize that Nazism only asserted the 'political' nature of the

1933 revolution and the future Reich in order to obscure its increasingly strong disavowal of the true political moment. In National Socialist discourse, 'political' was the prime signifier not of a power structure that could be situated in, and legitimized by, modern politics and political philosophy. Nazism merely took the shape of some institutions and adopted some titles during the early stages of its development, such as Hitler's 'Chancellorship'. The 'total state' or the total 'politicization' that it prided itself on was nothing but a folkloristic usage of the word 'political'. The very obsession with the political denoted the appearance of an ultra-political and extremely potent 'sovereignist-governmental' conglomerate. Consequently, the 'political science' ('politische Wissenschaft') that Heidegger feared was not political at all.

Hannah Arendt has argued that Adolf Eichmann was wrongly considered as 'normal' and therefore accountable at his trial in 1961, on the grounds that 'under the conditions of the Third Reich only "exceptions" could be expected to react "normally"' (Arendt, 1994: 26–7). In the same way, 'science' or 'philosophy' could not be made 'political' under Nazism, precisely because its aberrant homogeneity had already flawlessly brought them all 'into line', and thus weathered the very sense of those words. German philosophers blindly strove to legitimize as 'political' a revolution that was actually playing on a much more abstract level, maybe to be termed organizational. One part of the National Socialist revolution was governmental in the extreme and aimed at excessive normalization. Schmitt, Heidegger and others lacked the philosophical acumen to perceive this fundamental shift in social dynamics. Looking down to the 'homogeneous medium' that the new 'sovereign' regime was supposed to bring about, as Schmitt did, or looking up to the 'higher powers' that were guiding it, as Heidegger did, both resulted in the installation of illegitimizable instances of sovereignty. The sovereign had reappeared from the voting booth.

References

Allemann, B. (1969), 'Martin Heidegger und die Politik', in *Heidegger*, ed. O. Pöggeler (Köln: Kiepenheuer & Witsch).
Arendt, H. (1994), *Eichmann in Jerusalem* (London: Penguin).
Bodin, J. (1577), *Les six livres de la République* (Paris: Iacques du Puys).
Brecht, B. (2002), *The resistible rise of Arturo Ui*, trans. R. Manheim (London: Methuen).
Brogan, W. (2002), 'The community of those who are going to die', in *Heidegger and practical philosophy*, eds. F. Raffoul and D. Pettigrew (New York: SUNY Press).

Crombez, T. (2006), '"The sovereign disappears in the election box": Carl Schmitt and Martin Heidegger on sovereignty and (perhaps) governmentality', *Pli: The Warwick Journal of Philosophy*, 17: 61–83.
Domarus, M. (1973), *Hitler: Reden und Proklamationen 1932–1945* (4 vols.; Wiesbaden: Löwit).
Edler, F.H.W. (1990), 'Philosophy, language, and politics: Heidegger's attempt to steal the language of the revolution in 1933–34', *Social Research*, 57 (1): 197–238.
Faye, E. (2005), *Heidegger: L'introduction du nazisme dans la philosophie: autour des séminaires inédits de 1933–1935* (Paris: Albin Michel).
Fest, J. (1970), *The face of the Third Reich*, trans. M. Bullock (London: Weidenfels & Nicholson).
Ford, J.D. (1998), 'Sovereignty', in *Routledge encyclopedia of philosophy*, ed. E. Craig (10 vols.; London: Routledge).
Foucault, M. (1975), *Surveillir et punir: naissance de la prison* (Paris: Gallimard).
Foucault, M. (1994), *Dits et écrits 1954–1988*, eds. D. Defert, F. Ewald and J. Lagrange (4 vols.; Paris: Gallimard).
Foucault, M. (1999), *Les anormaux: cours au Collège de France 1974–1975*, eds. V. Marchetti and A. Salomani (Paris: Gallimard and Seuil).
Foucault, M. (2003), *'Society must be defended': lectures at the Collège de France, 1975–1976*, eds. M. Bertani and A. Fontana/trans. D. Macey (London: Allen Lane).
Gouldner, A.W. (1950), *Studies in leadership* (New York: Harper & Brothers).
Heidegger, M. (1975–), *Gesamtausgabe*, various eds. (102 vols.; Frankfurt a. M.: Klostermann).
Heidegger, M. (1985), 'The self-assertion of the German university', trans. K. Harries, *Review of Metaphysics*, 38 (3), 467–502.
Hirst, P. (1987), 'Carl Schmitt's decisionism', *Telos*, 72: 15–26.
Hitler, A. (1925–26), *Mein Kampf* (2 vols.; München: Franz Eher Nachfolger).
Lefort, C. (1986), 'The logic of totalitarianism', in *The political forms of modern society: bureaucracy, democracy, totalitarianism*, ed. J.B. Thompson (Cambridge: Polity).
Lefort, C. (1988), *Democracy and political theory*, trans. D. Macey (Minneapolis: University of Minneapolis Press, and Cambridge: Polity).
Minder, R. (1966), 'Heidegger, Hebel und die Sprache von Messkirch', *Der Monat*, 114: 13.
Monrose, L. (1986), 'The Elizabethan subject and the Spenserian text', in *Literary theory/renaissance texts*, eds. P. Parker and D. Quint (Baltimore: Johns Hopkins University Press).
Nicholson, G. (1987), 'The politics of Heidegger's rectorial address', *Man and World*, 20 (2): 171–87.
Pöggeler, O. (1985), 'Den Führer führen? Heidegger und kein Ende', *Philosophische Rundschau*, 32 (1–2): 26–67.
Pye, C. (1990), *The regal phantasm: Shakespeare and the politics of spectacle* (London: Routledge).
Safranski, R. (1998), *Martin Heidegger: between good and evil*, trans. E. Osers (Cambridge, MA: Harvard University Press).
Schmitt, C. (1912), *Gesetz und Urteil: Eine Untersuchung zum Problem der Rechtspraxis* (Berlin: Verlag Otto Liebmann.).

Schmitt, C. (1934a), *Der Begriff des Politischen* (2nd ed.; Hamburg: Hanseatische Verlagsanstalt).

Schmitt, C. (1934b), *Politische Theologie: Vier Kapital zur Lehre von der Souveränität* (2nd ed.; München: Duncker & Humblot).

Schmitt, C. (1940), *Positionen und Begriffe im Kampf mit Weimar-Genf-Versailles, 1923–1939* (Hamburg: Hanseatische Verlagsanstalt).

Schmitt, C. (1986), *Political romanticism*, trans. G. Oakes (Cambridge, MA: MIT Press).

Skinner, Q. (1978), *The foundations of modern political thought* (2 vols.; Cambridge: Cambridge University Press).

Sluga, H. (1993), *Heidegger's crisis: philosophy and politics in Nazi Germany* (Cambridge, MA: Harvard University Press).

Trachman, M. (2000), *Rethinking leadership: presidential leadership and the 'spirit of the game' of democracy* (unpublished doctoral thesis, York University, Toronto, Canada).

Žižek, S. (1999), *The ticklish subject: the absent centre of political ontology* (London: Verso).

Žižek, S. (2003), 'Learning to love Leni Riefenstahl', *In These Times*, September 10 (retrieved August 11, 2005, from http://www.inthesetimes.com/site/main/article/learning_to_love_leni_riefenstahl/)

Moshe Hellinger

The Criticism of Democracy in Rabbi E.E.M. Shach's Thought

I

Introduction

Rabbi Eliezer Menachem Mann Shach (1898–2001) served for several decades as head of the Ponevezh Yeshiva in Bnei Brak, Israel, one of the most prestigious higher institutes of Torah learning in the Jewish world. From the 1970s until the day he died, he was the preeminent leader in the world of the Lithuanian yeshivot, which has come to be associated with the ultra-Orthodox (*hareidi*) 'Torah World'. In the 1980s, R. Shach carved his way into a position of considerable political weight within wider Israeli society. He became one of the two leaders of the hareidi Agudat Israel Party and later on the uncontested leader of Degel haTorah Party, which seceded from the Aguda. He played a crucial role in the formation of Shas, the Sephardic hareidi party (Sephardi Torah Guardians), exerting great influence over its decisions for nearly a decade. Yet more than his institutional rank, he enjoyed an exalted personal status, especially in the last decades of his life. He was venerated by his adherents, who greatly admired his spiritual qualities and his moral virtues. Rabbi Shach stated his views loud and clear on numerous issues that were on the public agenda in the State of Israel and concerned the Jewish people as a whole. The major issues he addressed were his condemnation of Zionism and the secular character of the State of Israel; the utmost importance for Jewish life of constant Torah study within the yeshiva framework, whether in Israel or elsewhere; the negative impact of western culture; and the need for excessive territorial concessions for the sake of establishing a peaceful political settlement with the Arab world. With regard to all of these issues his teaching was clear-cut and unequivocal, placing great emphasis on the crucial importance of securing the existence of a separate hareidi community of Torah adherents. In his view, such a Torah-oriented community is the only guarantee for the survival of the Jewish people amidst the everlasting waves of human hatred that are dictated by the workings of divine providence.

This article focuses on Rabbi Shach's attitude toward democracy. Rabbi Shach declared war on any man-made system of ideas, believing that by its inherently human nature it would be contrary to the divine Torah, the only teaching that is eternal and immutable and absolutely true. In particular, he launched his attack on the democratic system, which he often presented as the rival of the Torah approach. Over the years, Rabbi Shach increased his attacks on democracy, treating it as a loathsome approach that entails moral and social corruption. For him, the shaping of Israel as a democratic state threatens to destroy the uniqueness of the Jewish people.

This article will introduce Rabbi Shach's major arguments against democracy—both as a general concept and as they are manifested in the Israeli context. Over the years, the concept of 'democracy' in R. Shach's teaching gradually came to be demonized, a tendency that is characteristic of various fundamentalist philosophies. Some of the meanings that R. Shach attaches to democracy are indeed representative of western democratic notions; others seem to betray conceptual confusion on his part. Regardless of this distinction, what emerges from his statements is a view of democracy as a limited human conception that aspires to bring about human progress but ends up in fundamental social corruption. Thus, as far as the State of Israel is concerned, the pervasive democratic influence is detrimental, undermining the unique and worthy character of the individual Jew and the Jewish people alike. In face of this destructive influence R. Shach strives to establish the centrality of Torah rule as a way of creating a worthwhile and valuable Jewish society.

II

R. Shach: Biographical Landmarks

Rabbi Shach was born in Lithuania. He attended various yeshivot in Lithuania and Poland and settled down in the Land of Israel in 1941. After successively serving as a rabbinic lecturer in several yeshivot, he was appointed as a senior rabbinic lecturer (Rosh Yeshiva) in the illustrious Ponevezh yeshiva, where he eventually became the central and dominant figure. In the 1960s, he joined the Agudat Israel Council of Torah Sages, thus gaining recognition as one of the outstanding rabbis in the hareidi camp. By the 1970s he was already one of the two senior leaders of the

Council, together with the Rabbi of Gur, the head of the largest Hasidic court. Thereafter he was acknowledged as *gedol hador*, 'the greatest rabbi of his generation', by the members of the Lithuanian-style yeshivot, who looked up to him for decisions on public affairs and consulted with him on personal matters, a custom that was widespread in the Hasidic world, but not in the Lithuanian yeshiva world with its strict Torah-study orientation and greater emphasis on personal intellectual development and accountability. Following the political turnaround (1977), in which power changed hands and for the first time the Likud Party of Menachem Begin superseded the Israeli Labour Party, the Agudat Israel Party became an important faction in the new right-wing government coalition and Rabbi Shach himself became a powerful political figure. In the 1980s, R. Shach reached the peak of his political power when he sanctioned and promoted the formation of Shas (an acronym for Sephardi Torah Guardians), for the Knesset (parliament) members of this Sephardic hareidi party used to consult with him on most important matters. In those years, even Rabbi Ovadiah Yoseph, the spiritual leader of the Shas movement, acknowledged R. Shach's seniority and was subservient to him. This cooperation came to an end in 1990, when under the initiative of Knesset member Arieh Deri, Shas's charismatic political leader, this party supported the 'stinky manoeuvre' (as described by Labour's Yitzhak Rabin) that led to the overthrow of Yitzhak Shamir's Likud government through a vote of non-confidence and to the ensuing unsuccessful attempt to establish a government headed by Shimon Peres, then the leader of the Labour Party. R. Shach was strongly opposed to raising the left to power, thereby creating a split between himself and the Shas Party. In 1992, the second Rabin government was formed. It was this government that led the Oslo Process and the negotiations with the PLO. In this government a great weight was given to Meretz, the ultra-liberal left-wing party, while at the same time Shas was a partner in the coalition. Now the attacks of R. Shach on the leftist government and on Shas became stronger, as will be shown below. At the end of the 1980s, R. Shach's influence led to the breaking away of the Yeshiva circles from Agudat Israel and to the formation of the separate hareidi political party Degel haTorah (The Banner of the Torah), as the spiritual leader of which he operated. Throughout this period he continued teaching in his yeshiva, though in the last years of his life he hardly left his house due to his physical frailty.[1]

Side by side with his scholarly works on the Torah, Rabbi Shach was involved in writing rabbinic responsa concerning personal questions and

---

1 On R. Shach's life and teaching, see Horowitz (1989); Ben Hayyim (2004); Taub (2004).

current issues. Collected in six volumes of *Mikhtavim u-Ma'amarim* (*Letters and Articles*), these texts serve as a plentiful source of learning about his political opinions and social outlooks. His teaching on various issues also finds expression in other of his works. It should be noted that although Rabbi Shach was not a thinker who presented a systematic thought in book form, a careful study of his writings, his yeshiva lectures and public deliberations (which were all collected and published by his students) suggests that not only is there a definite system at the heart of his conceptual world, but that in fact a small number of basic concepts underlie the whole range of his pronouncements and are repeatedly conveyed to diverse audiences. The following discussion of his attitudes toward democracy will make several references to this conceptual system and its impact on his outlook.

III

Judaism versus Democracy in R. Shach's World

In R. Shach's writings various aspects of the democratic system are subject to a scathing criticism. R. Shach addresses in his criticism both the procedural-institutional aspects of democracy and its value-oriented aspects. At times, however, his criticism is not relevant to western democracy, which he mistakenly associates with totally different regimes. At the basis of his critical approach is the notion that democracy is an unworthy system, and particularly so insofar as the Jewish people is concerned. Rather than democracy, it is the Torah (the expression of the divine will for humanity) that should govern Jewish life.

Democracy as a machinery of lies, false notions, the pursuit of narrow interests and deceit — as opposed to the Torah regime, which is based on seeking the ultimate truth

For R. Shach the basis of the democratic system is the give and take between competing interest groups for the purpose of passing parliamentary bills and meeting the material needs of both the administration and society in general. The democratic process involves no striving for real goals: 'The whole point of democracy is money. The one does what the other asks him to do in pursuit of his own interest, so as to be given what he himself asks for, and the whole purpose of the transaction is that each would get what they want' (2005: 205).[2] As opposed to this, says R. Shach, in Judaism 'the only appropriate thing is the divine Torah. As it is written

---

2   If not indicated otherwise, English translations are by Ms Ruty Bar-Ilan, the translator of this article.

(Deuteronomy 32:4): "He is the rock, His work is perfect for all, His ways are justice; A God of truth and without iniquity, just and right is He"' (205). Parliamentary democracy is based not only on bargaining within the confines of parliament, but also on pork-barrel politics: 'Consider what their democracy looks like. They appeal to the voter and convince him: "Vote for me so that I will give you a job"' (1988-95: V/126). Parliamentary deals are also affected by the need of the Knesset members to 'deliver the goods' to their electoral constituents: 'Whenever they pass a bill, do they really consider whether it is good or bad? Not at all. In fact, every one of them considers what is best for him and calculates how to please his electoral constituency through the proposed law'. Here, too, the Torah takes an opposite stand:

> For according to the Torah laws, whoever takes bribe is disqualified to pronounce judgement, whereas here all the members of the legislature take bribes. Only this week, the prime minister and his ministers convinced some of the factions to vote for them in exchange for a bribe, promising six million to this one, seven million to the other, and ten million to yet another one. And where did they take it? From the public funds and our money (V/126).

Rabbi Shach's criticism penetrates into the very core of parliamentary democracy. It presents the deliberations and the compromises made between parties and factions as a dubious process of stealing public funds. In the same breath, it attacks the practice of courting the voters, which takes place at the public marketplace of the democratic arena. By contrast, a regime based on the laws of the Torah is bound to conduct itself in an entirely relevant manner, guided only by considerations of the absolute good of the general public. The problem is that Rabbi Shach does not concede that, from a democratic viewpoint, different factions reflect the respective needs of different social groups, so that meeting these needs has nothing to do with stealing. Moreover, in the course of various election campaigns it was Rabbi Shach himself who urged his adherents to participate in the elections and vote for an ultra-Orthodox party so that the votes would not get lost, thus inadvertently reinforcing the secular parties (V/148-9, 160). This begs the question whether in doing so R. Shach was taking part in the same democratic process that he so vehemently denounced. For it was precisely Agudat Israel, the party he led for so many years, which was most associated with pursuing sectoral interests through the political power it wielded while sitting in the coalition. Be that as it may, R. Shach's criticism of democracy is still valid as far as the shortcomings of the democratic procedure are concerned.

According to R. Shach, one of the most acute problems in the politics of parliamentary democracy is that partisan interests even enter into the consideration of whether or not to wage war against the enemy. During the first Lebanon War (1982), R. Shach denounced those members of the religious-Zionist camp who viewed the war against the PLO as *milhemet mitzva* (an obligatory war of a religious value), arguing as follows:

> Is *milhemet mitzva* determined by a vote in the Knesset, with some members voting for this side and others for the other side, whereby the voting is based on conspiracies and mutual agreements — you'll back me now and I'll back you some other time — until finally a decision to engage in war is reached by a majority vote and as such is considered legitimate? Isn't it true that if the conspiracies had not taken place, the voting would have been different, so that a different decision would have been made? If so, how is it possible to rely on decisions that are based on such considerations? (2007: 116).

In his criticism, R. Shach addresses the two major foundations of democracy: (a) the sovereignty of the people, which finds its expression in a government by representatives; (b) abiding by the majority decision both in electing the representatives and in making parliamentary and cabinet decisions. It is noteworthy, however, that R. Shach neither offers an alternative model of government nor does he argue anywhere in favour of dictatorial regimes.

R. Shach's critique of the false basis of parliamentary democracy is inseparable from his overall critique on the falseness and superficiality that characterize modern western reality:

> The men of the world are attracted by superficial glitter and do not seriously look into the heart of the matter. For example, it is well known that old buildings are stronger than the new ones of our own time, although the latter are more attractive. ... The older generations looked for the roots and the innermost being, which are the essence, while the young generation is looking for glamour and outward appearance, for that which is enjoyable and pleasing and attractive (203).

A Jewish democratic law-governed state detaches the Jewish people from its religious roots

This argument specifically relates to the secular character of Israeli democracy, yet in part it is also relevant to the general issue of democracy. R. Shach was highly apprehensive of the secular character of the State of Israel and viewed it as disrupting the continuity of Jewish religious tradition and alienating the Jews in Israel from their roots. Most of the youngsters, he argued, 'are still raised without the Torah and its commandments. ... This is due to the grave situation in the secular schools and in the institutes of higher education, where there is no trace of the name of God' (1988-95: V/13). R. Shach connects this state of affairs to the problematics of Israel's democracy. In Israel, the democratic regime endeavours to offer an alternative to Jewish halachic (legal) tradition in the form of a law-governed state that does not abide by the laws of the Halakhah (Torah-derived law):

> The widespread view on the street: a "law-governed state" rather than a "state governed by the Jewish Law". Let's consider: should we be ashamed of the Halakhah that has been transmitted down the ages?! Our Torah is a Torah of life, a Torah that teaches us how to live a pure and holy life. The whole intent of these secular circles is to detach the Jewish people from its glorified past, to build a new nation by legislating new laws. As far as they are concerned, the Sabbath does not exist. The observance of the Sabbath was erased in the courthouse, the Knesset is fighting against the pure Halakhah, the High Court of Justice obliterates whatever has been agreed upon by the people of Israel from time immemorial. As far as they are concerned, the Nation of Israel was born merely a hundred years ago. Yet the Jewish people has existed for thousands of years in conjunction with the Halakhah, which has been transmitted down the ages, the very Halakhah that made it possible for the Jews to overcome the terrible decrees and the horrible slaughters. ... Does their new teaching offer any future guarantee for the security of Jewish people? (V/13)

R. Shach repeatedly equates the poor quality of democracy with the popularity of football games and contrasts both of them with the cumulative wisdom inherent in Jewish halakhic tradition. The following description is a caricature of the shallow figures at the head of Israel's democratic government, which itself is grossly alienated from Jewish tradition:

> Regrettably, what does this state look like? Whoever designated it a law-governed state would not merit Heaven. For here the verse of Scriptures (Jeremiah 2:5) has been fulfilled: "They have walked after vanity and have become themselves worthless". Whenever ball games are played, fifty thousand people attend the opening game, headed by the President of the state and the leaders of the nation. Now, if they happen to win, it is a good day for them. They have a toast and dance in the streets. What is this joy? The whole fuss is just because one of the players kicked a ball, and having a stronger foot, he managed to finish it into the net and win the game!! Is this the virtue and merit of the Jewish people—handling the ball? Is this how the strength or weakness of the people of Israel is measured? Doesn't our wisdom lie in the statutes and judgements given to us by God? As it is said (Deuteronomy 4:8): "And what nation is there so great that has statutes and judgements so righteous as all this Torah". It is these statutes and judgements, the laws of the Torah, which give vitality to man. This is what a Jewish state should look like—a state that abides by the law of the Torah, a state governed by the Halakhah rather than a law-governed state (2007: 186).

For R. Shach, the contrast between a law-governed state and a state that abides by the Halakhah has wide implications. One of the major issues on the agenda of the State of Israel is how to combine its identity as a Jewish state with its identity as a democratic state. From a national point of view, this involves a conflict between laws that give preference to the Jewish citizens, on the one hand, and the civil rights of the Arab and other non-Jewish populations, on the other hand. From a religious point of view, there is a clash between religious laws and liberal norms. On the whole, the Israeli public tends to stress the clash between laws regarding the personal status of Jews, which are within the exclusive jurisdiction of the religious courts and the Chief Rabbinate, and liberal values. For instance, in Israel formal marriages between Jews must be officiated only by an orthodox rabbi and divorce proceedings are conducted only in a rabbinical court (see Neuberger, 2000: 311-8). Rabbi Shach considers the matter from the opposite point of view. He argues that from a religious point of view the very existence of secular laws that go against religious tradition signifies the rebellion of Israeli democracy against its religious tradition, for the people of Israel is committed to the covenant with God, by force of which it received the Torah on behalf of all mankind. In response to a certain court ruling he said: 'In the State of Israel a female judge dares to say that when the laws of the state conflict with the laws of the Torah one must abide by the laws of the state. Well, this is worse than the gravest transgression' (1988-95: V/135). He points out that the Torah explicitly says that abandoning the covenant with God is bound to bring about the wrath of God. The nations of the world are free to build for themselves legal frameworks as they please, but not so the people of Israel. Laws that make it possible to desecrate the Sabbath in a Jewish state signify a rebellion against God (V/135-6).

The point he is making here goes beyond treating Israel as a shallow, law-governed state that deviates from the wisdom of previous generations. What he argues is that legislating laws in a Jewish state is strictly the prerogative of Jewish Halakhah. This is a fundamentalist notion par excellence (see Mayer, 1993).[3]

Democracy is a human system based on the notion of equality and like any other man-made system it leads to destruction, as happened under communism

One of the conspicuous motives in R. Shach's writings is contrasting the divine Torah with any humanly-devised ideological system, which is necessarily

---

[3] On the fundamentalist attributes of the hareidi world view of the yeshiva Torah world, see Rosenak (1993); Selengut (1993).

flawed by its very nature. The root of the problem lies in the human sense of self-glorification, the complacent feeling that 'my power and the strength of my hand have gotten me this might' (Deuteronomy 8:17). R. Shach deplores the fact that humans tend to cultivate an idolatrous belief in their power and creativeness instead of being humble in the presence of God (1988-95: I/46-7). In the context of Zionism and the State of Israel he finds this approach extremely detrimental. The new Israeli admires his military power and his technological capability. But this sense of triumphant arrogance — an outcome of the Six-Day War (1967) — was, according to R. Shach, one of the main causes for the Yom Kippur War (1973), which was brought upon the State of Israel in retribution and took a heavy toll on the soldiers (I/47). R. Shach's consistent opposition to the settlement in the so-called occupied territories (Judea, Samaria, and the Gaza Strip) was motivated by the view that the State of Israel should not discount the statements made by the nations of the world and defy them by flaunting its self-confidence in 'my power and the strength of my hand' (I/12).[4]

The glorification of human power is also at the basis of the new political systems invented by humans. At this point, R. Shach's criticism is reminiscent of Edmund Burke's conservative outlook. He protests that instead of relying on traditions that gradually unfold throughout the generations, various ideologues devise systems that look like a magic solution but actually shatter in the face of a complex and dynamic reality.[5] The wisdoms of the world are based on limited human inventions, whereas the wisdom of the Torah is eternal, being divine (III/168).

Only the wisdom of the Torah is certain, since it is based on a chain of transmission that goes back to the generation of the Sinaitic Revelation. As to the wisdom of the world, says R. Shach,

> [n]o one can establish that it is true wisdom, since the same ideology that is adjusted and accommodated by some philosopher according to the particular situation in his own time may not be relevant and appropriate forty years later, when times change. Indeed, we have witnessed with our own eyes how various systems and ideologies concocted by strangers were smashed overnight against the rock and all those millions of people who believed in them and became their followers lost their support and were smitten by a sense of futility and bewilderment (III/169).

In Burke's world, the French Revolution epitomizes the failure of an abstract, humanly invented ideology that was not put to the test through the historical process. In Rabbi Shach's world, the overwhelming example of the failure of

---

4   For an elaboration of this issue, see Brown (2003: 292 ff).
5   On Burke's conservative ideology, see Burke (2003).

ideological systems is the communist revolution in Russia. R. Shach is persistent in reminding us of the lessons of this revolution. Apparently, his personal experiences in Russia during the communist revolution and in its aftermath became forever imprinted in his memory as a particularly traumatic experience. The following words of his illustrate the shaky human foundation upon which the human system of communism was built in Russia:

> We have witnessed right in front of us how millions of people lived in error, being tempted by false visions of a "new world" and believing that "my power and the strength of my hand" would bring a change for the better—but now, alas, they are facing total bankruptcy. I still remember the days when the slogans of "equality" and "justice" were heard all over Russia, promising happiness to all mankind. I also remember that in order to fulfil their new ideas they threw people into the sea. They tried to persuade a whole nation to follow Stalin in blind faith. They brought up their children to be grateful to Stalin for the sun that shines thanks to him, as it were, and for the bread with which he feeds the hungry. Evidently, they should have learned a lesson from all that has happened but those of the young generation go on innovating new ways. The path followed by their fathers is no longer "suitable" for them. Yet we know that only the Torah sustains us (V/75).

R. Shach associates democracy with the communist regime in Russia: 'Do you know what "democracy" is? We are familiar with the democracy in Russia, whereby millions of people all around the world lost their lives! They were all Trotskyites' (2007: 174). It seems that the common basis of equality and public participation is what misled him to equate the two forms of government: western liberal democracy and the totalitarian regime in the Soviet Union. In any case, R. Shach bases his criticism of democracy on the fact that even the modern democratic form of government is founded on a system invented by humans out of a sense of power and autonomous authority that finds its expression in human, autonomous parliamentary legislation, which is independent of any religious tradition. In the following statement R. Shach presents democracy as a kind of a non-kosher food that is forbidden to religious Jews:

> We must know that as Jews we are not allowed to be swept up by any system. If you hear about new methods or new ways, bear in mind that they lead to the destruction of the Jewish community as a whole. God forbid that we deviate from the old path. Democracy is a non-kosher thing and their whole intent is to make use of it in order to eradicate the Jewish people. They consistently make laws in order to undermine the Torah (1988–95: V/124–5).

Furthermore, R. Shach sees democracy as a decision-making machinery that is separated from reality, as emerges from the following criticism, which blurs the boundary between western democracy and totalitarian democracy:

> Lo and behold, a number of people sat in the cabinet and invented a system of living, introducing it as a way of life for millions of people. Yet do they have sufficient knowledge about human capabilities and mental faculties to determine whether everybody can live by it? Do they know whether it is possible to endure such a style of life? And nevertheless millions were forced to suffer because of these systems (2005: 254).

A democratic state is a state 'like all the nations' and is incompatible with Jewish uniqueness

One of the striking characteristics of Jewish tradition is the tension inherent in it between universalistic and particularistic tendencies. The basis for the universalistic orientation is the notion that man was created in the image of God (see, for example, Genesis 1:26; Tractate Avot III, 6; Sifra on Genesis 5:1). On the other hand, the nature of the people of Israel as 'a kingdom of priests and a holy nation' (Exodus 19:6), which is 'a people that shall dwell alone' (Numbers 23:9) and is committed to mutual responsibility (Tractate Shevu'ot 39a, and others), suggests particularistic orientations.[6] Sometimes the same Biblical verse lends itself to opposite interpretations, following both directions. Such is the well-known verse 'Love thy neighbour as thyself' (Leviticus 19:18) (Simon, 1975). At times, a different formulation embodies a contrary underlying assumption. This is true, for instance, of the two mishnaic variants: 'Whoever preserves a single soul *of Israel/of the world*, it is as though he had preserved a whole world' (Sanhedrin IV, 5; see Maimonides, Hilkhot Sanhedrin XII, 3). The intricate combination of spiritual universalism and religious-national particularism reaches its peak in the messianic vision of the prophets (Isaiah 2, 11; Micha 4) and later on in Maimonides (Mishna Torah, Hilkhot Teshuvah, ch. 9; Hilkhot melakhim, chs. 11–12).

Various Jewish thinkers and various intellectual currents in Judaism disagree about how to treat non-Jews. Those who stress the universal elements of Judaism tend to adopt an open, moderate approach, while those who embrace the particularistic approach tend to hold negative stands that underline the gulf between Jews and non-Jews. These particularistic positions stand out in the kabbalistic world of the last few hundred years.[7]

---

6   On the idea of Israel as the Chosen People, see Urbach (1979: ch. 16); Novak (1995).
7   Particularistic views are typical of the thought of R. Yehuda Halevy, Maharal, and central voices in the Kabbalah and in Hasidism, see Hallamish (1983). On the universalistic foundations in Maimonides and Rabbi Menachem Meiri, see Blidstein (1987); Halbertal (2000). On this issue, see Greenberg (1985b, a, c).

The distinction between the universalistic and particularistic positions is important for understanding the difference between the various political attitudes that are prevalent in the contemporary Jewish world.[8]

Rabbi Shach clearly belongs to the particularistic camp. In his world, there is an abysmal contrast between Jews and non-Jews. Isaac's saying 'The voice is Jacob's voice but the hands are the hands of Esau' is interpreted by our sages as embodying the difference between Jews (Jacob's descendants) and non-Jews (Esau's descendants). For R. Shach this saying serves as the lynchpin around which he builds the contrast between the Jewish spiritual world and the non-Jewish physical world, which celebrates struggle, violence, and wars (1998: 19–20). This has always been the case, as stated by R. Simeon ben Yohai, the Talmudic sage: 'This is the ruling: it is known that Esau hates Jacob'. According to the Midrash, Mount Sinai derives its name from the hatred of the nations of the world toward Israel.[9] Israel, say the sages, is 'a sheep among seventy wolves' and for R. Shach 'this is not a metaphor but rather the reality, and it will continue to be so until the coming of the redeemer. For this reason the people of Israel was "a nation that dwells in isolation", both collectively and individually' (1988-95: I/11). The secular Zionists wanted to establish a 'normal' state that would be an integral part of the nations of the world for all intents and purposes, thus bringing an end to the problem of anti-Semitism. What they did not understand, however, was that anti-Semitism expresses the real and sharp difference between Jews and non-Jews, and as such it will continue to exist up to the complete redemption, when the non-Jewish world will change fundamentally (I/4–5).

R. Shach's particularistic stand has a bearing on his attitude toward western democracy. In his writings the democracy/Torah contrast corresponds to the contrast between the nations of the world and the people of Israel. Democracy embodies the general universal norms while the Jewish people must cling to its divinely ordained uniqueness. The secular state does not acknowledge the unique role of the Jewish people and hence its sole interest in maintaining a democratic state like all other western states:

> It is with great sorrow and a heavy heart that we must say that there is no denying of the obvious truth to anyone who is willing to face it, namely that the whole intent of the government is for us to be a state like all other states and that it makes no difference to them that this involves the people of Israel. They are interested in a free, democratic

---

8   For a discussion of this issue in relation to religious-Zionist thought in the twentieth century, see Hellinger (2008).

9   In Hebrew there is a phonetic resemblance between the words 'Sinai' (*sina'y*) and 'hatred' (*sin'ah*). The issue is discussed at length by Ben Hayyim (2004: ch. 1).

> state that has nothing to do with religion, with the past. They want the house of Israel to be like all nations. Concerning this issue the prophet has already stated: "This shall never come about" (Ezekiel 10:32) (V/122).

The secular way of life, says R. Shach, is no different from the non-Jewish way of life and Israel's secular education is grounded in modern notions of Social Darwinism and the like instead of drawing on the age-old Torah tradition (I/12). It follows that R. Shach's objection to establishing the State of Israel on democratic foundations is not merely a matter of the discrepancy between the laws of democracy and Jewish religious tradition. He is adamantly against sharing universal values with non-Jews and stresses the need to bring into sharp focus the abyss between the two worlds. In this context, the major democratic value that is subject to R. Shach's attack is that of democratic equality. In the last section we have seen that R. Shach equates democracy with communism on the basis of their common advocacy of democratic equality. R. Shach strongly believes that this value has no place in the Israeli context, where civil equality in the elections is likely to have a detrimental effect on major political decisions as a result of taking into consideration the votes of the Arab and other non-Jewish representatives. In this case, too, the reliance on democratic values undermines the Jewish character of the State of Israel:

> The prime minister governs by a majority of one or two votes, among them some Arab members of the Knesset. And I am asking, is this, in their opinion, the vision of the State of Israel? Is this what the Jews have been waiting for down the ages, sacrificing their souls over the fundamental belief: "I believe with perfect faith in the coming of the Messiah" — only to be privileged by having a Jewish government that is sustained by Arabs? ... This is the weakness of democracy, and in this respect it resembles communism, its counterpart sister, which also subscribed to "equality" and under its banner millions of people were killed in Russia (V/126).

Based on individual freedom, democracy entails terrible licentiousness

R. Shach's criticism of democracy and its reinforcement in the State of Israel sharpened during the second Rabin government (1992–95). As mentioned in section II, R. Shach strongly opposed this left-wing government, which was under the leadership of the Labour Party that had formed a coalition with ultra-secular Meretz, a leftist anti-religious party, on the one hand, and with Shas, the ultra-Orthodox Sephardi party, on the other hand. Note that the second Rabin government led a policy of reconciliation with the Palestinian people, which involved significant territorial concessions. Although R. Shach was long in favour of such positions (I/14–7), he did not want the ultra-Orthodox parties to join the coalition headed by Rabin, and once the government was formed with the support of Shas—the very party he had helped create—, he went against both of them.

One of the reasons for R. Shach's opposition to Rabin's government was his disapproval of Meretz, a clearly anti-hareidi party that called for the separation of religion from state affairs and for the military drafting of all yeshiva students. In addition, it seems that R. Shach was settling accounts with the Labour Party for its historic role in secularizing Israeli society. And since Rabin's government stressed liberal democratic values at the expense of Jewish values, R. Shach honed his attacks against democracy. If in the past he had targeted his attacks on the penetration of democracy into the State of Israel and on relegating Jewish values to the sidelines, now he made a frontal attack on liberal democratic values themselves. Furthermore, while his previous attacks concerned the egalitarian aspect of western democracy, now he directed his criticism against the value of freedom, which came to be strongly associated with liberal democracy:

> Let us not think that the system that is called "democracy" is a positive value. For what is democracy? Freedom, liberty, not to be restricted at all! But the truth is that only the Torah grants true freedom to humanity. For man must have restricting laws, because without guidance he is liable to destroy the world. ... And it is only God who can teach this, for He is well aware of the powers of man, and knows what man can withstand and what is above his powers (V/124).

He goes on to say that democracy 'is a disaster to the world. It imparts a false sense of "freedom" while actually amounting to nothing more than licentiousness. ... Democracy is a non-kosher thing, and their whole intent is to make use of it in order to eradicate the Jewish people' (V/124-5).

The sharp contrast he makes between the restrictions imposed by the Torah and the licentiousness nurtured by democratic freedom leads R. Shach to equate democracy with non-kosher food. Here too we can detect a clear-cut fundamentalist dimension. In another formulation R. Shach argues that precisely the Torah, which sets limits to humans, affords them happiness. In contrast, 'it is precisely democracy, which obliterates these limits, that destroys humanity' (V/126). 'In the name of "the freedom of the individual" they want to create a situation whereby everyone does as they please: permitting civil marriages, opening stores on the Sabbath day' (V/133). R. Shach equates democracy with assimilation, for the more widespread the notion that each individual is entitled to do what he or she pleases (as long as this does not harm others), the greater the number of people who choose to depart from the traditional religious framework. In the Jewish context this way of life threatens to destroy the Jewish people through the very nature of a democratic culture (V/133). Thus the secular, democratic education is catastrophic. At this point, R. Shach's attacks on democracy reach their peak:

> Torah teaches us the rule: "Jealousy, lust, and ambition drive a man out of the world". But nowadays, as far as the secular education is concerned, children are taught to pursue jealousy, lust, and ambition as much as possible. ... We pray to the Master of the World to rid us from the curse of the new democracy that was brought into the world, for it is as bad as the disease of cancer that was brought into the world. Only the holy Torah is true democracy (V/127).

IV

Conclusion

In Rabbi Shach's world, democracy is viewed as one of the worst diseases of the twentieth century. He objects to democracy mainly insofar as the character of the State of Israel and of Israeli society is concerned. His apprehension that Israel would become a liberal democratic state, detached from its Jewish roots, makes him treat democracy as a dangerous adversary. Its rule of law and its liberal democratic values defy the Torah and Halakhah, by which a 'kosher' Jewish state must be governed. Furthermore, its major values are deplorable. Equality is a false value, as demonstrated by the communist revolution. Democratic freedom leads to licentiousness and to the destruction of the Jewish people. Even the more technical and procedural aspect of democracy, namely the principle of majority decision in free elections and in parliamentary and cabinet decision making, serves as an instrument of manipulation, bribery, and intrigue and leads to political decision making that is immoral and harmful.

In contradistinction to democracy, R. Shach postulates the eternal Torah with its high spiritual and moral values. Only the Torah promotes the full moral and spiritual development of the human personality. As a 'Chosen People' of moral and ethical exemplars living in the light of Torah values, the Jewish people can offer an alternative to the shallowness that is inherent in democratic regimes.

References

In Hebrew

Ben Hayyim, A. (2004), *The man of vision: the ultra-orthodox ideology according to Rabbi Shach* (Jerusalem: Mosaics).

Brown, B. (2003), 'R. Shach: his veneration of the spirit, his criticism of nationalism, and the political decisions in the state of Israel', in *Religion and nationalism in Israel and in the Middle East*, ed. N. Horowitz (Tel Aviv: Am Oved).

Greenberg, M. (1985a), 'The integration of Israel into mankind according to Jewish sources', in *On the Bible and Judaism: a collection of writings*, ed. A. Shapiro (Tel Aviv: Am Oved).

Greenberg, M. (1985b), 'The value of man in the Bible', in *On the Bible and Judaism: a collection of writings*, ed. A. Shapiro (Tel Aviv: Am Oved).

Greenberg, M. (1985c), 'You are called man', in *On the Bible and Judaism: a collection of writings*, ed. A. Shapiro (Tel Aviv: Am Oved).

Hallamish, M. (1983), 'Several aspects of the question of the relation of the Kabbalists to the nations of the world', in *Israeli philosophy*, eds. A. Kasher and M. Hallamish (Tel Aviv: Papyrus).

Horowitz, M. (1989), *Rabbi Shach: holding the key* (Jerusalem: Keter).

Neuberger, B. (2000), 'Democracy with four blemishes', in *The state of Israel: between Judaism and democracy*, ed. Y. David (Jersualem: The Israel Democracy Institute).

Shach, E.M.M. (1988-95), *Mikhtavim u-Ma'amarm* (6 vols.; Bnei Brak: publisher not mentioned).

Shach, E.M.M. (1998), *Ba-Zot Ani Bote'ah: Iggrot u-Ma'amarim al Tekufat ha-Yamim u-Me'oroteha* (2nd ed.; Bnei Brak: publisher not mentioned).

Shach, E.M.M. (2005), *Mahshevet Musar, vol. 2: Sihot Musar*, ed. B.M. Shenkar (Bnei Brak: Rashbi Yeshiva).

Shach, E.M.M. (2007), *Mahshevet Zekenim*, ed. B.M. Shenkar (Bnei Brak: publisher not mentioned).

Taub, E. (2004), *Religious leadership in the political arena: leadership methods of Rabbis Eliezer Shach and Ovadiah Yoseph in theory and practice* (unpublished doctoral thesis, Bar-Ilan University, Ramat-Gan, Israel).

In English

Blidstein, G. (1987), 'Tikkun Olam', in *Tikkun Olam: social responsibility in Jewish thought and law*, eds. D. Shatz, C.I. Waxman and N.J. Diament (Northvale: Jason Aronson Inc.).

Burke, E. (2003), *Reflections on the revolution in France*, ed. F.M. Turner (New Haven: Yale University Press).

Halbertal, M. (2000), '"Ones possessed of religion": religious tolerance in the teaching of the Me'iri', *The Edah Journal*, 1 (1).

Hellinger, M. (2008), 'The tension between universal and particular orientations within religious Zionism and its consequences: the 'Torah and Labor' movement as a test case', *Review of Rabbinic Judaism*, 11 (1): 139-66.

Mayer, A.E. (1993), 'The fundamentalist impact on law, politics and constitution in Iran, Pakistan, and Sudan', in *Fundamentalisms and the state*, eds. M.E. Marty and R.S. Appleby (Chicago: University of Chicago Press).

Novak, D. (1995), *The election of Israel: the idea of the chosen people* (Cambridge: Cambridge University Press).

Rosenak, M. (1993), 'Jewish fundamentalism in Israeli education', in *Fundamentalisms and society*, eds. M.E. Marty and R.S. Appleby (Chicago: University of Chicago Press).

Selengut, C. (1994), 'Yeshiva fundamentalism in Jewish life', in *Accounting for fundamentalisms: the dynamic character of movements*, eds. M.E. Marty and R.S. Appleby (Chicago: University of Chicago Press).

Simon, E. (1975), 'The neighbor (*Re'a*) whom we shall love', in *Modern Jewish ethics*, ed. M. Fox (Columbus: Ohio State University Press).

Urbach, E.E. (1979), *The sages, their concepts and beliefs*, trans. I. Abrahams (Cambridge, MA: Harvard University Press).

Jalal Alamgir

State(ments) of Emergency
Anti-Democratic Narratives in Bangladesh

I
Introduction[1]

A veiled military takeover in early 2007 brought to an end about fifteen years of formal democracy in Bangladesh, during which power had rotated between two major parties through national elections held on schedule and deemed generally free and fair. This is not to say that all was satisfactory in those fifteen years. The quality of governance and democratic performance had declined considerably since 2001. The parliament was handicapped by a highly confrontational relationship between the treasury bench and the opposition, involving frequent walkouts and abuse of authority. By 2006, the norms of democracy had decayed so much that the Bangladesh Nationalist Party (BNP), the centre-right party that was in power, began openly to change electoral rules and institutions in order to engineer the coming national elections in its favour. Fierce protests by the opposition, led by the centre-left Awami League, spiralled into widespread street violence, paving the way for a military takeover — to the relief of most at that time.

The military regime promulgated a state of emergency and suspended all fundamental rights, including the rights of expression and organization. It initiated an 'anti-corruption' drive, under which it detained hundreds of political leaders. The regime formed summary tribunals outside the standard legal system, and handed out draconian prison sentences to many of the detained. Around the country, nearly half a million were imprisoned,

---

1 This paper was first presented at the Annual Conference of the Development Studies Association (DSA) in London, England, November 2008.

most without specific charges. The notorious military intelligence agency began operating torture cells in the dark of night, in which many critics were punished, including journalists and indigenous activists. According to foreign media, by September 2007 at least twenty-two people had been tortured to death (see *The Economist*, September 6, 2007). The media in Bangladesh remained subdued and controlled, not just through constant intimidation but also at times by the seizure, through carrot and stick, of substantial ownership of media companies. The strategy, in short, was to use force to mould political players as well as political discourse, allowing the number of regime supporters to grow as dissenters were silenced. The turn of events was dramatic indeed over the next two years: Bangladesh slid from a state of chaotic freedom marked by a vigorous exercise of political rights but not political responsibility to a state of extreme repression marked by an eradication of political rights under the guise of the military's responsibility to 'save the nation'.[2]

The *state* of emergency that gagged independent political voices and action was accompanied by *statements* of emergency, essentially anti-democratic narratives marketed deliberately to discredit democracy as a political system in the context of Bangladesh. These narratives emanated from a variety of sources that sprung up to take advantage of the political void. These sources included the military patrons and their clients, regime collaborators or 'reformists' within political parties, and sections of the urban civil society. This paper reviews the two major anti-democratic narratives. The first one, aired mainly in 2007, is a grand narrative claiming a wholesale failure of parliamentary democracy as a political system. The second one is a functional narrative. Publicized later, it views popular sovereignty as a form of tyranny, contending essentially that it needs to be functionally 'balanced' with new institutions not based on popular sovereignty. Together the two narratives form the basis of the recent anti-democratic thought in Bangladesh, the growing legitimacy of which, I will argue at the end, is rooted ironically in actions and non-actions of the democratic West.

The term 'narrative' is significant. With it I imply that the ideas and thoughts are propagated by fitting them in the backdrop of local events and local history, such that together they have 'a background or setting, a beginning, a sequence of scenes, and an ending' (Bates, Greif, Levi, Rosenthal and Weingast, 1998: 14). A narrative is accessible and understandable, and it is feasible; propagation of a narrative brings ideas down from loftier levels of philosophy and logic and inserts them into popular

---

2 'Saving the nation', of course, has been the foremost excuse for military power grabs around the world, see Alamgir (2007a).

imaginations. A narrative, thus, becomes the connector between anti-democratic thought and anti-democratic action — and that is what happened in the case of Bangladesh. To describe and analyze these anti-democratic narratives, we will (re)construct a dialog between government perspectives and popular reactions (mostly as expressed in the media), against a backdrop of political events. The purpose of narrative analysis is to expose and elaborate, more so than to explain, which is the aim of theories. In doing so, narrative analysis can provide rich details about a phenomenon or a process, and illuminate understandings not discerned as well by employing more formalistic approaches (see Alamgir, 2007b: 155). The goal of this paper, accordingly, is to give the reader a glimpse of anti-democratic thought in action by exposing the narratives marketed by the military regime in Bangladesh.

II

Backdrop: 1/11 and the Atmosphere of Control

The day that emergency was proclaimed in Bangladesh is now known simply as 1/11 (January 11, 2007). The night before, military movement had increased in and around the presidential palace. After pressured negotiations with diplomats and the military top brass, the President, Iajuddin Ahmed, declared — or rather, was forced to declare — a state of emergency. No specific reason was given. On the surface, it seemed that the President, who had earlier shown a strong bias toward BNP and thereby proven ineffective as a mediator between contending political parties, would be appointing an interim non-party civilian administration, formally known as a caretaker government (CTG), in order to organize elections. The constitution of Bangladesh requires the formation of a three-month caretaker government to organize national elections every five years. But such an interim administration had never before required a state of emergency. The present episode was unprecedented. The word 'coup' was whispered in some circles but never appeared in the public discourse until *The Economist* ran an analysis a week later (January 18) with the title *The coup that dare not speak its name*, stating directly: 'The army, not the politicians, now runs Bangladesh'. A caretaker government was formed the next day. It served officially as a cabinet, but eventually came to be understood in street parlance as the civilian facade of military decision makers operating behind the scenes. Joint Forces, a combination of police, paramilitary, and the army, usually led by an army major outside judicial oversight, began mass arrests of political activists soon after, under the guise of anti-crime, anti-terror, and anti-corruption drives. Amid rising speculation and insecurity, the major political parties apprehensively welcomed the imposition of the emergency as a temporary measure and urged the government to hold elections as shortly as possible in order to return the administration to elected representatives. As evident in the Bengali and English media at the time, there was neither public expectation nor demand for a prolonged suspension of fundamental rights, let alone a wholesale change in the system.[3]

The official rationale for the emergency was given on January 22, in a televised speech by the Chief Advisor, Fakhruddin Ahmed, who served as the civilian head of the caretaker government. Like in many other military-led takeovers, the rationale for the suspension of fundamental rights was, paradoxically, expressed in terms of a need to 'strengthen democratic rule'. But the Chief Advisor hinted at the creation of a changed environment, not just to hold free and fair elections but to prevent 'past excesses': 'The nation does not want to backslide once again and go fall back into past instability and intolerable situation' (*sic*). Aside from promising stern action 'against godfathers, listed criminals, terrorists, extortionists and anti-social elements', no clear indication was given on what exactly would constitute future changes in the political environment in order to strengthen democracy (in *The Daily Star*, January 22, 2007). Within weeks, a powerful task force called National Coordination Committee (NCC) against corruption and severe crimes was formed, with a serving hardliner army general and former head of military intelligence as its chief. Another retired general was appointed the chief of the Anti-Corruption Commission (ACC). For the first time in history, military personnel were appointed to the Election Commission. The public expectation, however, was not one of militarization but that an anti-crime and anti-corruption drive, led essentially by the army, would continue for some time.[4] This was consistent with statements made regularly by the government, which emphasized, using the military rhetoric of a 'war' on corruption, that a 'cleanup' of the political space is a must before power could be handed over. While the government did not announce when elections would be held, many in the polity expected that the elections would be announced, if not held, within ninety days, since the constitution of Bangladesh does not allow a caretaker government to prevail beyond ninety days, nor does it allow the

---

3   See news reports published between January 11 and 22, 2007, in the leading dailies *The Daily Star* and *New Age* (both English), *Shamokal*, *Inqilab*, *Sangbad*, *Prothom Alo* and *Jugantor* (all Bengali).

4   It was about a year later that the prospect of long-term militarization became a concern. Amnesty International noted in a press release 'the creeping role of the armed forces in a range of functions, with no clear rules of accountability, that should rightly be carried out by the civilian administration' (2008).

CTG to undertake policy decisions except those that are required to conduct elections.

Doubts about these expectations of a short-lived suspension of the erstwhile political system began to emerge as the military top brass became more visible across the country, giving speeches at highly publicized events, offering ideas on politics, political problems and their solutions. Virtually all of these events were vetted and approved by the Directorate General of Forces Intelligence (DGFI), the national intelligence agency that usually operates with impunity and served, according to a report by the International Crisis Group, as 'the driving force behind military rule' (2008: 16). Anonymous Internet bloggers reported that journalists, speakers and participants often had little choice regarding their reports and speeches. The draconian Emergency Power Rules (EPR) imposed severe restrictions on press freedom. On the surface, the CTG allowed some dissent to appear, thus providing a sense of openness, but most dissent was carefully controlled. Some journalists vocal against military intervention in politics were imprisoned and tortured, in order to send a signal to all others (see Human Rights Watch, 2008). A highly controlled atmosphere thus had been created for the dissemination of anti-democratic thought.

III

The Grand Failure of Democracy

The first serious exposé of anti-democratic thought was broadcast just over two months into emergency rule, in March 2007. In a tea party organized to commemorate Bangladesh's independence day, the Army Chief, Lt. Gen. Moeen Uddin Ahmed, remarked in his speech: 'In the 36 years since independence, politicians have not given us anything good' (in *The Daily Star*, March 28, 2007). This invective was carried prominently in all national newspapers, and made headlines in the international media as well. The BBC reported, for instance: 'Bangladesh's army chief has launched a scathing attack against the country's politicians, saying they have offered nothing but corruption and division' (Sudworth, 2007). Nevertheless, prominent politicians who at that time remained outside the net of the government's anti-graft drive hailed the speech by the Army Chief the following day. The General Secretary of the Awami League, Abdul Jalil, noted that the speech would 'inspire the nation' (in *The Daily Star*, March 29, 2007). Much of the media also accepted it, partly because elements of it rang true to many in the public. But cynics whispered that most politicians did not oppose these remarks because they were indeed corrupt—and the only way that they could protect themselves from being exposed or detained by the dreaded Joint Forces was by showing a favourable disposition to the powers at the helm. In fact, the only public criticism against this wholesale lambasting of the political class came from the leftist political leaders, who, though politically relatively marginal, are deemed to be much 'cleaner' and principled than mainstream politicians. Rashed Khan Menon, a respected leftist veteran, commented:

> Unfortunately, the fact is [that] history was distorted by the army-backed post-1975 governments who had ruled the country for more than one and a half decades out of the 36 years [of the country's independence] …. It is not wise to blame politicians for every fault. Though the politicians have failed to run the country properly, they should also be recognised for a number of achievements (in Ruhin, 2007).

This dialogue constituted the initial volleys of what was to become a narrative of grand failure. The narrative acquired more shape in the next few days. The Army Chief continued a provocative political role, criticizing the political class and the political process in frequent public speeches. He argued, to the assent of most observers, that 'money and muscle' had become endemic to politics. Labelling Bangladesh as a derailed train, he asserted that 'the nation needed an efficient administrator to bring it to the right track for ensuring progress and prosperity' (in *New Age*, March 29, 2007). The allusion about 'an efficient administrator' was too clear to be lost.

The most significant propagation of the narrative took place a few days later. The Army Chief was asked to present the keynote address at a regional conference of the International Political Science Association (IPSA) held in Dhaka. In what became his most talked-about address, he continued the delegitimization of Bangladesh's political class, arguing for its replacement with 'a new concept' and 'new leadership':

> [We now have] an opportunity to develop a new concept and find a new sense of direction to the future politics of Bangladesh. … [T]he country has a principle to live by and a purpose to strive for, and this needs rethinking so that we can reinvent a system of governance with new leadership at all levels (Ahmed, 2007b).

Indeed, speaking from within a non-transparent emergency government that had suspended all fundamental rights, the Army Chief advocated a rethinking of Bangladesh's 'elective democracy' on the grounds of its non-transparency and violation of rights: 'We do not want to go back to an "elective democracy" where corruption in society becomes all-pervasive, governance suffers in terms of insecurity and violation of rights, and where political "criminalisation" threatens the very survival and integrity of the state' (Ahmed, 2007b).

This delegitimization, interestingly, went back to the political and theoretical relevance of the city-states of ancient Greece, as though democratic theory had not developed or progressed since then: 'the democratic ideal established by the ancient Athenians and successively modified by Cleisthenes and Pericles ... is not remotely achievable today' (Ahmed, 2007b). The speech noted that Pericles had reformed democracy to introduce merit and efficiency as criteria for holding office, but that these ideals are no longer displayed by democracies today. No mention was made of the evolution of more modern norms, such as civil and political rights, representation, or checks and balances. In other words, the two straw models that the speech identified in order to deride democracy were the direct democracy of Athenian city-states two thousand five hundred years ago and the 'oligarchic and plutocratic governmental system' in Bangladesh between 1991 and 2006.

In the context of Bangladesh, the address pointed out that both parliamentary and presidential systems had failed to deliver. And therefore, what was needed was a new, homegrown, institutional arrangement in the future, the opportunity for which was now at hand: 'We cannot copy, we must deliberate and reinvent our own style in the light of our social dynamics and economic potential. ... I reckon Bangladesh will have to construct its own brand of democracy'. The only two criteria given for this alternative system were that it needs to be consistent with 'social, historical, and cultural conditions, with religion [Islam] being one of several components of [the] national identity', and that it needs to elevate security in its emphasis: 'I perceive that both democracy and security are complementary features of the system now being put in place by the current initiatives' (Ahmed, 2007b).

These remarks and their implications made front page headlines in national media, were broadcast on local television channels, and made it to many regional and international outlets, being taken, in the following days, as an indication that the military-led caretaker administration was planning political changes far beyond simply holding elections and returning power to elected representatives (see *BBC News Online*, April 2, 2007; *Dawn*, April 2, 2007; *Hindustan Times*, April 2, 2007; *Gulf News*, April 3, 2007; *People's Daily*, April 3, 2007; *The Economist*, April 4, 2007). Indeed, the acknowledgment throughout the speech was that the 'current initiatives', comprised of political purging and political reconstruction, were not geared merely to hold elections but to fundamentally change the political system of the country. To some observers, the intention and the moves were parallel to what Pakistan's Pervez Musharraf had done to consolidate the military's role in politics by delegitimizing democracy as dysfunctional and ineffective and political leaders as wholly corrupt (see Saleh, 2007; Siddiqa, 2007a; Siddiqa, 2007b). Over the next few months, the government attempted to send into exile the chiefs of the two major political parties, both former Prime Ministers of Bangladesh, Khaleda Zia (BNP) and Sheikh Hasina Wazed (Awami League), further drawing striking parallels to Musharraf's strategy, in discourse and action (see *The Economist*, September 6, 2007). It should be noted that DGFI, Bangladesh's intelligence agency running the anti-democracy show, was set up to closely follow the model of the Pakistani intelligence services (International Crisis Group, 2008: 16).

Delegitimizing the status quo ante was a strong part of (and indeed the foremost rationale for) the anti-democracy narrative that was beginning to take shape. Simultaneously, the narrative aimed to legitimize the new regime's existence and actions. To establish its legitimacy, the regime and its collaborators, including some prominent local constitutional experts, pointed to two sources.[5] The first was the pretext of the emergency: the political impasse and the violence had left no other option than to resort to rule by decree. The event of 1/11 was no doubt constitutional, since the constitution provides, in extreme situations, an option to declare a state of emergency under which democracy, along with all fundamental rights, is temporarily suspended. However, the combined existence of a state of emergency and an unelected caretaker government was constitutionally dubious. More problematic was the constitutionality of the broad range of policy measures that the government had begun to undertake. According to Article 58D (1) of the constitution:

> The Non-Party Care-taker Government shall discharge its functions as an interim government and shall carry on the routine functions of such government with the aid and assistance of persons in the services of the Republic; and, except in the case of necessity for the discharge of such functions its [*sic*] shall not make any policy decision (Government of Bangladesh, 2004).

A strict application of this provision would have jeopardized the government's large-scale arrests as well as other major policy decisions, including large-scale purchases, which it was beginning to make every week. Unable to draw unequivocal support from the constitution despite repeated blessings from the country's best-known constitutional lawyer, the emergency government placed the legitimacy of its ongoing 'reform' programmes and political pogroms in the supposed will of the people, as though it was

---

5   Ullah (2007) points to the role of certain political scientists in shaping the anti-democratic political thought emanating from the regime: 'a host of intellectual collaborators [are] lining up to offer endorsements just to get a share of the podium'.

somehow more representative of the popular mandate than what was enjoyed by any previous elected government. The government went on to claim that even its highly repressive measures enjoyed overwhelming popular support. The Army Chief asserted, for instance, that 'the emergency gave a respite to the people. It has provided an opportunity to the administration to work unitedly with the people. People are happy with the actions of the joint forces in coordination with the administration' (in *New Age*, March 29, 2007).

The narrative on democratic failure continued for almost a year, with the Army Chief being the main spokesperson on its behalf. He made similar remarks on trips he took abroad. In February 2008, at the launch of a book containing his essays, he reiterated that the country had tried 'Westminster-type parliamentary democracy', but it had failed to work. Instead, the country needed to establish 'a form of democracy that is suitable for us' (in *BBC News Online*, February 20, 2008). The specifics of this new form of democracy were still not clear, even a year after the initial need for a new system had been announced. The other major gap in this narrative was oversight of the fact that Bangladesh's incipient democracy had been interrupted by a string of military dictatorships since 1975; the country was under military rule for sixteen out of thirty-six years. It was during these sixteen years that most of the democratic institutions and norms of the country were destroyed and the holding of engineered processes to elect militarized governments in civilian garb became fashionable.[6]

While not stated explicitly in public discourse, specifics about the type of system envisioned by the military leadership can be deduced from the political actions of the government. The foremost set of actions was not about institutions but about individuals. The mass arrests since 2007 were, in every essence, a large-scale political purging. The government's intent was to wipe out most of the mid-level organizational bedrock of the two major political parties, as due to the grassroots presence of these parties it would be virtually impossible for the government's preferred candidates to win free and fair elections. Such purging was accomplished at times by issuing, preposterously, a blanket warrant to arrest thousands of unnamed 'suspects'. In August 2007, for example, following campus violence against army rule, the government issued a mass warrant in which 82,000 unnamed persons were made accused—essentially giving the police and the military a *carte blanche* to persecute and prosecute anyone at will (see *New Age*, September 10, 2007). This *carte blanche* was used violently to purge political

---

6   Newspaper articles by the London-based veteran Bengali columnist Abdul Gaffar Chowdhury provided details of this contradiction throughout 2007.

activists from the university campuses. The government created summary tribunals to convict the detained, and then passed ordinances to make convicts ineligible to run in future elections. It branded selected political leaders as corrupt even before cases, however sham, were disposed, and prevented the media from printing arguments of the defence. The goal, as before, was to delegitimize individual politicians. Under a plan called 'The Minus-Two Solution' the government tried to clear the field by sending the two major party chiefs into exile and then encouraged a few preferred candidates, including Muhammad Yunus, the 2006 Nobel Peace Laureate, to launch new political parties. It allowed the newcomers to organize themselves while banning political activity for all others under the state of emergency. The first preference of the regime, in other words, was to attack career politicians and political activists verbally, legally, and physically and to install new faces while keeping most of the system intact. Anti-democratic narratives were given expression through stern action against active participants of the status quo ante.[7] It seemed that any alternative system would be acceptable to the military leaders as long as it prevented a certain range of individuals from gaining power. That plan did not work fully. Political parties over time became uncooperative with the regime's heavy-handed ways. There was a strong international backlash against the Minus-Two Solution. Human rights watchdogs became increasingly vocal, pointing out the severe persecution of opponents and installation of favoured candidates or puppets through all branches of the government (see Samad, 2008). Anti-democratic thought consequently shifted emphasis from individuals and began to offer, alongside its political purging, institutional arrangements designed to keep the former political class permanently out of power. Through that process, the anti-democratic thought leaders began to betray a strong distaste for popular sovereignty.

IV

The Discourse of Functional Alternatives

While promoters of the 'grand failure' narrative did not lay out comprehensive 'solutions' in the public space, they influenced regime collaborators to propose alternatives in order to test the water. Three such ideas gained prominence. The anti-democratic element common to all three is a distrust or disregard for publicly elected representatives. In other words,

---

7 The Army Chief clarified in a recent interview with *Time* magazine: 'No systems of government are bad in their own right [sic] .... It's the human beings who make it so' (in Tharoor, 2008).

all of these ideas focus on curtailing the extent of popular sovereignty, arguing that committing most power in the hands of an elected government in the status quo ante led to gross abuses. Power will need to be distributed and balanced not just between the executive, the legislature, and the judiciary, as in the traditional approach, but between elected and non-elected institutions.

National charter

The first of these ideas involves the creation of a national charter. Fakhruddin Ahmed, an ex-World Banker who, as Chief Advisor, came to serve the military regime as its civilian figurehead, vaguely aired the need for such a document shortly after 1/11. He made a stronger demand for it in an address to the nation on May 12, 2008, stating: 'Efforts will be made to formulate [a] "National Charter" on the basis of consensus on relevant matters prior to the polls so [that] qualitative changes are [ensured] in government and political systems after the election' (in *The Daily Star*, May 13, 2008). Ostensibly, such a charter was meant to be an agreement between all political players to abide by certain ground rules in the greater interest of the nation. In extreme forms it could be a foundational document to rival the constitution. As one of the supporters of this idea put it:

> [T]here should be an agreement on a set of things that must not happen anymore. Some of them are related to amendment of the Constitution, and the politicians are right when they say that it cannot be done by this government. So, a priori consensus must be reached so that this document, signed by all concerned, remains in hand for the elected government to act on (Ahmad, 2008).

The narrative to support this charter included proposals not just to accept electoral outcomes, whatever they may be (see Quader, 2008), but to formally legitimize all of the anti-politics drives and economic policies undertaken by the caretaker government. In addition, the charter's proponents advocated key constitutional amendments, using two venues. First, the Election Commission, which is technically supposed to only oversee elections, began proposing major institutional changes for the sake of conducting 'better' elections. All of these changes, such as replacing the current unicameral system with a bicameral parliament, increasing the number of parliamentary seats, and the introduction of proportional representation, would require constitutional amendments (see *New Age*, May 23, 2008). Second, the government began talk of forming a constitutional commission to review the constitution with a substantial goal: 'removing inconsistencies and contradictions in the state's guiding principles' (in *New*

Age, June 5, 2008). While the specifics were not made clear, they would also, in all likelihood, involve curtailing the power of elected representatives.

Essentially, a national charter would formalize the political discourse, democratic as well as anti-democratic, into a legal agreement and summarize the above-mentioned recommendations toward achieving 'consensus' on legislative issues before the election of a legislature. One of the advisors (ministers of the caretaker government), Hossain Zillur Rahman, explained the move as follows: 'The issue of concentration of power ... by the constitution was discussed at the meeting [of advisors]. It may be taken to the next parliament, but for that there should be a consensus' (in *New Age*, May 23, 2008). In its dialogue with political parties, the government tried to impose its reform ideas on them, under duress.[8] The resumption of political activity, the holding of elections, and their escape from 'anti-corruption' lawsuits and summary punishment would be conditional upon not only acceptance of the charter but its speedy promulgation as law once a parliament was elected. What is interesting is that this charter was being enumerated and imposed by an *unelected* emergency government for the sake of strengthening democracy. With its justification wedded to democracy, parties not assenting to the charter ran the risk of being branded 'anti-democratic'. As one columnist urged: 'To restore democracy through a free, fair and credible election, it is essential that the politicians agree to reforms done by the CTG' (Zahur, 2008).

The idea of a charter was rejected by all major political parties from the left to the right — but the most principled opposition came once again from the left, which argued that the caretaker government had no authority to promulgate anything of this magnitude and that discussions of any such document had to take place in an elected parliament (see *New Age*, May 18, 23 and 24, 2008; *The Daily Star*, May 19 and 27, 2008). Khandker Delwar Hossain, the Secretary General of BNP, noted that the idea was being used essentially to impose conditions on free political activity, summarizing his party's opposition to a charter as follows: 'It ... is unacceptable and contrary to the existing laws and the constitution. It could be an evil strategy to delay the elections' (in *New Age*, May 29, 2008).

National government

The second key idea to re-organize politics was the formation of a national government. Two variants of this idea made the rounds. The first idea was to bypass the parliament altogether and form an appointed leadership for

---

[8] Government spokespeople, of course, denied the imposition of the charter by force (see *The Daily Star*, May 14 and 19, 2008).

a certain period of time. One observer defined it as 'government composed of eminent people belonging to different political ideologies, intellectuals, educationists, social activists, diverse professionals etc.' (Ahmed, 2007a). Another promoter urged 'a national government under universal law of necessity with honest and courageous people who are willing to take the political heat of the reforms' (Kabir, 2007).

The two most vocal advocates of the idea of a national government were Kamal Hossain, a lawyer, and Badruddoza Chowdhury, a doctor — both discards from larger political parties, the former from the Awami League and the latter from BNP. Hossain had been promoting the idea of a national government for years (see *The Daily Star*, September 12, 2005, February 10, 2006, and March 27, 2008). Chowdhury's advocacy became strong in October 2006, at the height of the political crisis prior to 1/11. He proposed that a national government should run the country by consensus for ten years.

This idea, supported to some degree by the regime, was born out of a great distrust of the role of elections and representative government. It is a 'solution' to the problem laid out in the narrative about the grand failure of democracy: politicians, along with the current system, have simply not worked. The idea is also consistent with a merit- or efficiency-based system of governance, a notion supported by the Army Chief. As such, this idea of a non-elected government was an extension of the caretaker government in power. In fact, one advisor, Mainul Hosain, alluded to that in a statement in August 2007: 'Our present government is a national government, army-backed government. That means it is a collective government' (in *The Daily Star*, August 28, 2007). The effort was to append the word 'national' as a prefix in order to qualify a non-democratic government as acceptable.[9]

Most observers saw the promotion of the idea of a national government in collaboration with the regime as a ploy to gain power, since the two formerly influential politicians who were the principal peddlers of the idea had little scope to gain power electorally, having weak constituencies. It was advertised strongly during the first year of the emergency government, when political parties were severely repressed. It was supported by sundry regime collaborators among the urban elite who too would have no means to gain power democratically. Initial reformists (that is, turncoats) within the Awami League and BNP also endorsed the idea of a national government, toeing the line of the regime. But unlike Hossain or

9   The statement was reportedly considered a gaffe by the Army Chief, who was not pleased by the allusion to the prominent role of the army in the government. The advisor was sacked from his job shortly thereafter.

Chowdhury they argued that such a government should be formed *after* holding elections (see *The Daily Star*, April 22, 2007). In early 2008, Jatiya Party, headed by a former military dictator, Hussain Muhammad Ershad, also proposed that a '"national government" comprising all political parties and civil society members is required as it's not possible for the caretaker government to tackle the present political and economic crises' (in *The Daily Star*, January 25, 2008). This quasi-democratic power-sharing idea was raised when it became apparent that fully dismantling a parliamentary system would not be possible, nor would it be politically and internationally tenable to install such a government without holding elections. By February 2008, thus, the caretaker government's Law Advisor dispelled the notion of a national government, noting that there is no constitutional provision for it (see *The Daily Star*, February 8, 2008). In the modified conception that followed, an all-party coalition with proportional representation would govern in lieu of a traditional winner-take-all administration (see Chowdhury, 2008). The role of an appointed leadership was left vague.

What is important to note is that the source of all of these ideas was confined to a small coterie of the elite. The government intellectually engaged mostly pre-selected supporters, while dissenters and public discourse remained shackled. The goal of the ideas as well was to curtail the power of the public. The representative nature of all of these ideas was seriously in doubt. But few, if any, raised this fundamental point. Muhammad Zamir, one of the exceptions, in a regular newspaper column called this approach of consulting with a few key supporters—essentially the same faces—'a very restrictive bandwidth of engagement', explaining it thus:

> [The government's] approach has been decided upon on the basis of a continuing perception that reforms to the political process, the electoral dynamics and changes within the election laws and within political parties can be achieved through limited dialogue, urban in nature and scope, within the matrix of emergency provisions. Restrictions accordingly have continued to be in place through emergency provisions and the broader picture overlooked. This in turn, has denied opportunity for discussion and knowledge sharing in the non-urban areas inhabited by nearly 75 per cent of our total population (Zamir, 2008).

Regardless, hardliner parts of the military intelligence agency supported a 'permanent solution' through these changes in order to protect their elevated political role, for the constitution would not allow these unelected institutions and persons to exert as much influence. In order to perpetuate their presence, they proposed and then 'approved' a third institutional innovation: a National Security Council.

National Security Council

A narrative centred on a security urgency was promoted soon after 1/11. While it was true that the internal law and order situation had deteriorated precipitously between October 2006 and January 2007 due to political violence, it was also plain that no major security threat had arisen since then. The country faced no external enemies or internal insurgencies. Regardless, the initial discourse emanating from the government, as seen in section III, emphasized security as a need on par with democracy, with the insinuation that democratic norms and institutions should be compromised on a permanent basis in order to maintain security in a troubled global environment. The crucial 'vision speech' of the Army Chief in April 2007 was titled *The Challenging Interface of Democracy and Security*. And with the military at the helm of governance, perhaps it should be accepted that security needs would become more prominent than usual. But a possibly deeper reason reveals itself once we look at the institutional structure being designed at the nexus of democracy and security.

The narrative for a National Security Council (NSC) made the initial rounds in March 2007, corresponding to the other 'vision' statements made by various generals and civilian advisors. In the initial incarnation, simply the idea, and not any specifics, was circulated. Government spokesmen remained reserved and mysterious about the NSC's role. The brief justification given at that time was that it would help coordinate security matters, and that some version of it had existed before. An advisor (minister) of the regime, Maj. Gen. (retired) Mohammad Abdul Matin, noted that under the broad umbrella of security the NSC would also deal with issues of 'corruption and accountability' (in *The Daily Star*, March 8, 2007), which suggested that sweeping powers were envisioned for this body. What was certain is that all the military, paramilitary, and intelligence chiefs would be in the council. What was uncertain is whether elected civilians would play any meaningful role in its decisions. Sarcastically, a newspaper columnist wrote about the need to form an NSC: 'Since the army came to our rescue last January, it is only fair that a grateful nation should find them a rightful place at the nation's table' (Ahsan, 2007).

Under the radar, the Law Ministry was directed to prepare the legal structure for a powerful council run essentially by the military with representation from some civilian administrators. In August 2007, the Foreign Affairs Advisor, Iftekhar Ahmed Chowdhury, confirmed that a process was underway to form the NSC, but gave neither details nor a timeframe (see *The Daily Star*, August 13, 2007). A draft for a 24-member NSC was reportedly prepared by December. In early 2008, the Army Chief stated in a television interview when asked about this mysterious council: 'It's there in India and Pakistan — so why not in Bangladesh?' (in Saleh, 2008). Then, in a sudden announcement on March 10, 2008, the government approved the set up of an NSC (see *New Age*, March 10, 2008). The Law Advisor, A.F. Hassan Ariff, said that the NSC would deal with broad issues, 'not only regarding law and order but also about other national crises like disasters and food security issues' (in *The Daily Star*, March 21, 2008). But he too gave no other details nor the chance for public input into the process. In May 2008, the Home Ministry circulated a document to other ministries recommending the formation of two other bodies to help the NSC: a Cabinet Committee on National Security and a Joint Intelligence Unit (see *The Daily Star*, May 25, 2008).

Unlike the other two ideas, that is, national charter and national government, the idea of a council to formulate and implement national security policy was not allowed space for much public discourse. The public was kept in the dark throughout its design and formation, and was informed summarily by the caretaker government that the decision had been taken to form the NSC. Details of the structure of the NSC were never made public. The hushed nature of the NSC's development suggests its importance: it could not be derailed or demeaned through public debate. All that analysts had was a set of hints, at various times of the government's tenure, about the necessity of the council. In August 2007, a newspaper columnist asked a simple question about the rush (and hush) to create an NSC: 'Why not wait until the next parliament so that people are also convinced that it is a council for their security?' (Ahsan, 2007). Even those close to the military did not know fully what the plan was, and some moderate voices were raised, asking for more public information. A former Air Force officer made an appeal for public discourse: 'If we wish to have the NSC, the best would be to debate it on public forum as well as in the Parliament. Unless an organisation enjoys popular support, it is bound to wither away; NSC will be no exception' (Choudhury, 2008). Finally, when the approval of the NSC was announced, the editor of *The Daily Star*, the largest English language daily in the country, wrote an unusually critical front page column:

> Since we know nothing about it [the NSC], it is not possible for us to comment on the substantive aspects of the idea. However, we can and do intend to comment on the process so far followed. Bluntly put, whatever thinking has gone behind the NSC idea has been behind closed doors. Nothing has been shared with the public, and that is where our biggest objection lies. Why a matter of such importance has been worked at in such a hidden manner [sic]? (Anam, 2008)

The political parties engaged in this discourse strategically. Having lost significant parts of their national and local leadership to detention by the emergency government, those who were left outside (including many collaborators) were careful not to irk the government and thereby invite persecution. Even in June 2008 it was difficult for party spokespeople to speak their mind. As a local human rights group pointed out to a reporter from *Time* magazine: 'Everywhere you look there are watchmen outside your door .... Just open your mouth and you're liable to be jailed' (in Tharoor, 2008). In addition, the remaining leaders of political parties, like everyone else, were in the dark about the structure and workings of the NSC. Given the situation, they were careful to support the council and the need to coordinate security issues, but pointed out that such a body could be formed with better legitimacy only after an elected government had assumed power. A BNP leader summarized the position tactfully: 'I don't deny the necessity of forming the National Security Council, but this is not necessary at the moment' (in *The Daily Star*, June 4, 2008). Although expected, their lukewarm support sent signals about potential future problems, especially with the durability of the institution. As one supporter of NSC, himself a former military man, observed:

> The cause of concern is neither its composition nor its timing of formation. What concerns me most is that how will our political leaders react to it [*sic*]; and when they come to power how they will use this organization. It is evident from the past record that our political leaders are averse to such organizations (Ahmad, 2007).

A few political analysts and writers tried to inject criticism of the idea of an NSC, publishing either in Internet blogs outside the country or, when possible, sneaking in commentary in media that remained under a certain degree of control and oversight by the intelligence agencies. The concerns were primarily about the dilution of popular sovereignty through the creation of a high-powered non-transparent institution and, alongside, the potential of a permanent political role for the military. As one commentator, the head of Drishtipat, a human rights organization, wrote:

> No matter how free and fair the election, there is a risk that it will not be meaningful as the government will constantly be dictated in the name of "advice" by NSC. The risk is there that democratic institutions will always remain subservient and weak, leading to prolonged de facto military rule in the country (Saleh, 2008).

Another writer feared that, in the absence of a credible external security threat, the NSC would be used primarily to quell domestic dissent. It would offer 'a protected exit' for the emergency rulers, ensuring that human rights abuses committed by the regime go unaccounted for. And, very dangerously, it would politicize the military by inducting the armed forces formally into domestic political decisions (Khan, 2008). The discourse on the National Security Council, however, remained limited primarily to the English language media, assuring that the bulk of the population was in the dark about the formation of this powerful new institution shrouded in mystery. The possible reason is not difficult to guess. The vernacular media in general were under greater control and oversight from the intelligence agencies, while the English media, consumed mainly by the diplomatic community, were given a less restricted roam in order to show western observers that press freedom was unhampered in the country.

V

Conclusion: Cloaking and Selling Anti-Democratic Narratives

Given the precarious political situation between October 2006 and January 2007, it is difficult to imagine that there was any alternative left other than to declare a state of emergency. The military-led administration took over amid cheers from almost all political parties and observers. At the same time, 1/11 and its aftermath constituted an ominous turn of events in the third-largest Muslim country in the world, for it not only brought the military back in charge of the polity, but also opened space to initiate a troubling delegitimization of democracy.

To be sure, important parts of the narrative of democratic failure are well deserved. While formally democratic, the reign of BNP between 2001 and 2006 was anything but democratic. The opposition was persecuted relentlessly, corruption skyrocketed, parliamentary bipartisan committees were made defunct, power was centralized, the judiciary was severely compromised, and violation of human rights, including extra-judicial killings, reached an all-time high. Moreover, unlike the Awami League, BNP failed during both of its tenures to transfer power smoothly and peacefully through free and fair elections. What specifically failed in Bangladesh was not democracy but governance by one of the main parties, BNP. Created by a military dictator in the 1980s, the party, once elected to power, showed utter disregard for democratic norms, especially during 2001–06. Both quantitative and qualitative indicators of democratic performance demonstrate wide differences in democratic performance between the two parties (see Alamgir, 2008). Going farther back, Bangladesh's institutions of democracy and norms of human rights and good governance suffered tremendously during a protracted period (1975–91) of dictatorships, assassinations, and violence, overseen by competing military leaders. Therefore, a grand narrative that ignores decades of military-led destruction of democratic institutions and extends the particular failure of one party into a condemnation of all politicians and all forms of democracy practiced in Bangladesh is heavily suspect in terms of both veracity and motive.

The cloak

This invective, nonetheless, formed the heart of the anti-democratic thought propagated in Bangladesh since 2007. At first brush, the anti-democratic narratives seem remarkably successful because of two simple reasons: recent memory provided strong evidence for them, and their potential opponents were forcibly silenced. But two additional reasons also helped: a civilian cloak and a democracy cloak, so to speak. First of all, the military takeover was done cleverly. The Army Chief admitted during a trip in London that proclaiming martial law was an option, but would not be easily acceptable. Moreover, unlike previous takeovers, there was neither a direct usurpation of power nor an ousting of any political leader from power (see Harun, 2007). So, on January 12, 2007, the high command appointed a primarily civilian administration as the Council of Advisors, a civilian Chief Advisor was the head of the government under a civilian President who was the nominal head of the state. While the military top brass became visible and chaired powerful committees, it ensured that all major policies were formally decided by the civilian side, thus cloaking its role especially during the formative first few months. Of course, there were strong suspicions that the army was running the show, but the public remained confused for a fairly long time about who actually held sway. Many in the international media were similarly befuddled. In March 2007, *Time* magazine, for example, profiled the Chief Advisor as *The Boss of Bangladesh* and the main protagonist in the government's major drives and policies (Abdullah, 2007). Moreover, the Army Chief made it a point to periodically deny the army's primary role (see Harun, 2007). The subject role of the military became clearer with time. *Time*'s next major article on Bangladesh, in June 2008, was titled *General Command*, and it noted plainly: '[F]ew in Dhaka doubt that anybody but the generals are calling the shots behind the scenes in this interim government' (Tharoor, 2008).

The second cloak for the anti-democracy narratives was democracy itself. Everything—from the declaration of the state of emergency to the suspension of fundamental rights to launching invectives and mass arrests to proposing a national charter and a National Security Council—was done for the sake of strengthening democracy. In his book of essays, the Army Chief noted the goal of his regime: 'Frankly we are working tirelessly to bring [about] a pure and sustainable democracy in Bangladesh' (in Harun, 2008). Fakhruddin Ahmed, the civilian figurehead, explained away all the policies in his interview with *Time* in March 2007 in similar fashion: 'The objective is strengthening Bangladesh's democratic order' (in Abdullah, 2007). The Law Advisor noted in June 2007 that the goal was not holding 'an election for election's sake but rather to restore democracy' (International Crisis Group, 2008: 5).

The usage of a pro-democracy language was at least ironic: none other than the government had a right to speak freely and express his or her opinion during the propagation of all of the correctives to democracy envisioned by the regime. But the use of democracy as the excuse was served obviously to legitimize the CTG's rule not to the local populace—who, out of previous bouts of military rule, were well-aware of these machinations—but to the international community. Here, we can draw a distinction between elections and representation. The regime's claims of legitimacy were derived not only by the goal of restoring democracy through elections, but also from representing, until then, a strong popular mandate. Though unelected, claimed the regime, it represented the true interests of the people. The Army Chief declared that 99.8 percent (!) of the population was supporting the caretaker government's moves (see *The Daily Star*, September 6, 2007). The government simply assumed, and successfully convinced the diplomats, that the local populace had had enough of the usual politicians and were looking for completely new faces in politics. Overlooking the hundreds of thousands imprisoned and the draconian laws that kept all muzzled, the Chief Advisor went as far as to observe: 'I don't think the common people are facing any problems due to continuation of the state of emergency' (in *New Age*, November 15, 2007). Whether it was the ostrich syndrome or a fiddling-Nero syndrome, such remarks claiming popular support contradicted the regime's proposed agenda toward the curtailment of popular sovereignty. But few were left outside the jail to speak in protest.

The sale

By imbuing its narrative with claims of popular representation, the regime tried to bolster the legitimacy of its programme to a key constituency: western diplomats. The West had reacted strongly—and understandably so—to Bangladesh's political crisis prior to 1/11. The European Union had threatened to 'reassess its trade relations' and the United Nations had threatened to cut back Bangladesh's lucrative peacekeeping role if it went ahead with holding sham elections, as BNP was planning to do. The envoys of the United States, United Kingdom, Japan, EU, Canada, Australia held frequent closed-door meetings with major political parties (see *The Daily Star*, January 12, 2007). After the 1/11 coup, they welcomed the new emergency administration. The US ambassador noted 'a lot of goodwill' for the administration. Even after the military's crackdown began and human rights violations began to rise, they supported the regime. By the end of January, the British High Commissioner, Anwar Choudhury, remarked: 'We are pleased with the approach that has been taken and the progress that this government seems to be making .... We hope that it continues that way' (in *The Daily Star*, January 23, 2007). Amid outcries about violations of due process in the summary imprisonment of politicians in mid-February, the EU envoy, Stefan Frowein, stated: 'I think this government is doing the right thing. They are doing what they have to do' (in *The Daily Star*, February 13, 2007). Multilateral donors, including the World Bank, Asian Development Bank, and the UNDP, but also the British DFID, quickly declared funds to bolster the anti-corruption drive. This level of support is not surprising. Based on interviews with diplomats posted in Bangladesh as well as Bangladeshi military officers, the International Crisis Group concluded that outside powers had been 'proactive' in bringing the military into power. At that time, they saw the military as 'a necessary evil' — and, given the political risks in the country, 'the only way to protect our [that is, the western donors] development investments' (in International Crisis Group, 2008: 7–9).

While the CTG claimed that its acts to redefine democracy in Bangladesh by force drew legitimacy from popular will, it was the backing of the West that provided legitimacy and staying power. This strong support from the presumably rights-conscious democratic West is what drove the caretaker government to continue committing its rights abuses, market its anti-democratic narrative, while claiming to do all this in order to restore 'pure' democracy. Once the West began to put light pressure to announce an election schedule, from the middle of 2007, at the peak of the regime's arbitrary use of power, the regime negotiated a two-year long emergency, during which the military would undertake its wide-ranging political reforms in order to strengthen democracy. The public was subjected to vision statements and policy decisions from the government, but not involved in the negotiations regarding polls and tenure in power; those were done with the West. High officers of the military wielded skillfully sophisticated presentations and scenarios of a security crisis to justify a prolonged stay in power. Even ideas such as the National Security Council and other functional alternatives to curtail popular sovereignty drew support from the West. As an international official noted ominously:

> When or if the dust settles in Bangladesh, we may see a retired army chief as president, another retired army chief as the anti-corruption czar, a retired general administering elections and a security council

which takes the advice of three or more generals as to how to manage the country. And this could be the best case scenario for Bangladesh's civilian democracy (in International Crisis Group, 2008: 17).

At the end of the day, anti-democratic narratives in Bangladesh could not be expected to invite broad public engagement while all rights of expression remained suspended in the country. In this situation, the diplomats representing the democratic West could have been the only source of pressure.[10] Moreover, they held the crucial card of international legitimacy sought by the caretaker regime. But the democratic West failed to come to the support of democratic institutions in Bangladesh. In fact, it had subscribed to the exact same storyline: all politicians in Bangladesh were corrupt and messy to deal with. They did not speak good English; their interests were complicated; they were not as presentable as polished military officers. As one Awami League politician noted: 'We have lost some trust in the diplomats .... They think we are all criminals' (in International Crisis Group, 2008: 28). The West refrained from casting a discerning historical eye that could separate those administrations that governed well from those that did not and instead employed the same wholesale mentality that was being propagated in the public by the new regime. Accordingly, the West hardly voiced concerns about the gross violations of human rights and the systematic destruction and militarization of crucial public institutions that took place. Through its inactions, the West joined the regime in denying the possible universality of democratic norms, and supported in essence the argument that the particularity of Bangladesh's context required a different mode of governance. With such a willing buyer, the selling of anti-democratic narratives in Bangladesh could not have been more successful.

References

Abdullah, A. (2007), 'Fakhruddin Ahmed: the boss of Bangladesh', *Time*, March 22.
Ahmad, M. (2008), 'Country and democracy more important than individuals', *The Daily Star*, May 24.
Ahmad, S. (2007), 'National security council for Bangladesh', *The Daily Star Strategic Issues*, March 24.
Ahmed, K.A. (2007a), 'Liberty of talking at random', *The Daily Star*, September 17.
Ahmed, M.U. (2007b), *The challenging interface of democracy and security* (keynote address at a regional conference of the International Political Science Association, April 2; retrieved September 28, 2008, from http://www.thedailystar.net/2007/04/04/d704041501137.htm).

---

10 It is important to note that legislative organs of western powers, such as the US Senate and the European Parliament, criticized the heavy-handed ways of Bangladesh's caretaker government. But executive branches remained steadfast in supporting the CTG.

Ahsan, M.B. (2007), 'Whose security and whose council?', *The Daily Star*, August 17.
Alamgir, J. (2007a), 'Bangladesh: democracy saved or sunk?', *Foreign Policy* (retrieved September 28, 2008, from http://www.foreignpolicy.com/story/cms.php?story_id=3765).
Alamgir, J. (2007b), 'Narratives of open-economy policies in India, 1991-2000', *Asian Studies Review*, 31 (2): 155-170.
Alamgir, J. (2008), 'Democratic performance in Bangladesh, 1991-2006: a political measurement', *Journal of Bangladesh Studies*, 9 (2): 1-12.
Amnesty International (2008), *One year on: human rights in Bangladesh under the state of emergency* (press release, January 10; retrieved September 28, 2008, from http://www.amnesty.org/en/for-media/press-releases/one-year-human-rights-bangladesh-under-state-emergency-20080110).
Anam, M. (2008), 'Nat'l security council: make ideas public', *The Daily Star*, March 12.
Bates, R.H., A. Greif, M. Levi, J.-L. Rosenthal and B.R. Weingast (1998), *Analytic narratives* (Princeton: Princeton University Press).
Choudhury, I.I. (2008), 'National security council for Bangladesh—not for now', *The Daily Star Strategic Issues*, April 12.
Chowdhury, A. (2008), 'National government: some thoughts', *The Daily Star*, February 8.
Government of Bangladesh (2004), *Constitution of the People's Republic of Bangladesh* (Dhaka: Ministry of Information).
Harun, N.M. (2007), 'Popularity is the litmus test of a political leader', *New Age*, October 21.
Harun, N.M. (2008), 'General Moeen gets extension: time for the court to act', *New Age*, April 13.
Hossain, M. (2007), *Broken pendulum: Bangladesh's swing to radicalism* (Washington, DC: Hudson Institute Press).
Human Rights Watch (2008), *The torture of Tasneem Khalil: how the Bangladesh military abuses its power under the state of emergency* (New York: Human Rights Watch).
International Crisis Group (2008), *Restoring democracy in Bangladesh* (Asia Report no. 151; Dhaka and Brussels: International Crisis Group).
Kabir, J. (2007), 'We need a national government', *The Daily Star*, September 1.
Khan, S.H. (2008), 'The five dangers of a national security council', *The Daily Star*, March 24.
Quader, G.M. (2008), 'Dialogue and its future', *The Daily Star*, June 11.
Ruhin, O.H. (2007), 'Army chief's speech draws mixed reaction from politicians', *New Age*, March 29.
Saleh, A. (2007), 'Four months of emergency government: a progressive FAQ', *The Progressive Bangladesh*, May 16 (retrieved September 28, 2008, from http://www.progressivebangladesh.org/index.php?option=com_content&task=view&id=26&Itemid=34).
Saleh, A. (2008), 'Say "no" to national security council', *New Age*, February 2.
Samad, S. (2008), 'The international audit of Bangladesh', *The Progressive Bangladesh*, March 18 (retrieved September 28, 2008, from http://www.progressivebangladesh.org/index.php?option=com_content&task=view&id=121&Itemid=26).

Siddiqa, A. (2007a), 'Bangladesh's sleeping Frankenstein', *The Daily Times*, January 1.
Siddiqa, A. (2007b), 'Fighting for the soul of Bangladesh', *The Daily Times*, December 17.
Sudworth, J. (2007), 'Army chief lambasts politicians', *BBC News Online*, March 27 (retrieved September 28, 2008, from http://news.bbc.co.uk/2/hi/south_asia/6500615.stm).
Tharoor, I. (2008), 'General command', *Time*, June 19.
Ullah, A.H.J. (2007), 'Democracy recalled by military wisdom', *The Progressive Bangladesh*, April 27 (retrieved September 28, 2008, from http://www.progressivebangladesh.org/index.php?option=com_content&task=view&id=21&Itemid=27).
Zahur, A.B.M.S. (2008), 'Adopting a national charter', *The Daily Star*, May 21.
Zamir, M. (2008), 'Looking for a "healthy and stable" democratic process', *The Daily Star*, May 24.

Pauline C. Westerman

From Democracy to Accountability

I

Introduction[1]

According to John Stuart Mill, one of the reasons justifying the importance of democracy is 'that the rights and interests of every or any person are only secure from being disregarded when the person interested is himself able, and habitually disposed, to stand up for them' (1861: ch. III). If someone wants to be sure that his interests are taken into account, he should better be where the decisions are made. Although this view does not strike us as very unusual or original, I want to maintain that Mill's wisdom is far from shared in present-day political discourse. The idea that democratic debate and decision making should include a wide range of interests and rights, and should be conducted by all those who are affected by the outcomes of such debates and decisions, seems on the decline. If we understand democracy as entailing inclusive participation of all involved, anti-democratic thought is not a phenomenon that surfaces only in exotic or extremist circles but characterizes much of present-day thought on how society should be run. Much of it is however couched in democratic-sounding language, which makes it hard to detect.

In this article I will try to reveal the anti-democratic elements in the current pleas in favour of accountability. I will do so by drawing examples from areas as diverse as legal theory, political theory and political studies and show that the notion of accountability is widespread even in circles that do not use the term explicitly. Accountability effectively postpones the moment of control. It is only after decisions have been reached and

---

[1] This paper was first presented at the UK IVR Conference in Edinburgh, Scotland, May 2008.

policies are devised or even carried out, that control is allowed to be exercised. Furthermore, this *post hoc* control is to be exercised on the basis of mainly substantive criteria, which cause control to be delegated to — different kinds of — experts. After having analyzed accountability as a form of 'outcome-oriented' legitimacy, the question arises what we exactly mean by 'outcome'. For that reason, I will distinguish three senses of 'outcome' and investigate the relation between outcome and procedures in each of these three senses. This analysis will enable me, finally, to explain the reasons for the current distrust in democratic procedures and the resultant pleas in favour of accountability.

II

Giving Reasons

The cry for accountability is commonly heard in the context of discussions of governance, an umbrella term for new forms of 'governing without government' (Rosenau and Czempiel, 1992; Rhodes, 1996) or 'policy making without politics' (Kazancigil, 1998). The term governance, whether 'corporate', 'regional' or 'global', indicates forms of governing that lack the formal structures provided by the nation state and consequently lack formal procedures of democratic representation. It is claimed that this absence of democratic representation should be compensated for by alternative mechanisms of control. Institutions should account for what they are doing by other means. Governing without government should be accompanied by a system in which 'no one controls an agency', but in which 'the agency is yet "under control"' (Majone, 1994: 2-3).

This is also the reason why accountability is deemed especially important in the context of EU politics. In the Commission of the European Communities' *White Paper on European Governance* (2001), accountability is advocated as one of the five principles of good governance. It is claimed that by improving accountability a form of democratic control is ensured even though a clear constituency is lacking. The fact that Europe has *no demos* does not necessarily lead to *no democracy*, as long as mechanisms of accountability are safeguarded and strengthened. The principle of accountability is not tied up with the nation state, and not even reserved to public institutions. Not only governmental institutions should account for what they did, private and semi-private institutions can and should rely on mechanisms of accountability too.

The abundant literature on accountability (see Davies, 2001; Harlow, 2002; Fisher, 2004) reveals that the term in itself is rather uninformative. Accountability mainly refers to the obligation to give reasons for one's doings. The term in itself does not stipulate to whom, why or how this should be done. An institution may account for its doings internally, to its own members, or externally. It may do so only to those who provided it with a budget or to the public at large. The motives for accountability may also differ: it may be that an institution or firm poses as an accountable one because it thereby hopes to increase its credibility or respectability, or because it is the only way to attract funding. And finally, the mechanisms used may be widely different. Accountability may require an elaborate and formal audit system or may rely solely on peer review and/or professional competition. Giandomenico Majone (1994) refers to mechanisms as diverse as professionalism, budgetary discipline, expertise, monitoring by interest groups, inter-agency rivalry, and judicial review.

But in all its forms and manifestations accountability is giving reasons *after the fact*. It is only after the decisions have been reached, the policies have been carried out and the results have or have not been obtained that an institution accounts for what it did. The kind of transparency that is required by accountability is transparency of the steps that were taken and the results that have been obtained. These steps and results are then presented in a report, a tangible and visual proof of one's past performance. In the report past performance is presented and justified at the same time.

If we define accountability as the requirement to give reasons for past performance it is clear that such a requirement presupposes that there is an identifiable set of standards or criteria which serve as points of reference for those who give the account as well as for those to whom one accounts. This implies that accountability presupposes the existence of *shared* standards, at least shared by those who account and to whom is accounted. The necessity of developing shared criteria means that most of the time a specific audience (set of institutions, professionals, peers) is addressed that shares the standards that differentiate good outcomes from bad outcomes and good reasons from bad reasons. In the absence of such a specific audience—for instance, if an institution professes to be accountable to the public at large by means of results published on the Internet—, this means that such a wider public should be informed of the relevant standards and criteria. They should be 'educated' and taught to judge matters according to *the* relevant criteria, established by expert groups.

A common way of developing, spreading and instilling the relevant values and standards is by clarifying one's mission. The mission statement is indispensable in a system of accountability. It may be written by the institution itself, or else dictated or prompted by subsidy givers who draw up a list of desirable goals and objectives that should be reached by the institution that has to account for its doings. These goals serve as the starting point from which the standards and criteria are derived (Westerman, 2007b).

It is important to note that these criteria may be substantive as well as procedural. Hospitals may account for how they handled waiting lists by referring to substantive criteria, either medical or moral, but may also refer to protocols and procedures—to the steps that were taken before arriving at decisions. That does not alter the fact that *what is accounted for are not the procedures, but the outcomes*. Procedures only figure in the arguments that are used in order to account for and to justify outcomes.

We may end this section by proposing a somewhat more precise definition of accountability than we noted at the beginning. Accountability is more than just giving reasons for one's doings. Diversity of forms and mechanisms notwithstanding, the principle of accountability requires a *post hoc* justification of past performance in accordance with shared criteria, derived from an identifiable goal or set of goals.

III

Consequences for Thinking about Democracy

The assumptions underlying accountability recur in much contemporary theorizing about democracy. They lead to anti-majoritarianism, an emphasis on results, *post hoc* justification, and reliance on expertise. I will give three examples, borrowed from three completely different areas, each favouring a different kind of expertise as better suited to the task of control than bodies of democratically elected representatives.

Accountable to the technical expert

Perhaps the best example of how accountability is linked to technocracy is furnished by Majone, a political economist and influential theorist of the EU. Majone is well-known for his advocacy of what he calls independent and non-majoritarian institutions. His favourite example is the European Central Bank. He argues that independent institutions are more efficient in pursuing policies that serve the common interests of European nation states than any representative body of member states is capable of. Moreover, since these institutions are not dependent on short-term political gains such as re-election, they can afford to consistently pursue policies that may be unpopular but are beneficial in the long run (Majone, 1994; 2001).

The independent agencies Majone has in mind are mostly single-purpose. They are organized around a single central aim, e.g. environment, consumer regulation, etc., for which a lot of expertise is required and for which bureaucratic governmental institutions are ill-equipped. The agencies should engage in fact-finding, distributing information, rulemaking as well as in adjudication, while 'protecting the citizen from bureaucratic arrogance' (1994: 5). Confronted with the criticism that these non-majoritarian institutions are cut loose from control by (representatives of) member states, Majone retorts that alternative forms of accountability are better instruments of control than traditional forms of representative democracy.

Legitimacy is gained here by judging results rather than procedures. It does not depend on the question whether decisions are taken according to well-defined procedures, but

> on such factors as expertise, problem-solving capacity and accountability by results. ... In the final analysis the democratic legitimacy of non-majoritarian institutions depends on their capacity to engender and maintain the belief that they are the most appropriate ones for the function assigned to them (77).

In Majone's writings, accountability is not only seen as a substitute for (procedural) democracy but also as a better alternative. We see here all the abovementioned characteristics recur: the idea that there are shared standards as well as the notion that these are derived from identifiable institutional goals about which there is no disagreement. The sole criteria that count are the effectiveness and efficiency with which these goals are pursued and realized. They can best be applied by the experts who are trained in the field that is defined by the objectives and purposes of the institution at hand. Only they can know what the 'appropriate function' of these agencies and institutions is, only they have the criteria at their disposal to judge the results they obtained.

Leaving aside for the moment the question whether democratic institutions are suited to carry out the complex tasks of rulemaking and standardization required in the modern European context, we might agree with Fritz W. Scharpf (1999) that there is a tendency towards what he called 'output'-oriented legitimizing beliefs. In output-oriented legitimacy, political choices are legitimate if they effectively promote the common welfare of the constituency. In output-oriented legitimacy, democracy is seen as 'government for the people' rather than as government 'by the people'. In such a view, there is no room for Mill's citizens. If citizens are allowed a say on the matter, they should do so as members of organized 'interest groups'. This is significant. Only these groups—and not the ordinary individual citizen—are capable of hiring the required (counter-)expertise to speak in favour of their particular interests.

What is conspicuously missing from Majone's account is the problem of enforcement. The question what happens if the institutions fail to perform adequately, or if they fail to give good reasons for their failure, is not addressed. This is not only the case in Majone's work. The earlier mentioned *White Paper* of the EU, although advocating the virtue of accountability, also fails to point out the consequences if accounts turn out to be unconvincing or unsatisfactory. Andreas Føllesdal criticizes this omission by remarking: 'Accountability must go beyond transparency, to ensure that citizens are able to hold the various agents accountable and if necessary to replace them' (2003: 79). We should, however, keep in mind that that extra step is usually not taken because the requirement of accountability relies on experts rather than on the citizenry at large.

Accountable to the legal expert

Majone is well acquainted with EU politics. He is a man of practice and has definite ideas about the direction Europe should take. In this sense, it is not amazing to find him elaborate on the main tenets of the European governance creed. It is more amazing to come across the same ingredients in the work of those who do not mention the term 'accountability' at all, and who may not even be aware of the way this requirement is advocated and practiced in regulatory politics.

Far removed from European governance experiments a parallel version of accountability can be found in the work of what may be the most influential legal theorist of our time: Ronald Dworkin. Working in a different field, situated in a different context, Dworkin's theory is clearly not meant to answer the question how we can compensate for the democratic deficit of the European Union. Yet, he struggles with a similar question: how to deal with the democratic deficit of judicial review.

A common objection against judicial review is that since courts are not democratically elected we should be cautious to allow judges to give a final verdict on matters that were decided by democratically elected representatives. The dominant viewpoint nowadays is in favour of judicial review and many of the arguments serving to minimize the dangers this might pose to democracy are influenced by the writings of Dworkin. According to Dworkin, the claim that judicial review is undemocratic cannot plausibly be defended. On the contrary, he maintains that judicial decision making is often *more* democratic than decision making by the legislature.

Dworkin defends this bold position by asking whether there are 'institutional reasons why a legislative decision about rights is likely to be more accurate than a judicial decision' (1985: 24). The answer is that there are no such reasons. According to Dworkin, 'legislators are subject to pressures that judges are not, and this must count as a reason for supposing that, at least in such cases, judges are more likely to reach sound conclusions about rights'. Moreover, given the inequalities of power between democratically elected representatives, the judiciary is better equipped to preserve the rights of minorities than the legislature (27–8). Judicial review will therefore promote rather than retard the 'democratic ideal of equality of political power' (28).

It is not my intention to rehearse the debate on judicial review here. I only want to point to the concept of democracy which underlies his position. The first element that catches the eye is then that legislation is identified with 'decisions about rights'; secondly, that Dworkin seems to suppose that it is possible to arrive at 'accurate answers' about those rights; and finally, that democracy is seen here mainly as an ideal.

I will briefly comment on these assumptions.

Democracy as an ideal. In Dworkin's view, democracy is an ideal which is derived from the basic norm that requires 'equality of concern and respect'. Throughout Dworkin's writings, the adjective 'democratic' is used to indicate that a certain thing *agrees* with this norm of equal concern and respect. 'Democratic' is no longer an attribute of procedures here (like 'democratically elected', or 'democratically controlled'), but of outcomes: democratic institutions are institutions which embody the democratic norm of 'equal concern and respect' and democratic decisions are decisions that agree with the basic norm of 'equal concern and respect'. Jeremy Waldron has criticized this view so eloquently, that I can confine myself to a mere quote:

> Notice how it turns on an elision between a decision *about democracy* and a decision *made by democratic means*. Dworkin seems to be suggesting that if a political decision is about democracy, or about the rights associated with democracy, then there is no interesting or interestingly distinct question to be raised about the way in which the decision is made. All that matters is that the decision be right, from a democratic point of view (1999: 292).

Legislation as decisions about rights. But what are these decisions 'about democracy'? We have seen that Dworkin formulates these issues as decisions *about rights*. This seems to me an unnecessarily reduced idea of legislation. Legislation is about the sizes of meshes in fishermen's nets, about the permitted emission levels of toxics or the required temperature of cooling systems at grocery stores. Although it is undoubtedly true that these decisions have profound effects on the lives of fishermen and customers of grocery stores, these issues cannot be reduced to rights matters alone. They are *not only* about rights and obligations; they are also about how we would like the world to become, and the goals we set ourselves. Whether we think of reduction of emission levels as more important than economic innovation is a political choice. The political debate that should precede that choice is here reduced to a legal question.

Accurate answers. Once the political domain is reduced to matters of rights, it is clear that the ground is prepared for the final conclusion that these matters should be entrusted to those who are trained to deal with those matters, legal experts. They are better suited to give 'accurate answers' than the fishermen, grocers, and their representatives themselves. It is the legal expert who is more democratic than democratically elected representatives because he is better trained to deal with the rights that are derived from the basic norm of equal concern and respect. Whereas Mill thought that rights are best defended by the rights owners themselves, Dworkin wants to delegate these issues to the legal expert.

One might be tempted to object to this that we should differentiate here between the rule of law and democracy. Lawyers may be better trained to uphold the rule of law *against* the majority of representatives who might be trampling upon the rights of minorities. But this is not Dworkin's view. He does not want to allow for any tension between the concept of the rule of law and democracy. Both ideals, he says, 'are rooted in a more fundamental ideal, that any acceptable government must treat people as equals' (1985: 32). Both ideals are in the end reducible to the basic norm of equal concern and respect and the rights that are derived from this norm. In Dworkin's view, it is possible to consider the judge a true democrat if he defends the rule of law and to deny that title to elected representatives who trespass the fundamental norm of equal concern and respect.

All the ingredients that we discerned in the notion of accountability are present in Dworkin's notion of democracy. Here again we see anti-majoritarianism coupled with an emphasis on outcomes which are judged in a *post hoc* manner (judges always come in after the fact). These outcomes are evaluated by reference to criteria shared by experts. The only difference is that for Dworkin the appropriate experts are not technical specialists but legal experts. Only they have access to the right answers and criteria which are derived from the fundamental goal (equality) of the institutions to be judged.

Accountable to the moral expert

Confronted with the abundant literature on the importance of experts, legal or otherwise, for democracy, it comes as a kind of relief to turn to the literature on deliberative democracy. There, it seems that an attempt is made to revitalize the notion of democracy as a forum for ongoing discussion: it is maintained that democracy is more than just voting according to fixed preferences and interests. Rather, the citizens are thought to shape their preferences in a consensus-seeking debate. In truly deliberative debates, everything revolves around the *soundness of arguments*. Here at last, there seems to be hope for the ordinary citizen, the rights owners Mill had in mind to speak up for themselves and to deliberate on the priority of aims. Here at last, there seems to be scope for a political, not only a technocratic debate.

But there is reason for doubt. Confining myself to the work of Amy Gutmann and Dennis Thompson (2004), it seems that in the end deliberation boils down to a form of accountability: providing arguments that mainly serve to justify—in a *post hoc* manner—the outcomes/decisions that have been reached. The good arguments that are required by these deliberative theorists are not thought to be of any help to *find* compromises or optimal solutions, they are at best put forward to *influence* decisions and they are mainly invoked to *justify*. And what is justified are not opinions or preferences, but *decisions*. If we read Gutmann and Thompson carefully, we get the impression that deliberation is advocated not as a way to arrive at good decisions, but as a means to justify decisions already taken. Deliberation does not play a role in what philosophers of science call the 'context of discovery' but in the 'context of justification'. This analogy with science is noticed by the authors themselves when they compare their requirements to the requirement of replication in science. They write that just as 'a finding of truth in science requires replicability, which calls for public demonstration', 'a finding of justice requires reciprocity, which calls for public deliberation' (2004: 101). They haste to add here that this is not needed all the time: just like established truths in science need not be replicated endlessly, repeated deliberation is unnecessary with well-established moral principles.

In itself, this limitation might not seem shockingly novel. Since J.S. Mill, it is generally conceded that large assemblies do not lend themselves easily to doing things, let alone to drafting complex pieces of legislation. Parliaments are there mainly to control. Proponents of deliberative democracy seem to connect themselves to this tradition, and their only novelty is then that good arguments should be provided by the officials who took the decisions. But appearances mislead. Traditional theory (and practice) starts from the assumption that whereas the preparatory work is done by committees of expert legislative jurists, it is the approbation of the representative body that turns the proposals into statutes. In Mill's words: in parliament, the 'element of will' is attached to the 'element of intelligence' which is introduced by a commission of codification. If parliament withholds its consent, there are no decisions taken at all. This implies, furthermore, that in the traditional model, there is good reason for officials to justify their proposals, for if they don't, they are sanctioned by disapproval: their proposals remain void.

In the book of Gutmann and Thompson, this threat of withholding actual consent has disappeared. In line with the American political situation, in which the President can decide matters on his own, the authors write:

> The participants ... intend their discussion to influence a decision the government will make .... At some point the deliberation temporarily ceases and the leaders make a decision. ... Once he decided, deliberation about the question of whether to go to war ceased. Yet deliberation about a seemingly similar but significantly different question continued: was the original decision justified? (5-6).

The entire book revolves around the quality of the arguments used by officials in their justification of decisions. Here, relations are reversed: 'intelligence' as a product of deliberation is joined to the 'will' of the executive. Just like in the European context sketched in the *White Paper*, there are no serious consequences attached to bad reasons or bad performance.

The fact that deliberation seems mainly to serve as justification of outcomes rather than guiding the heuristical process of finding solutions and compromises is, I think, the reason that the authors emphasize the importance of substantive criteria. According to them, '[n]o decision-making method ... should be able to justify a war of aggression' (19). We are on familiar ground here. Like Dworkin and Majone, these authors emphasize the rightness of outcomes rather than the soundness of procedures. To Gutmann and Thompson, only those outcomes which are morally just can count as democratic answers.

One might object that Gutmann and Thompson, despite their emphasis on outcomes, are nevertheless unwilling to delegate matters to experts. It is here that the citizen might play a role. But we should not be too optimistic. Only preferences which are morally just count as good arguments. The citizen is only granted a platform if he or she is reasonable. And the criteria for reasonableness are mainly identified by (moral) philosophers. Although the debate envisioned is not a technocratic one, it can still not be considered a political one. Deliberative theorists turn politics into a moral debate in which moral philosophers are the experts. It is up to them to decide whether the decisions reached can survive the test of critical morality.

There seems to be only one aspect in which the theory on deliberative democracy differs from other attempts to reshape democracy into accountability: deliberative democracy does not seem to rely on the notion that there is an identifiable set of goals from which the basic standards and criteria are derived. But we should be cautious here. Underneath its apparent liberalism we can feel the pressure of the 'basic opportunities' that must be fulfilled in order to count as morally defensible. We are but one step removed here from John Finnis' set of basic goods without which human nature cannot flourish (1980). This is not surprising. In order to derive standards and criteria, the supposition of one or more goals is simply indispensable. Normative statements cannot be developed out of the blue, they need to rest on an assumption about the goals that are served by institutions and societies. Developing substantive moral criteria, therefore, necessarily starts from the assumption that there are 'proper' goals to be distinguished from the goals that frame ordinary people's preferences.

IV

Three Types of Outcome

We have seen that in different areas people tend to reshape democracy into a form of accountability — the requirement to justify outcomes in a *post hoc* manner, according to criteria which are accessible to experts rather than to lay citizens. I have argued that these theories inevitably end up turning political debates into legal, technocratic or moral debates. But the question arises whether there is a viable alternative. Is it really possible and desirable *not* to stress the importance of good outcomes? What would be the advantage of procedural legitimacy? Niklas Luhmann described procedural legitimacy as the general willingness to abide by whatever outcome as long as procedures are followed (1969). But what is the basis for this willingness? Is it sensible to rely on procedures alone, which, if followed by potentially wicked, passionate or downright silly people, may lead to very bad outcomes? *How can we make sense of procedural legitimacy in the first place?*

In order to answer this question and to understand the importance of procedures, I think we should start from the other end and inquire first into what we should understand by 'outcome'. Most theorists speak about procedures and outcomes without specifying the kind of outcomes they have in mind, and I think that leads to unnecessary confusion (the discussion between Arneson, 1993, and Estlund, 2003, is an example in point). Let me try to bring some order to the discussion by distinguishing three possible candidates for what counts as 'outcome'. In each of these senses, I shall ask myself whether we might view the procedures that lead to this (sense of) outcome as being capable of generating legitimacy by their intrinsic value.

A. Specific consequences in individual cases

We might view as outcome the result of any procedure or set of rules when applied to a concrete case. Outcome here is concrete outcome: the outcome of elections, the verdict of the judge in an individual case, but also the knee operation conducted according to the strict rules of a medical protocol, or the gains and losses of the players who play according to the rules of the game. According to John Rawls, who analyzed this kind of outcome (1971: 86) by means of the example of gambling, such outcomes cannot be evaluated independently from the rules of the game. He meant to say that in these cases there are no criteria for judging the fairness of outcomes other than those provided by the procedures themselves. The rules of the game give legitimacy to *any* outcome.

This may be true in the closed universe of games, although even there I can think of instances in which one may deplore an outcome and even judge it as unfair, despite the fact that procedures and rules were followed. But in most cases, I believe, this kind of what Rawls called 'pure proceduralism' collapses into what he called 'imperfect proceduralism', defined by him as the situation that arises where procedures cannot be designed in such a way that they always generate the correct outcome. Despite having followed protocol, based on medical evidence, this particular patient dies. Despite fair and reasonably reliable rules concerning evidence in court, this particular innocent man is sentenced to prison. In all these cases there is a tension not between procedure and outcome, but between what is *generally* taken to be the outcome of the procedure (for which reason the procedure was adopted in the first place) and the *specific* outcome in this particular case. Generally, the protocols and procedures launch reasonably fair results, but fail to do so in this particular instance.

There are then three possible sources for arguing that, adverse effects in particular cases notwithstanding, we should stick to the procedures. The first is the one already hinted at: that a certain set of rules *in general* lead to fairly adequate results. Just as it is no good to forsake the advantages of evidence-based medicine because of one dead patient, it would be unwise to give up general rules of procedure because of one judicial error (see Schauer, 1991). This argument does not commit us to the view that there is an intrinsic value to a specific kind of procedures. Procedures owe their *raison d'être* here to the fact that in general they generate good outcomes.

A second possible source of arguments in favour of sticking to the rules and procedures even where they fail to generate the right outcomes is by pointing at problems of coordination and inefficiency which may arise if we don't follow procedures and judge each case on its own merits. These are interesting arguments in favour of the use of rules and procedures, but they only point out that *some* rules and procedures are needed, not that a particular set of rules should be followed—despite adverse effects—because of its intrinsic quality. Arguments that point to the importance of legal certainty, reliability of the judicial system, and the protection rules can offer against arbitrary power are all arguments in favour of some form of rule of law, but they do not argue in favour of democratic rules and procedures (and, unlike Dworkin, I would like to maintain the difference between the two).

A third possible argument is that democratic procedures have intrinsic value not because they are rules, and not because as such rules they tend to produce good outcomes in general, but because they were agreed to by free and equal people in conditions that were fair. The problem with this answer is that it does not argue in favour of intrinsic value of democratic procedures. Rather, it *shifts* the burden of legitimacy from the procedures to *the initial conditions* in which agreement was reached. The procedures (rules of the game) owe their fairness to the fact that they were devised in conditions that were fair. Here, the procedures are not valued for the fact that they are procedures, but because they are outcomes of a previous process of fair deliberation. This argument brings us to the next possible meaning of outcome.

B. Institutional arrangements

A different concept of 'outcome' can be discerned if we focus our attention on the deliberations conducted in a fictional pre-contractual situation. For what is the 'outcome' of deliberation and consent in this stage? Not the individual losses and gains, but the very procedures, rules, rights and obligations the contracting parties consent to live by. That which figures under A as 'procedures' is here the 'outcome' of the pre-contractual deliberations. Which testifies to the fact that procedures and outcomes are relative terms: it depends on one's point of view what is to count as procedure or outcome.

By institutional arrangements I mean the arrangements that shape the way people relate to one another. It comprises what Rawls called the basic institutions of society: the main rules, principles and practices regulating the distribution of rights and duties, benefits and burdens. It also comprises the allocation of rights that Dworkin had in mind.

To what extent is the legitimacy of this kind of outcome safeguarded by the preceding procedures? It is here that contract theory comes in. For here it might be expected that the fairness of institutional arrangements is at least *furthered* by procedures (the deliberations in the pre-contractual stage) that tend to include the weak and the poor as well, and which minimize differences in freedom and equality. This does not mean that fair procedures inevitably lead to just results, nor that unfair procedures inevitably lead to unjust outcomes, but at least there is a link between procedure and outcome to the extent that the *chance* of a fair institutional arrangement is *maximized* by initial conditions (including the freedom and equality of parties) that are fair.

This link should not be conceived of as another kind of invisible hand theory in which procedures automatically channel selfish interests into a fair distribution of rights and duties (see Griffin, 2003). They only do so if we suppose the consenting partners to act behind a Rawlsian veil of ignorance. But as far as this type of outcomes are concerned, we may say (with Rawls) that in order to maximize the chances of a fair distribution of rights, duties, burdens and benefits, we should try to design procedures that come as close as possible to this hypothetical situation of free and equal citizens. Mill's inclusiveness of interests and rights is one way of approaching that hypothetical situation (but not the only one).

I believe that this is the closest we can get to defending the intrinsic value of democratic procedures. It is not immune to rejection. If some day we would find out that a fair distribution of rights and duties is better realized by, for instance, organizing a lottery, there is no way to escape the conclusion, on the basis of this very argument, that a lottery should be preferred.

C. *Goals and enterprises*

A third possible reading of 'outcome' is the enterprise or course of action on which a given society embarks. This calls for clarification and I can think of no better example than that furnished by Hugo Grotius, who (for different reasons) adduces the shipping companies that joined forces in seventeenth-century Holland and formed an Admiralty in order to minimize the risks of piracy attached to the great voyages to the Indies (Grotius, 1901: ch. XII). One might call the enterprise of defending oneself against pirates (but also the 'less worthy' goals to which Grotius alludes) 'outcome' of this third type. This example lends itself nicely to capturing the three different senses of 'outcome' I discern here. The shipping companies, which were not equal but differed in size and strength, consented to an institutional arrangement (outcome type B) which rested on the principle that those who took greater risks should have a greater share in the revenues. They did so in order to defend themselves against pirates (outcome type C). This resulted eventually in a distribution of gains and losses according to the rules (outcome type A).

It is important to see that the relation between procedure and outcome of type C is different from the relation between procedure and outcome of type B. Whereas there is a certain link between the reasonableness of an institutional arrangement and the initial situation in which the consenting partners find themselves, no such link can be discovered between procedures and enterprises. If, for instance, the Admiralty has to choose between fighting pirates or enslaving African inhabitants, they are not really helped in that choice by the fact that the participating associations are free and equal. The fairness or reasonableness of the outcome (type C) is not *in any direct way* furthered by the fair and reasonable relations of the consenting partners. In fact, terms like reasonableness and fairness do not apply here at all. These terms generally refer to how relations between participants are ordered. But here we are not dealing with *how* people relate to each other but *what* they are going to do.

However, what does help to further an informed choice between different enterprises is someone who has the required knowledge to sum up the pros and cons of enslaving Africans versus fighting the pirates. It is here that the expert is called for. Procedures which guarantee inclusiveness of rights and interests are important *only* insofar as a diversity of perspectives is instrumental in getting a better view of the enterprises and goals. (In fact, this is the argument Waldron, 1999, supplies in favour of democracy.) But this link is contingent upon the nature of the enterprises themselves. If they are complex enough, it is more useful to call in the expert than a multitude of equal but also equally ignorant people.

V

Boundaries between Arrangements and Enterprises

We are now able to locate the specific legitimacy generated by democratic procedures. It does not reside in the fact (mentioned under A) that they are procedures (for that would only be an argument in favour of the rule of law), nor does it reside in the fact (mentioned under C) that multiple perspectives generate better knowledge (Waldron's argument is dependent upon the complexity of the subject matter). Democratic procedures are only a source of legitimacy insofar as they are likely to generate fairer institutional arrangements than non-democratic procedures.

If this is true, it might explain much of the current distrust in democratic procedures and the predilection for a *post hoc* justification of outcomes. It is not because the procedures themselves are felt to be worrisome and suboptimal (although there is also a trend to downplay the importance of the rule of law for this very reason: see Westerman, 2007b), but because the *subject matter* does not lend itself easily to democratic deliberation. The dominant issues of present-day political debate are very much like the goals and enterprises of type C. Not pirates but terrorists should be fought, not loss of cargo should be prevented but unemployment, not bad winds and tempests but a polluted environment or global warming. The contemporary 'shipping companies' that have come together to form admiralties like the WTO or the EU did so in order to be better able to cope with external risks and threats. Like the Dutch seventeenth-century shipping companies they joined forces because of a keenly felt common interest, analyzable as type C outcome. The institutional arrangements (type B) that deal with how the partners relate to one another are thought to be of secondary importance, or at best merely instrumental in order to cope as efficiently as possible with these external dangers.

In this respect, Majone draws an interesting and revealing distinction between 'efficiency' and 'redistribution'. The former deals with positive-sum games in which common interests are at stake, while the latter has to do with potentially conflict-ridden matters which need the support of direct democratic legitimacy (1994: 23). Majone uses this distinction to pave the way for anti-majoritarian independent institutions. The idea is that democratic procedures, although indispensable in matters where distribution of rights and duties, burdens and benefits is at stake, are not appropriate, and even cumbersome and inefficient, in dealing with 'positive-sum games' such as beating Asian competition or reducing emission of toxics.

However, having grasped the difference, it is time to immediately question the firmness of the boundaries demarcating B from C. We should trespass them from both sides. In the first place, we should realize that type B outcomes cannot be reached without reference to desirable C outcomes. It is an illusion to think of institutional arrangements as being wholly determined by fair and reasonable procedures followed by free and equal persons without any regard for enterprises type C. This explains why various different arrangements are imaginable. If we think once again of Grotius' shipping companies, we see at once that, although most of them were approximately equal to each other, they *could* have designed a different arrangement. Instead of allocating gains on the basis of risk, they could have agreed to an institutional arrangement in which the greatest revenue was given to those who had invested most labour in the enterprise. Even where consenting parties are free and equal, or probably just *because* they are free and approximately equal, all kinds of institutional arrangements could have been designed, none of them totally just or unjust. The choice of 'risk' as the determining criterion rather than labour may be inspired but is not completely dictated by internal power relations. It is also partly determined by the enterprise of fighting pirates for which the shipping companies had joined forces. It is possible that the allocation of benefits on the basis of risk turned out to be the institutional arrangement that was the most conducive to efficiently fighting the pirates, for instance because such an arrangement is better suited to attract the bigger, stronger and richer companies than allocation on the basis of labour. So, considerations concerning type C outcomes enter into the deliberations. And that is precisely the reason why fair procedures do not *guarantee* fair institutional arrangements.

But the boundaries between B and C can also be crossed in a different direction. Grotius' example of the shipping companies makes clear that underneath the boundary between 'institutional arrangement' and 'enterprise' there is another boundary which divides 'us' from 'them'. Fighting pirates can count as an enterprise because we define piracy as an external threat; as outsiders, pirates can figure as an enterprise 'out there'. But as soon as we include pirates in our discourse—a possibility as remote to my seventeenth-century ancestors as the inclusion of the Taliban in our contemporary moral discourse—, they become part of the world to which we should *relate*. Then, suddenly, the Taliban or pirates move from C to B. Our relations to them become part of our institutional arrangements. At that stage, they should take part in the deliberations that lead to the establishment of these institutional arrangements. One and the same issue can therefore figure either as 'fighting terrorism' or as a 'human rights issue' (Koskenniemi, 2007). Where outsiders become insiders, outcomes type C become outcomes type B.

If we think of issues such as education or the improvement of infrastructure, it is clear that they can be regarded *both* as external states of affairs to be promoted *and* as issues that have to do with how we define our relations with other members of the community. They can be seen as common enterprises in the sense that everyone profits from good education and a good infrastructure. But as soon as one has to decide which goal should gain priority and the (scarce) resources that should be allocated to these goals, these matters move clearly to B-type outcomes. As soon as the available and limited resources should be distributed between students and teachers, or between both these groups and transport companies, C-type outcomes turn into B-type outcomes.

However, it is significant to note that issues are nowadays more easily defined in terms of external enterprises than in terms of relationships. There is a tendency to regard matters mainly as C-issues serving the common interest—as 'positive-sum games'. Such a representation ignores the fundamental political choices that have to be made between the different enterprises to embark upon. It is only by hiding from view the choices that have to be made between desirable goals and enterprises that outcomes B can be converted into outcomes of type C (see also Westerman, 2007a).

VI

Conclusion

It is time to put the threads together. I argued that in different areas we can witness a growing distrust of democratic procedures. Instead of attempting to improve procedures where they are found unreliable, critics try to reshape democracy into 'accountability', which I defined as the requirement to give a *post hoc* justification of past performance (outcomes) in accordance with shared criteria, derived from an identifiable goal or set of goals. I argued that in different areas this tendency entails a reliance on control by experts, whether technical, legal or moral. Debates are de-politicized. Government *by* the people is replaced by government *for* the people, mainly designed and implemented by experts.

In order to appreciate this change more fully, different senses of 'outcome' were distinguished: A) the gains and losses in individual cases, B) institutional arrangements, and C) common goals or enterprises. Each of these senses of 'outcome' turned out to entertain a different relationship with preceding procedures. The possible problems pertaining to type A outcomes may be brought about by the fact that general procedures were followed but do not tell us anything about the kinds of procedures that should be adopted. Type B outcomes, on the other hand, are more directly linked to the kind of procedures by which they are generated. The chance that the institutional arrangements that figure under B *fairly* distribute rights and duties as well as burdens and benefits is enhanced or diminished by the possibilities for the citizens to defend their own interests. This link between procedures and outcomes is absent in outcomes of type C, the enterprises or shared goals of a society. The quality of this type of outcome is not directly linked to the degree of inclusiveness of preceding procedures and seems to be more dependent on expertise.

The current distrust of democratic institutions can now be understood more fully as a result of the *reformulation* of B-type outcomes as C-type outcomes. Problems tend to be interpreted as problems about which there is a shared understanding, the solution of which is in the common interest. This interpretation seems to be supported by the way these type C outcomes are presented. First, they are generally presented in highly *abstract* terms, e.g. many so-called framework directives, issued by the European Commission, require the addressees to 'further an innovative economy', to 'improve labour conditions' and to 'aim at a reduction of emission of toxics'. Who would be against these noble aims? No one in their right mind should oppose such 'positive-sum outcomes'! Shouldn't any policy designed to further these universally shared goals be embraced and welcomed? Disagreement arises only if these abstract and noble aims are translated into more concrete measures and rules. But this very process of concretization takes place in largely expert circles. If a political debate is conducted there, it is usually couched in technical language, accessible to the expert only.

Second, these positive-sum results are generally represented in splendid isolation. In themselves, the aims are all valuable. But they are not *equally* valuable. Preferences about whether we should give more attention to (and spend more money on) an aim like the 'improvement of mental health' (to mention just a recent EU target) or to a further 'reduction of traffic accidents' may differ. And this problem how to prioritize aims is effectively hidden from view — and consequently from public debate — by the organization of the regulative landscape into many single-purpose agencies and committees (see Smismans, 2004). Within these agencies and committees, the choice between and the consequent coordination of different aims necessarily plays a more modest role than in parliamentary debates, and even if it arises is again largely restricted to debates among experts. These mechanisms all contribute to the reduction of political debates into technical ones.

This sets the stage for the major battle that, according to Martin Shapiro, is to be fought in the coming years: 'the battle between those who envision transnational regulation as properly placed in the hands of technically expert deliberators and those who seek a gate through which politics may enter' (2005: 354).

That Shapiro — and with him many others, e.g. Martti Koskenniemi — tries to open that gate by invoking legal expertise (judicial review!) is not a very reassuring sign to those who would rather see citizens stand up for themselves.

References

Arneson, R. (1993), 'Democratic rights at national and workplace levels', in *The idea of democracy*, eds. D. Copp, J. Hampton and J.E. Roemer (Cambridge: Cambridge University Press).

Commission of the European Communities (2001), *European governance: a white paper* (Brussels).

Davies, A. (2001), *Accountability: a public law analysis of government by contract* (Oxford: Oxford University Press).

Dworkin, R. (1985), *A matter of principle* (Cambridge, MA: Harvard University Press).

Estlund, D. (2003), 'The democracy/contractualism analogy', *Philosophy and Public Affairs*, 31 (4): 387–412.

Finnis, J. (1980), *Natural law and natural rights* (Oxford: Oxford University Press).

Fisher, E. (2004), 'The European Union in the age of accountability', *Oxford Journal of Legal Studies*, 24 (3): 495–515.

Føllesdal, A. (2003), 'The political theory of the white paper on governance: hidden and fascinating', *European Public Law*, 9 (1): 73–86.

Griffin, C.J. (2003), 'Democracy as a non-instrumentally just procedure', *The Journal of Political Philosophy*, 11 (1): 111–21.

Grotius, H. (1901), *The rights of war and peace: including the law of nature and of nations*, trans. A.C. Campbell (New York and London: M. Walter Dunne).

Gutmann, A., and D. Thompson (2004), *Why deliberative democracy?* (Princeton: Princeton University Press).

Harlow, C. (2002), *Accountability in the European Union* (Oxford: Oxford University Press).

Kazancigil, A. (1998), 'Governance and science: market-like modes of managing society and producing knowledge', *International Social Science Journal*, 50 (155): 69–79.

Koskenniemi, M. (2007), 'The fate of public international law: between technique and politics', *The Modern Law Review*, 70 (1): 1–30.

Luhmann, N. (1969), *Legitimation durch Verfahren* (Neuwied am Rhein and Berlin: Luchterhand Verlag).

Majone, G. (1994), *Independence versus accountability? Non-majoritarian institutions and democratic government in Europe* (EUI Working Paper SPS No 94/3; Florence: European University Institute).

Majone, G. (2001), 'Nonmajoritarian institutions and the limits of democratic governance: a political transaction-cost approach', *Journal of Institutional and Theoretical Economics*, 157 (1): 57–78.

Mill, J.S. (1861), *Utilitarianism, liberty, and representative government*, ed. A.D. Lindsay (London: Dent & Sons).

Rawls, J. (1971), *A theory of justice* (Oxford: Oxford University Press).

Rhodes, R. (1996), 'The new governance: governing without government', *Political Studies*, 44 (4): 652–67.

Rosenau, J.N., and E.-O. Czempiel (1992), *Governance without government: order and change in world politics* (Cambridge: Cambridge University Press).

Scharpf, F. (1999), *Governing in Europe: effective and democratic?* (New York: Oxford University Press).

Schauer, F. (1991), *Playing by the rules: a philosophical examination of rule-based decision-making in law and in life* (Oxford: Clarendon Press).

Shapiro, M. (2005), '"Deliberative," "independent" technocracy v. democratic politics: will the globe echo the E.U.?', *Law and Contemporary Problems*, 68 (3–4): 341–56.

Smismans, S. (2004), *Law, legitimacy, and European governance: functional participation and social regulation* (Oxford: Oxford University Press).

Waldron, J. (1999), *Law and disagreement* (Oxford: Clarendon Press).

Westerman, P.C. (2007a), 'Governing by goals: governance as a legal style', *Legisprudence: International Journal for the Study of Legislation*, 1 (1): 51–72.
Westerman, P.C. (2007b), 'The emergence of new types of norms', in *Legislation in context: essays in legisprudence*, ed. L. Wintgens (Aldershot: Ashgate).

Erich Kofmel

Fighting Capitalism and Democracy

I

Introduction[1]

Since the 1950s, political scientists, historians, sociologists, and economists have been attempting to prove scientifically common-sense observations about an inherent linkage between democracy and capitalism ('Any causal glance at the world will show that poor countries tend to have authoritarian regimes, and wealthy countries democratic ones': Przeworski, Alvarez, Cheibub and Limongi, 2000: 78). They built upon arguments presented in the literature that emerged in the wake of the Second World War and the independence of former colonies on the economic development of so-called underdeveloped or developing countries. Soon this body of literature led to the academic discipline of Development Studies and a scientific theory of development, usually called 'modernization theory', which was of major influence in the 1950s and 60s and again, along with neo-liberalism, in the 1980s and 90s. While many of the early authors of modernization theory were only concerned with the economic side of capitalist development, others, such as Seymour Martin Lipset, assumed that economic development—capitalism—, would lead to political development—democracy.

[1] The research underlying this paper was undertaken in partial fulfilment of the requirements for the degree of Master of Management in Public and Development Management (MM–PDM) at the Graduate School of Public and Development Management (P&DM) of the University of the Witwatersrand in Johannesburg, South Africa, from which I graduated with distinction in November 2004. Abbreviated versions of the paper were presented at the Fourth Annual Conference 'Workshops in Political Theory' in Manchester, England, and at the Fourth General Conference of the European Consortium for Political Research (ECPR) in Pisa, Italy, both in September 2007.

> Concretely, this means that the more well-to-do a nation, the greater the chances that it will sustain democracy. From Aristotle down to the present, men have argued that only in a wealthy society in which relatively few citizens live in real poverty could a situation exist in which the mass of the population could intelligently participate in politics and could develop the self-restraint necessary to avoid succumbing to the appeals of irresponsible demagogues (Lipset, 1959: 75).

This observation, embedded in contemporary modernization theory, according to Adam Przeworski *et al.*, 'has generated the largest body of research on any topic in comparative politics' (2000: 78–9).

Nevertheless, there still remain questions that have not been answered. Maybe they have not even been asked.

In the mid–1990s, shortly after the fall of communism, it was hardly possible to question the legitimacy of capitalism and market economy. That was the time when Francis Fukuyama posed the now famous question if 'the end of history' had arrived (1989, 1992). With the simultaneous emergence of anti-capitalist democratic movements such as the anti- and alter-globalization movements and non-democratic movements such as the terrorist network of *al-Qaeda* this threshold was taken. The linkage between democracy and capitalism, and its deeper meaning, remain however a taboo.

The research from which this paper emanates aimed at exploring the linkage between democracy and capitalism, particularly in relation to phenomena of 'globalization' such as (a) the rise of anti- and alter-globalization movements and their worldwide fight against capitalism, (b) the fight of terrorist movements all over the (primarily underdeveloped) world against western values such as capitalism and democracy, and (c) the 'Fighting Democracy' as it emerged during the US-led 'War On Terrorism' (or 'The Long War').

The title of the paper, *Fighting Capitalism and Democracy*, can thus be read in two ways: as meaning the attempt to fight those western philosophical-political concepts or as their fight to gain influence all over the world.

The first problem I encountered in my research was that few have taken a close look at the linkage between democracy and capitalism. Only once in twenty years a major liberal author bothered to write about the linkage of democracy to capitalism at all, and then, as Milton Friedman put it, 'to keep options open until circumstances make change necessary …, to keep them alive and available until the politically impossible becomes politically inevitable' (1982: ix).

Thus, there is not a single theoretical book, it seems, that concerns itself exclusively with the linkage between democracy and capitalism. Most authors discuss the issue within the scope of a broader interest. My research may have been the first attempt to systematically gather evidence for such a linkage from different bodies of literature (including empirical evidence) and to review what major authors of all provenance throughout history had to say about it.

To give an indication of the scope and findings of my research, I will proceed to present and discuss (in section II) the linkage between democracy and various forms of capitalism throughout history, (III) the liberal tradition arguing an inextricable linkage between democracy and capitalism, (IV) (a) the existence of an intrinsic linkage between democracy and capitalism as it has been argued in the literature on the economic and political development of underdeveloped countries, particularly in modernization theory, and (b) the findings of empirical, historical and sociological studies that tried to demonstrate this linkage over the course of the last fifty years, (V) (a) the counter-argument in the socialist tradition arguing against an inevitable linkage between democracy and capitalism as made most recently by the anti- and alter-globalization movements, and, finally, (b) socialist authors contradicting this and arguing in favour of a linkage between democracy and capitalism once more.

This review has since been complemented by a separate study gathering and analyzing statements posted by representatives of terrorist movements on the Internet, as part of a research project comparing the socio-political analyses of radical Islam and Christian 'political theology', respectively (Kofmel, 2009).

Between sections IV and V, I will pause to discuss one of the central questions to Political Science: can there be a democracy, at national level, that is not capitalist? To answer this, we will need to look at deviant cases in which democracy exists in not-yet-capitalist circumstances. I will argue that the reasons for the survival of democracy in these cases lie outside of capitalism and democracy.

I will conclude this paper by arguing that if someone wants to fight capitalism, and maybe sees globalization as today's primary manifestation of it, they need to abandon democracy and its values first. One cannot fight capitalism, it seems, and replace it with some non-liberal democracy because every form of democracy, if sustained long enough, will in turn give rise to some form of capitalism. That is why grassroots-democratic anti- and alter-globalization movements are contradictory in themselves and therefore bound to fail.

Being anti-capitalist, it appears, one must be anti-democratic too.

II

In History

The notion that democracy is intrinsically linked to money, and democratic power is linked to material wealth, is as old as democracy itself.

In the very first democracies, in ancient Greece, as James Bryce writes, '[t]he power of money and the greed for money appears from the prevalence of bribery and the frequent embezzlement of the public funds' (1921: I/206).

Democracy, it appears, cannot exist without some form of 'capitalism' being in place, while capitalism can, and does, exist in countries without democracy.

> Materialism is a dangerous malady of the human mind in all nations, but one must dread it particularly in a democratic people because it combines marvelously with the most familiar vice of the heart in these people. Democracy favors the taste for material enjoyments. This taste, if it becomes excessive, soon disposes men to believe that all is nothing but matter; and materialism in its turn serves to carry them toward these enjoyments with an insane ardor. Such is the fatal circle into which democratic nations are propelled (Tocqueville, 2000: 519).

Socrates, in Plato's *Republic*, speaks of markets and shopkeepers, mercantilism, export and overseas trade as well as the 'capitalist mode of production' (long before Marx gave it that name): 'hired labourers, as we call them, because they sell the use of their strength for wages' (1941: 370–1). The latter existing beside the exploitation of bought and sold slaves. Aristotle speaks of the 'class of labourers' (1988: 1291a6) and Cicero, in *De Republica*, of the origins of the term *'proletarii'* in an early Roman voting order whose major concern it was 'that the voting strength lay in the hands of the wealthy, rather than in the hands of the majority'.

> Servius [Tullius] provided carefully even for the very terminology to accompany this scheme. On the wealthy he conferred the name "assidui" because they contributed money; then he called those "proletarii" who either had not entered in their census returns more than fifteen hundred asses worth of property or had made no return at all except of their civil status (n.d.: 174–5).

We ought not to forget that 'democracy' in Greek polities often excluded the vast majority of people: male inhabitants who did not own property (Athens 'has been well described as a property-owning democracy', 'made up mainly of persons not dependent on employment by others': Macpherson, 1977: 13), resident aliens, slaves, and women. 'In Athens all citizens took part in public affairs; but there were only twenty thousand citizens out of more than three hundred fifty thousand inhabitants' (Tocqueville, 2000: 450).

> When the class of farmers and of those who possess moderate fortunes have the supreme power, the government is administered according to law. For the citizens being compelled to live by their labour have no leisure; and so they set up the authority of law, and attend assemblies only when necessary (Aristotle, 1988: 1292b25–9).

Aristotle — himself a resident alien in Athens who was refused the right to political participation — knew, as well as we know, that a large and well-off middle class is a prerequisite for a stable democracy (1295b–1297a). 'The city which is composed of middle-class citizens is necessarily best constituted in respect of the elements of which we say the fabric of the state naturally consists' (1295b26–9).

Both Plato and Aristotle view democracy as being established by the poor, against the ruling elite, 'whether by force of arms or because the other party is terrorized into giving way' (Plato, 1941: 557). Plato suggests however that the poor will swiftly lose interest in politics, though remaining the supreme power when in assembly (564), and 'promote to honour anyone who merely calls himself the people's friend' (558).

> Now, ... in the last form of democracy the citizens are very numerous, and can hardly be made to assemble unless they are paid, and to pay them when there are no revenues presses hardly upon the notables (for the money must be obtained by a property-tax and confiscations and corrupt practices of the courts, things which have before now overthrown many democracies) (Aristotle, 1988: 1320a17–22).

It was common in Greek polities that only very rich men were allowed (or able) to hold high (and time-consuming) office since they did not need to be paid and were, once elected, less prone to corruption. At times, they would bear the state expenses, finance wars and social welfare.

> The career of office in Rome from the time when its course took form as a series of elections, required so large a capital that every politician was the debtor of his entire entourage. ... Dinners were offered to the electors of whole wards, or free seats for the gladiatorial shows, or even (as in the case of Milo) actual cash, delivered at home — out of respect, Cicero says, for traditional morals (Spengler, 1971: II/458).

Plato and Aristotle were convinced that democracies would finally be overthrown at the hands of ruthless demagogues, leading to despotism (Plato, 1941: 562A–572; Aristotle, 1988: 1305a). Rather, money prevailed. Julius Caesar, who brought the Roman Republic to its end, was the richest man of his time — after having conquered Gaul with money borrowed to pay his legions. 'Caesar grasped the fact that on the soil of a democracy constitutional rights signify nothing without money and everything with it' (Spengler, 1971: II/459).

Both democratic Athens and the Roman Republic were military empires, exploiting the 'colonies' and provinces affiliated to them. The initial criterion for gaining Athens' citizenship had been the ability to equip oneself for the hoplite infantry. Athens' and Rome's power was based on their warships as much as on commerce. While Athens did not treat her subjects in other cities as equals, Rome generously granted Roman citizenship — which meant the duty to military service rather than political participation.

Political decisions were taken in Rome or Athens, respectively, and demanded personal presence. In the Roman Republic, as Cicero writes in his *Pro Sestio*,

> five people for each tribe attended plebiscites, and these really belonged to tribes other than that which they were representing. But these five were present only in order to have themselves bought by the possessors of the real power. Yet it was hardly fifty years since the Italians had died in masses for this franchise (Spengler, 1971: II/432).

The democratization of the Italian city republics from the eleventh century onward was equally due to the rise of a new middle class in the wake of 'capitalist' development: migration from the countryside to towns, centralized production and wage labour in the textile and shipbuilding industries, banking and credit arrangements, the setting up of large international companies and seafaring partnerships, import and export relations with far-off regions, and the invention of double-entry bookkeeping at that time (Luzzatto, 1961: 97–120).

> It was commerce more than anything that raised Italy to undisputed supremacy in the economy of the medieval world. Indeed, it was to satisfy the needs of the international commerce that technology and legal institutions were improved and business organization put upon a rational basis, that the spirit of initiative and enterprise was developed to the highest degree and a new social type, the modern entrepreneur, was brought into being (109).

Where the city aristocracy and the landed nobility of the surrounding areas lost influence, the town councils and consulate were thus dominated by merchants and master craftsmen — while in some communes property qualifications excluded the mass of manual workers as late as the thirteenth century (67).

Historically, it appears, democracy always emerged in a 'capitalist' context. The same is true, I argue, for Switzerland which may be the longest-standing democracy in the world.

In 1291, according to Switzerland's foundation charter, the 'ur-cantons' — Uri, Schwyz, and Unterwalden — declared that they would no longer accept foreign 'judges' (officials) in their valleys, and archaeological evidence speaks of a popular uprising at that time in which a number of castles were destroyed. Romantic legend wants it that '[t]hey lived off the produce of their own fields and woods and pastures, governing themselves by gatherings of the people in which every householder was the equal of every other' (Bryce, 1921: I/368).

As remote as the valleys of central Switzerland in which Swiss democracy originated may seem, they had benefited from the transit over the Alps since antiquity. And the opening of the St Gotthard pass promised the abutting valleys and their peasant population, once independent, a lucrative share of the increasing revenues from transalpine trade between Germany and Italy.

For the next few centuries the confederates engaged successfully in war with the European superpowers of their time and in the expansion of their territory — incorporating the wealthy town of Lucerne, the industrial town of Zurich and the regional military power of Berne as early as 1332, 1351 and 1353, respectively. 'The preservation of good order on the road from the St Gotthard pass to Zurich was to be the general concern of all the cantons' signing the Priests' Charter (*Pfaffenbrief*) of 1370 (Bonjour, Offler and Potter, 1952: 88–102).

At the same time the Swiss became famous for mercenary services rendered all over Europe. 'What could not be obtained by labour could be, almost must be, obtained by loot. ... [L]and, stores of food, cities, and gold were theirs for the taking' (121). They would fight for any power that paid them, and change sides as soon as someone offered more. 'It was thus possible to hire, buy, or corrupt high and low; the wisdom or justice of the quarrel mattered little in comparison with its proceeds. ... *Pas d'argent, pas de Suisses*, first used by the Swiss themselves, ... became a proverb' (142, 177).

When the introduction of artillery changed the trade of war, though, the Swiss turned to other profitable enterprises. Zurich had long been a centre of the silk and wool industry, and the rural areas of Switzerland offered an inexhaustible reservoir of cheap labour for 'capitalist production' — be it young men who came to town to work in manufactories, or people knitting, embroidering, making lace, spinning, or weaving at home. Switzerland, after the Thirty Years War, was 'the most highly industrialized corner of Europe' and the industrial revolution in Switzerland greatly preceded that in England.

> Like Great Britain in a later century, Switzerland must either export or decline. ... Equally necessary was knowledge of where foreign markets were to be found, and this was among the chief benefits brought back by those who served in foreign armies and visited many lands and peoples (187–8).

Basle was another stronghold of the wool textile industry, Geneva added watch and clock making and jewellery industries, and from the nineteenth century on the tourism industry and the production of machinery began to contribute to the country's revenues (189–204).

In the absence of a federal authority (which was not introduced until 1830) the level of democracy varied widely among the cantons that constituted the Old Swiss Confederacy. Grassroots democracy existed in the valleys of central and eastern Switzerland. In Zurich, the craft guilds ('trade unions') of 'industrial workers' had achieved constitutional participation in the town council, equal to the joint representation of nobility and merchants, as early as 1336 (91). In Lucerne and Berne, the councils were made up of merchant-patricians until the nineteenth century (104). 'Some cantons had by conquests in war acquired territories whose inhabitants they ruled as subjects, and to whom they granted none of the freedom they claimed for themselves' (Bryce, 1921: I/369).

The democratic movement that swept across Europe in the second quarter of the nineteenth century led finally to the setting up of the modern federal state in 1848. 'With the promise of economic freedom, large sections of the population were won over to the liberal movement' (Bonjour *et al.*, 1952: 251). Still, however, for some years to come, men without property or higher education did not qualify to hold office (252).

> In general the wealthier classes in the rural districts and the upper middle class in the towns were the ruling classes. Protected by the freedom of trade and industry, they strengthened their positions as leaders of commerce and industry and promoted the growth of capitalism and individualism. It was these classes which formed the shareholders into great limited companies for the railways and on the stock exchange. Members of the same classes sat in the cantonal and great councils. In this way economic and political liberalism entered on a close alliance (299).

In 1882, the St Gotthard railway tunnel was opened, once more the 'most important route between the north and the south of Europe' (311).

It was not until 1971 that women were granted the right to democratic participation at the national level.

The English Republic of Oliver Cromwell was short-lived not least because of her poor economic performance, her neglect for debt service, and rising taxes. Despite London merchants' influence on politics and elections, they were not prepared to fund the commonwealth with their money (Barnard, 1982: 18).

The impact of English Puritanism which, 'in that century, was rife with democratic ideas' (Macpherson, 1977: 14) and Cromwell's 'Independents' on modern-day democracy can nevertheless not be overestimated.

> Among the Puritans who formed the bulk of the parliamentary party in the Civil War, the Independents were the most consistent and most energetic element. In their view all Christians were, as Christians, free and equal, and therefore entitled to a voice in the affairs of a Christian State as well as of a Christian congregation. ... [S]o the seed of the Independents' doctrine, carried across the ocean, fell on congenial ground in the minds of the New England Puritans, and there sprang up, two generations later, in a plentiful harvest (Bryce, 1921: I/32).

In England herself, Fukuyama writes, economic and political 'liberalism ... emerged in direct reaction to the religious fanaticism of the English Civil War. Contrary to those who at the time believed that religion was a necessary and permanent feature of the political landscape, *liberalism vanquished religion in Europe*' (1992: 271).[2]

Thus, both the religious ardour of contemporary America and the insignificance commonly ascribed to religion in contemporary Europe may be directly attributed to the legacy of the English Republic.

The American Revolution was preceded by a hundred and fifty years of economic development. It took place, it appears, only once there was a 'capitalist' cause to fight for. 'The American republics in our day are like companies of merchants, formed to exploit in common the wilderness lands of the New World' (Tocqueville, 2000: 272–3).

American democracy was always exclusive. Early New England townships knew popular assemblies, though public affairs were conducted largely by a few influential men (40, 54). Later, property qualifications restricted the franchise. After the revolution, every American citizen was a voter, and eligible for office and juries (261), excluding slaves — even 'freed Negroes' (266) —, Indians, and women, although '[w]omen themselves often go to political assemblies and, by listening to political discourses, take a rest from household tedium' (230–2).

When in 1920 women's suffrage was extended over the whole Union, more than four fifths of blacks were still excluded by State provisions

---

2   All emphases in quotes are the original authors'.

(Bryce, 1921: II/51) which only in 1965 would be overruled by the federal Congress (Rueschemeyer, Huber Stephens and Stephens, 1992: 122).

All Americans, however, were united in their love and desire for, as Alexis de Tocqueville calls it, 'material well-being'. It was the prevalent motive behind everything they did. Even the Puritans were 'seeking with an almost equal ardor material wealth and moral satisfactions, Heaven in the other world and well-being and freedom in this one' (2000: 43).

> The passions that agitate the Americans most profoundly are commercial passions and not political passions, or rather, they carry the habits of trade into politics. ... One must go to America to understand what power material well-being exerts on political actions and even on opinions themselves, which ought to be subject only to reason (273).

Most men in the American Congress were 'wealthy property owners' (270), many of whom had made their fortunes by moving westward into the wilderness, 'impatient with every kind of yoke, greedy for wealth, often thrown out by the states that saw them born' (361). In later days, election campaigns were so costly as to 'give an advantage to wealthy men and to those who command the support of powerful newspapers' (Bryce, 1921: II/64). Bribery of voters was also not uncommon (II/55).

> Every year sees the distribution from what is called "the Pork Barrel" of grants of money to particular districts or cities for so-called "local public works" — it may be for making harbour which is sure to be silted up, or improving the navigation of a stream where there is just enough water to float a canoe (II/68).

As soon as parties became influential, 'open recognition was given to the principle that elections were a business, and state offices from top to bottom the "spoils of the victors"' (Spengler, 1971: II/451). Each party's funds were 'replenished by contributions exacted from business firms or corporations which its power over legislation and administration can benefit or injure' (Bryce, 1921: II/41).

> The power which money inevitably carries with it went on growing as the means of using it multiplied. Railroads and other business enterprises came to be worked on so vast a scale that it was worth while to obtain facilities for starting or conducting them by the illegitimate expenditure of large sums. The number of persons rich enough to corrupt legislators or officials increased, and as the tempters could raise their offers higher, those who succumbed to temptation were more numerous (II/25-6).

Overall, de Tocqueville assesses, 'those charged with directing the affairs of the public in the United States are often inferior in capacity and morality' (2000: 223), and '[t]he power of wealth, and particularly of great incorporated companies, to influence both legislatures, and the choice of persons to sit in legislatures and on the judicial Bench, has been formidable' (Bryce, 1921: II/169).

While the prosperity of the citizens in any democracy makes for its stability (Tocqueville, 2000: 267), in America just about 'everybody could find means of sustenance. Among the earlier settlers and almost down to our own time there was no economic distress, no pauperism nor ground for apprehending it' (Bryce, 1921: II/5).

> This double movement of emigration never stops: it begins deep in Europe, it continues over the great ocean, it follows across the solitudes of the New World. Millions of men advance at once toward the same point on the horizon: their language, their religion, their mores differ, their goal is common. They were told that fortune is to be found somewhere toward the west, and they go off in haste to meet it. ... Almost everywhere they encounter fortune, but not happiness. Among them the desire for well-being has become a restive and ardent passion that increases while it is being satisfied (Tocqueville, 2000: 268–70).

I cannot even attempt to penetrate the surface of the 'capitalist' constitution of all ancient, medieval, pre- and early modern democracies. Maybe one day a historian will be writing the 'economic history of democracy'. Our interest lies with modern-day democracies and modern-day capitalism. It lies with what we have come to call 'globalization'—the global spread of *the two of them*: capitalism and democracy.

And with the fight against them.

It is reasonable, I will suggest, to fight democracy.

If one wants to fight capitalism, it appears to be inevitable.

'It is the tragic comedy of the world-improvers' and freedom-teachers' desperate fight against money that they are *ipso facto* assisting money to be effective' (Spengler, 1971: II/401).

III

From Bentham to Fukuyama

The notion that democracy is intrinsically linked to money, and democratic power is linked to material wealth, is as old as democracy itself.

> The typical state of mankind is tyranny, servitude, and misery. The nineteenth century and early twentieth century in the Western world stand out as striking exceptions to the general trend of historical development. Political freedom in this instance clearly came along with the free market and the development of capitalist institutions. So also did political freedom in the golden age of Greece and in the early days of the Roman era (Friedman, 1982: 9–10).

Reviewing the literature concerning itself with *modern* democracy reveals that two implicit 'traditions' can be identified — apparently never stated as such: a tradition, which for want of a better term we may want to call 'liberal', that acknowledges that democracy cannot exist without some form of 'capitalism' being in place. And another tradition, let us call it 'socialist', dating back to Marx and even beyond (to the Chartist movement, some may argue to the days of early Christianity), arguing that the two of them are separable, and that one can fight capitalism without harming democracy.

However, while capitalist democracy continues, all attempts at socialist democracy collapsed at an early stage. The concept of socialist democracy has, too, no predecessor in ancient, medieval, or pre-modern history. We will discuss arguments in this tradition later.

Philosophical ideas may hardly ever originate in an author without being influenced or initiated by the outside world, namely by other writers. Most academic authors will reference such influences. Unfortunately, the books and articles written on the linkage between democracy and capitalism in the liberal tradition are often not scholarly products, but rather of a popular nature. Hardly an author acknowledges that someone before him has treated the topic, or if doing so they do not specify in what way such readings may have influenced their own views.

The genealogy of what I call the liberal tradition is thus somewhat obscured. According to C.B. Macpherson, liberals ('from Locke and the Encyclopédists down to the present') have supported 'the market freedoms of a capitalist society', but in the seventeenth and eighteenth centuries ('from, say, Locke to Burke') 'were not at all democratic' (1977: 20). Some British writers of the nineteenth century, staying in the succession of Jeremy Bentham — but also de Tocqueville (2000: 514-5) —, wrote about the linkage between economic freedom and political freedom (Friedman, 1982: 10-1). Now, the confusion of democracy and freedom is a common one. Political freedom is not the same as democracy and economic freedom is not the same as capitalism. There can be more or less political as well as economic freedom in a non-democratic state.

I am not going to give a definition of capitalism, democracy, or globalization either (although my own understanding may become manifest from reading my comments and the excerpts I have chosen). All authors quoted in this paper have their own, often time-bound, definitions which may be at variance with mine. They also differ among themselves, so that I have consequently waived their definitions too. It would lead too far for this paper to establish for each author his or her premises. The important finding, and my ongoing argument, is that, independent of their premises, all authors studied here have come to the same conclusion: democracy and capitalism are inextricably linked.

Macpherson came up with the intriguing suggestion that it was Bentham himself who discovered in the early nineteenth century the linkage between democracy and capitalism when contemplating the ideal political form for an advanced capitalist market society.

> The political problem was to find a system of choosing and authorizing governments, that is, sets of law-makers and law-enforcers, who would make and enforce the kind of laws needed by such a society. It was a double problem: the political system should both produce governments which would establish and nurture a free market society and protect the citizens from rapacious governments (for by the grand governing principle of human nature every government would be rapacious unless it were made in its own interest not to be so, or impossible to be so) (Macpherson, 1977: 34).

Macpherson calls this 'Protective Democracy'. Its main function was to protect class division and private property rights as the basis of capitalism, a system 'justified by its high level of material productivity' (44).

Following the laws of classical political economy, Bentham's Utilitarianism was built on 'a model of man (as maximizer of utilities) and a model of society (as a collection of individuals with conflicting interests)' and was 'both fundamentally egalitarian and thoroughly businesslike' (24–5). Because he had 'created his model of man in the image of the entrepreneur or the independent producer' (29), he took 'power over others' — incessantly sought by man —, to be just a means 'to maximize his own wealth without limit' (26), and thus assumed that 'whatever body has the power to legislate and to govern' (35) is 'governed altogether by its conception of what is its interest, in the narrowest sense of the word interest: never by any regard for the interest of the people' (Bentham, 1843: IX/102). 'The only way to prevent the government despoiling all the rest of the people is to make the governors frequently removable by the majority of all the people' (Macpherson, 1977: 35).

Indeed was Bentham speaking of 'democracy' — for instance 1830 in *The Constitutional Code* (1843: vol. IX) — while others spoke of 'freedom'. Since Great Britain already had a parliamentary system at that time (dominated by the 'narrow landed and moneyed class': Macpherson, 1977: 39), what made for 'democracy' was 'the extent of the franchise, along with certain devices such as the secret ballot, frequent elections, and freedom of press' (34). Bentham was, however, at different stages between 1791 and 1820, satisfied with something far short of universal franchise. 'Bentham was not enthusiastic about a democratic franchise: he was pushed to it, partly by his appraisal of what the people by then would demand, and partly by the sheer requirements of logic as soon as he turned his mind to the constitutional question' (35). Capitalist market economy depends on a class-divided society and 'security of property elevated to a "supreme principle" absolutely overriding the principle of equality' (33).

> Without security of property in the fruits of one's labour, Bentham says, civilization is impossible. No one would form any plan of life or undertake any labour the product of which he could not immediately take and use. Not even simple cultivation of the land would be under-taken if one could not be sure that the harvest would be one's own. The laws therefore must secure individual property. And since men differ in ability and energy, some will get more property than others. Any attempt by the law to reduce them to equality would destroy the incentive to productivity (30).

Unlimited private property, 'along with unlimited desire, ... while perpetuating inequality', maximizes the 'productivity of the whole system' (33). Thus, in introducing democracy, 'security of any kind of established property, including that which could not possibly be the fruits of one's own labour, must be guaranteed' (31).

Bentham only backed the democratic franchise 'when he had become persuaded that the poor would not use their votes to level or destroy property' (37).

> In the Anglo-American United States, the class who ... are without property—that is to say, without property sufficient for their maintenance—have, for upwards of fifty years, by means of the right of electing the possessors of the supreme operative power, had the property of the wealthy within the compass of their legal power: in what instance has any infringement of property ever been made? (Bentham, 1843: IX/143).

The poor, Bentham argued, 'have more to gain by maintaining the institution of property than by destroying it' (Macpherson, 1977: 37).

Bentham's disciple, James Mill, at the same time, 1820, held that the universal franchise 'would not be dangerous because the vast majority of the lower class would always be guided by the middle class' (39), and 'follow the advice and example of "that intelligent, that virtuous rank"' (43) of aspiring capitalists, petty tradesmen, and entrepreneurs. And anyway, as he wrote six years later in *On the Ballot*, 'the business of government' will always be 'the business of the rich'. The only question was whether they obtained it by good or bad means. The good means being 'the free suffrage of the people' (42) whose

> advocacy is based on the assumption that man is an infinite consumer, that his overriding motivation is to maximize the flow of satisfactions,

or utilities, to himself from society, and that a national society is simply a collection of such individuals. Responsible government, even to the extent of responsibility to a democratic electorate, was needed for the protection of individuals and the promotion of the Gross National Product, and for nothing more (43).

Other liberal authors trace the notion of a linkage between democracy and capitalism back to Friedrich August von Hayek's *The Road to Serfdom* (for example Friedman, 1982: vii).

There are however at least two earlier authors to consider.

First and foremost a German who links democracy and capitalism more vigorously than anyone who wrote later: Oswald Spengler. It is likely that von Hayek, a native Austrian, 'in close touch with German intellectual life' (Hayek, 1962: 2), read *The Decline of the West* at the time of its publication in German, 1918-22. As Spengler's translator remarks, 'it happened that this severe and difficult philosophy of history found a market that has justified the printing of 90,000 copies' (Atkinson, 1971: ix).

Von Hayek would come to denounce Spengler as one of 'the intellectual leaders of the generation which produced Nazism', one of 'the immediate masters of National-Socialism' (1962: 131). That is wrong, I argue. Spengler certainly was not a liberal, though this term does not make sense in the realm of Spengler's philosophy. For him, there is no such thing as an absolute truth, only truths that are true in their time. He analyzed what he believed to be historically true for Germany at that time, the years around 1920. He did not invent nationalism, he merely explained why it was there, and he did not invent 'socialism', he merely described it. He did not call for National Socialism, but described the Prussian *Amts*-Socialism of those years. He explained why English liberalism and Prussian socialism (Spengler used the term 'socialism' in a sense much different from other authors) were in constant conflict with each other. And although he distinguished ethical socialism and economic socialism throughout history (1971), he forecast, as much as did von Hayek, that socialism would always be authoritarian (Hayek, 1962: 132).

Sometimes, a later author may be unaware of an influence he received. Such might be von Hayek's case.

Spengler was a powerful voice who did not support liberalism, but argued the liberal case for a linkage between democracy and capitalism. He was no socialist (in the classical sense) either and did thus not need to hold that the two were separable. It is to assume that the liberal tradition of the linkage between democracy and capitalism up to Friedman and Fukuyama—moving from Europe to America once more—in no small manner was influenced by this great German philosopher who is as brilliant as he is controversial.

It is highly noteworthy that Spengler died in 1936, long before the Second World War. As much as Ernst Jünger, whom von Hayek denounces as well (131) and who stood in high honours when he died in 1998, Spengler deserves a re-evaluation based not on his unfortunate place in time and his untimely death, but on the merits of his philosophy.

'In the form of capitalism, money has won', Spengler says (1971: II/431).

According to him, two things emerged in the aftermath of rationalism and the Enlightenment: 'intellect' and 'money'. The former expressing itself in 'science' and particularly in 'general theories upon politics', 'abstract systems' — ideologies such as liberal democracy and communism. 'Along with abstract concepts abstract Money, — money divorced from the prime values of the land' — appeared as a political force. 'The two are inwardly cognate and inseparable ... under the two aspects of wish and actuality, theory and practice, knowing and doing.' 'Of the two, moreover, it is the Money that, as pure fact, shows itself unconditionally superior to the ideal truths' which are 'set in effective motion only by money' (II/400-1).

The relation of the 'rationalistic catchwords' such as 'Liberty' 'to the principles of the Manchester School was intimate — Hume was the teacher of Adam Smith' (II/403). Furthermore, both ideologies and capitalist economy 'emerge out of the chaotic mass of the Non-Estate', the leading bourgeoisie (II/401) — or middle class — and the mob (II/399-400) of 'the great city', defining itself as 'the unit of protest against the essence of Estate', particularly the landed aristocracy of the countryside, traditional feudalism (II/448-9), and the dominant religion (II/399). Liberalism ('in the broad sense') thus 'is freedom from the restrictions of the soil-bound life ... — freedom of the intellect for every kind of criticism, freedom of the money for every kind of business' (II/403).

'The powers of intellect and money set themselves up against blood and tradition. In place of the organic we have the organized; *in place of the Estate, the Party*', rejecting 'everything that cannot be rationally grasped'. 'Noble ideas are no longer recognized, but only vocational interest. Hence it is that on the soil of burgher equality the possession of money immediately takes the place of genealogical rank' (II/449).

Spengler holds that there is only one really legitimized parliamentary party, 'that of the bourgeoisie, ... that of money and mind, the liberal, the megalopolitan'. All other parties, the conservative as much as the communist, are only copying the liberal party, 'dominated completely by the latter's forms, bourgeois-ized without being bourgeois, and obliged to fight with rules and methods that liberalism has laid down' (II/449–50). He goes as far as to assert that

> [t]here is no proletarian, not even a Communist, movement that has not operated in the interest of money, in the directions indicated by money, and for the time permitted by money—and that, without the idealist amongst its leaders having the slightest suspicion of the fact. ... The great movement which makes use of the catchwords of Marx has not delivered the entrepreneur into the power of the worker, but both into that of the Bourse [stock exchange] (II/402).

Parlimentary democracy, for Spengler, is an empty form, 'reminding men of the fact that one can make use of constitutional rights only when one has money' (II/456). 'With the franchise comes electioneering, in which he who pays the piper calls the tune. The representatives of the ideas look at one side only while the representatives of money operate with the other' (II/402). He is particularly critical of the role the media (foremost the press in his time) play in a democracy.

> In actuality the freedom of public opinion involves the preparation of public opinion, which costs money; and the freedom of the press brings with it the question of possession of the press, which again is a matter of money .... The press serves him who owns it. It does not spread "free" opinion—it generates it (II/401–3).

The media thus, controlling, 'through money, all the intellectual machinery of speech and script, ... guide the people's opinions as they please *above* the parties' (II/456). They

> keep the waking-consciousness of whole peoples and continents under a deafening drum-fire of theses, catchwords, standpoints, scenes, feelings, day by day and year by year, so that every Ego becomes a mere function of a monstrous intellectual Something. Money does not pass, politically, from one hand to the other. It does not turn itself into cards and wine. It is turned into *force*, and its quantity determines the intensity of its working influence (II/460).

'What is truth?', Spengler asks. 'For the multitude, that which it continually reads and hears' (II/461). 'The thought, and consequently the action, of the mass are kept under iron pressure' (II/464). It is true, '[i]t is permitted to everyone to say what he pleases, *but* the Press is free to take notice of what he says or not' (II/463).

> The will-to-power operating under a pure democratic disguise has finished off its masterpiece so well that the object's sense of freedom is actually flattered by the most thorough-going enslavement that has ever existed. ... The reader neither knows, nor is allowed to know, the purposes for which he is used, nor even the rôle that he is to play. A more appalling caricature of freedom of thought cannot be imagined.

> Formerly a man did not dare to think freely. Now he dares, but cannot;
> ... and this is what he feels as *his* liberty (II/461-3).

'To-day Parliamentarism is in full decay' (II/415). Political power 'is passing *de facto* ... to unofficial groups and the will of unofficial personages' (II/416). 'As then sceptre and crown, so now peoples' rights are paraded for the multitude, and all the more punctiliously the less they really signify' (II/464).

Another writer, Henry C. Simons, predated von Hayek in spelling out the linkage between democracy and capitalism. He was the first of the many professors that were to turn the University of Chicago into a centre of so-called neo-liberal thought, directed against the adversary twentieth-century ideologies of National Socialism and communism. Von Hayek and Friedman were among those holding chairs in later years.

In his essay *A Positive Program for Laissez Faire*, first published in 1934, Simons took the 'preservation of democratic institutions' to be one of the 'objectives of economic policy' in America in the face of communism and fascism (1948: 40). He states that

> [m]uch significance has been, and should be, attached to the simultaneous development of capitalism and democracy. Indeed, it seems clear that *none of the precious "freedoms" which our generation has inherited can be extended, or even maintained, apart from an essential freedom of enterprise* (41).

He wishes thus to see 'economists, as custodians of the great liberal tradition out of which their discipline arose', protect 'political and economic freedom' (76-7) by championing 'the cause of economic liberalism and political democracy' (56).

Friedman sees Simons as much as von Hayek and himself as 'intellectual descendants' of Bentham and the Philosophical Radicals (1982: 11).

In 1944, twenty-two years after Spengler, von Hayek, a professor at the London School of Economics, published *The Road to Serfdom*. The central argument of that book had been presented earlier, in a 1938 article *Freedom and the Economic System*, and, somewhat enlarged, in 1939 in the same series as Simons' essay, as a 'Public Policy Pamphlet', printed by the University of Chicago Press.

Von Hayek does not as blatantly as Spengler and Bentham (according to Macpherson) give away the knowledge of the linkage between democracy and capitalism to criticism. Rather, he makes his point indirectly by criticizing the illiberal alternative of his time: socialism (the root of National Socialism and communism alike) and the centrally planned economy.

When saying that socialism leads to 'enslavement', he implies that there can be no socialist democracy.

> It is now often said that democracy will not tolerate "capitalism". If "capitalism" means here a competitive system based on free disposal over private property, it is far more important to realise that only within this system is democracy possible. When it becomes dominated by a collectivist creed, democracy will inevitably destroy itself (Hayek, 1962: 52).

Democracy and liberalism are western ideals connected to individualism ('freeing the individual from the ties which had bound him to the customary or prescribed ways in the pursuit of his ordinary activities'), and individualism is opposed to socialism. 'What the nineteenth century added to the individualism of the preceding period was merely to make all classes conscious of freedom' (11–2). 'We know that we are fighting for freedom to shape our life according to our own ideas' (4). For von Hayek 'political freedom' in liberalism is the same as democracy (as we have seen that was not always true), though '"[f]reedom" and "liberty" are now words so worn with use and abuse that one must hesitate to employ them to express the ideals for which they stood during that period' (11).

Capitalism and democracy constitute what he calls the 'free system'. The two of them together achieved that 'by the beginning of the twentieth century the working man in the Western world had reached a degree of material comfort, security, and personal independence which a hundred years before had seemed scarcely possible' (13).

However, he says, in the early twentieth century, people 'progressively abandoned that freedom in economic affairs without which personal and political freedom has never existed in the past' (10) — in favour of socialism — and forgot about 'the way in which the "free system" worked' (15).

The most influential of the authors of the neo-liberal 'Chicago School' of thought is undoubtedly Friedman. His book *Capitalism and Freedom* was first published in 1962. He named Simons and von Hayek, among others, as those to whom he owed 'the philosophy expressed in this book and much of its detail' (1982: xi).

Friedman describes 'competitive capitalism ... as a system of economic freedom and a necessary condition for political freedom' (4). He is 'deeply concerned about the danger to freedom and prosperity from the growth of government, from the triumph of welfare state and Keynesian ideas' of state interventions in the economy (vi). In his view, these policies are threatening the freedom of the individual as much as do socialism and communism which centralize economic and political power in the government.

'Welfare' and 'equality' are dismissed as the 'catchwords' of paternalistic politics against which classical liberalism fought (5–6).

> Bentham and the Philosophical Radicals ... believed that the masses were being hampered by the restrictions that were being imposed upon them, and that if political reform gave the bulk of the people the vote, they would do what was good for them, which was to vote for laissez faire. In retrospect, one cannot say that they were wrong. There was a large measure of political reform that was accompanied by economic reform in the direction of a great deal of laissez faire. An enormous increase in the well-being of the masses followed this change in economic arrangements (10).

With Bentham, Friedman holds that 'political freedom' is freedom of the individual from coercion 'by his fellow men' and requires the elimination of any 'concentration of power' in government 'to the fullest possible extent and the dispersal and distribution of whatever power cannot be eliminated—a system of checks and balances' (15). Again, democracy is only a means to achieving this overarching goal. It is the political system least obstructive to economic and individual freedom. In a democratic capitalist market economy, '[b]y removing the organization of economic activity from the control of political authority, the market eliminates this source of coercive power. It enables economic strength to be a check to political power rather than a reinforcement' (15).

Friedman insists that not 'any kind of political arrangements can be combined with any kind of economic arrangement' (7),

> that there is an intimate connection between economics and politics, that only certain combinations of political and economic arrangements are possible, and that in particular, a society which is socialist cannot also be democratic, in the sense of guaranteeing individual freedom (8).

For these reasons, Friedman advocates the limitation of government activity to the bare minimum. Any government activity interferes with individual freedom insofar as 'action through political channels ... tends to require or enforce substantial conformity. The great advantage of the market, on the other hand, is that it permits wide diversity' (15). Nevertheless, there must be a 'general customary and legal framework' (25) within which 'voluntary co-operation and private enterprise, in both economic and other activities' (3), can take place. '[A] good society requires that its members agree on the general conditions that will govern relations among them'. 'These then are the basic roles of government in a free society: to provide a means whereby we can modify the rules, to mediate differences among us on the meaning of the rules, and to enforce compliance with the rules' (25). The market cannot do this by itself (27). Besides the promotion of competition (34), in capitalist market society democratic government must provide particularly

> for the maintenance of law and order to prevent coercion of one individual by another, the enforcement of contracts voluntarily entered into, the definition of the meaning of property rights, the interpretation and enforcement of such rights, and the provision of a monetary framework (27).

As for further government activities, Friedman only wants to permit us 'to accomplish jointly what it is difficult or impossible for us to accomplish separately through strictly voluntary exchange', and contemplates the building and maintenance of roads or the care of 'madmen' ('we are willing neither to permit them freedom nor to shoot them': 32-3).

The market, however, reduces 'greatly the range of issues that must be decided through political means' (15), and thus

> reduces the strain on the social fabric by rendering conformity unnecessary with respect to any activities it encompasses. The wider the range of activities covered by the market, the fewer are the issues on which explicitly political decisions are required and hence on which it is necessary to achieve agreement. In turn, the fewer the issues on which agreement is necessary, the greater is the likelihood of getting agreement while maintaining a free society (24).

'An impersonal market separates economic activities from political views': 'No one who buys bread knows whether the wheat from which it is made was grown by a Communist or a Republican, by a constitutionalist or a Fascist, or, for that matter, by a Negro or a white' (21).

Capitalism, Friedman suggests, thus protects minority groups who 'can most easily become the object of the distrust and enmity of the majority' against discrimination (21). Economic freedom protects the 'freedom of speech, of religion, and of thought' (3). '[I]t is a mark of the political freedom of a capitalist society that men can openly advocate and work for socialism' or any other radical change as long as they do not employ 'force or other forms of coercion' (16). It is true that money is needed 'to hold public meetings, publish pamphlets, buy radio time, issue newspapers and magazines, and so on'. However,

> [r]adical movements in capitalist societies ... have typically been supported by a few wealthy individuals who have become persuaded — ... by a Friedrich Engels, to go farther back. This is a role of inequality of wealth in preserving political freedom that is seldom noted — the role of the patron (17).

If the propagation of anti-capitalist ideas in the form of a book or newspaper or other venture promises to be profitable, it will be seen as a business like any other and even be financed by capitalists. 'In a free market society, it is enough to have the funds. The suppliers of paper are as willing to sell it to the *Daily Worker* as to the *Wall Street Journal*' (17-8).

Finally, Friedman suggests, 'it is important to preserve freedom only for people who are willing to practice self-denial, for otherwise freedom degenerates into license and irresponsibility'. While in a capitalist state capitalists may profit from political as much as from economic freedom, '[i]t is entirely appropriate that men make sacrifices to advocate causes in which they deeply believe' — other than capitalism —, because 'no society could be stable if advocacy of radical change were costless' (18).

Consequently, Friedman advocates the individual pursuit of (non-radical, many might say public) interests which in the neo-liberal state of his are not to be pursued by the government. Such interests, according to Friedman,

> include the whole range of values that men hold dear and for which they are willing to spend their fortunes and sacrifice their lives. The Germans who lost their lives opposing Adolph Hitler were pursuing their interests as they saw them. So also are the men and women who devote great effort and time to charitable, educational, and religious activities. Naturally, such interests are the major ones for few men. It is the virtue of a free society that it nonetheless permits these interests full scope and does not subordinate them to the narrow materialistic interests that dominate the bulk of mankind. That is why capitalist societies are less materialistic than collective societies (200-1).

The forty years since Friedman have seen an array of minor authors as well as politicians advocate the linkage between democracy and capitalism in the liberal tradition. Either by now it was considered safe to do so, or with increasing experience with alternative systems, such as actually existing fascism and communism, the linkage between democracy and capitalism became clearer. As the journal *Commentary* put it in 1978: 'The idea that there may be an inescapable connection between capitalism and democracy has recently begun to seem plausible to a number of intellectuals who would once have regarded such a view not only as wrong but even as politically dangerous' (29).

Increasingly, citizens were seen as 'political consumers' 'with very different wants and demands' which in a market model of democracy 'had a choice between the purveyors of packages of political goods' or 'suppliers of political commodities', the 'entrepreneurial political parties ... of which the voters by majority vote choose one' (Macpherson, 1977: 78-81). '[P]oliticians and voters were assumed to be rational maximizers, and to be operating in conditions of free political competition, with the result that the market-like political system produced the optimum distribution of political energies and political goods' (78).

Underlying this was the pluralist conviction that modern society was 'a society consisting of individuals each of whom is pulled in many directions by his many interests, now in company with one group of his fellows, now with another' (77). According to this view, 'it is *because* men are on the whole such maximizing calculators that most of them may well decide not to spend much time or energy in political participation' (85).

Again, '[i]n the political market the purchasing power is to a large extent, but not entirely, money—the money needed to support a party or candidate in an election campaign, to organize a pressure group, or to buy space or time in the mass media (or to own some of the mass media)' (87).

Speaking of what he calls 'democratic capitalism', Michael Novak holds that 'political democracy is compatible in practice only with a market economy. In turn, both systems nourish and are best nourished by a pluralistic liberal culture' (1982: 14). Being in favour of this system, he nevertheless lists a whole range of shortcomings, stating that its 'ironical momentum heads toward hedonism, decadence, and that form of "self-fulfillment" which is like gazing into the pool of Narcissus'—for example, '[t]he leaders of the economic system permit advertising to appeal to the worst in citizens. They encourage credit-card debt, convenience purchasing, the loosening of restraint' (32). Politicians are

> clothing themselves in symbolism and wishes. Their promises of benefits have become a special form of bribery endemic to democracy. ... The careers of political leaders are shorter than the consequences of their actions. ... The political leader spends, spends—... bribes, bribes—since votes are seldom to be won by *lowering* benefits. ... The structural flaw in all welfare democracies is the desire of every population to live beyond its means (32-3).

One politician, former President of the United States, Ronald Reagan, a neo-liberal in Friedman's following, said in 1984—speaking of capitalism and democracy—that 'there's increasing realization that economic freedom is a prelude to economic progress and growth and is intricately and inseparably linked to political freedom' (1988: 117). 'Free people', Reagan pointed out, 'build free markets' (111).

Michael Mandelbaum underscores the more common liberal view of history that rather '[f]ree markets make free men' (2002: 265). In politics as in market economies 'individual choices are paramount', and '[t]he popular sovereignty by which governments are selected in democracies corresponds to the principle of consumer sovereignty in the market, by which individual preferences determine what gets produced and the prices at which products are sold' (268).

In general, 'the barrier between politics and economics is less an iron wall than a permeable membrane. Ideas and habits from one seep into the other' (269). 'Parties are organized to represent interests and the most important interests they represent are economic ones' (270).

> Property is, of course [sic] an economic concept. It is also a right. ... Property was the spawning ground not only of the rule of law but also of constitutionalism itself. It was the protection of property that gave birth, historically, to political rights. ... At the heart of both property and liberty, therefore, and underpinning both economic and political rights, is the rule of law. ... Applying the rule of law publicly and privately is the task of, indeed is impossible without, the state. ... Logically and historically, the rights-protecting state, without which functional democracy is not possible, comes into being to protect property, and property is the sine qua non of a market economy (271).

Furthermore, 'the creation of the welfare state bestowed property, in the form of entitlements, upon every citizen, thereby diminishing opposition to the principle of private property by making it less unequally distributed' (457).

The latest major liberal author to write about the linkage between democracy and capitalism was Francis Fukuyama, in his rightly famous book *The End of History and the Last Man*, published in 1992 and preceded by his 1989 article *The End of History?*

Fukuyama, unlike earlier liberal writers, was no longer concerned mainly with the dangers of socialism. At the time he wrote, almost fifty years after the end of National Socialism, the second major competing ideology of the twentieth century, communism, had finally lost its struggle for world domination. Fukuyama, in the tradition of Hegel, Marx and Spengler (1992: 68), undertook it thus to write once more a 'Universal History of mankind'. Contrary to Spengler (whose popular success and influence on statesmen of all political provenance Fukuyama attributes to the fact that he described 'the decline and decay of Western values and institutions': 68–70), Fukuyama proposed that liberal democracy and capitalism might constitute the 'end point of mankind's ideological evolution' and the 'final form of human government' — in short, the 'end of history' (xi).

Notwithstanding this 'catchphrase', Fukuyama shares much of Spengler's criticism of capitalism and democracy ('of course, many things could be improved': 46) and leaves a wide opening for an ultimately anti-liberal development of world history as prophesied by Spengler. Both of them drew greatly on Nietzsche.

'Today', however, Fukuyama writes, 'we have trouble imagining a world that is radically better than our own, or a future that is not essentially democratic and capitalist' (46).

> From the beginning, the most serious and systematic attempts to write Universal Histories saw the central issue in history as the development of Freedom. History was not a blind concatenation of events, but a meaningful whole in which human ideas concerning the nature of a just political and social order developed and played themselves out. And if we are now at a point where we cannot imagine a world substantially different from our own, in which there is no apparent or obvious way in which the future will represent a fundamental improvement over our current order, then we must also take into consideration the possibility that History itself might be at an end (51).

While 'the natural cycle of birth, life, and death' would go on, important events still would happen, and newspapers report them, Fukuyama observes a 'growing uniformity of modern societies' (xv). In a 'fundamental process' of a 'remarkable worldwide character' 'that dictates a common evolutionary pattern for *all* human societies' (48), there seems to be emerging a 'universal homogenous state' which combines 'a liberal democracy in the political sphere … with easy access' to consumer goods 'in the economic' (1989: 8).

> All countries undergoing economic modernization must increasingly resemble one another: they must unify nationally on the basis of a centralized state, urbanize, replace traditional forms of social organization like tribe, sect, and family with economically rational ones based on function and efficiency, and provide for the universal education of their citizens (1992: xiv–xv).

As for the linkage between democracy and capitalism, 'the spectacular abundance of advanced liberal economies and the infinitely diverse consumer culture made possible by them seem to both foster and preserve liberalism in the political sphere' (1989: 8).

> Just as impressive as the growth in the number of democracies is the fact that democratic government has broken out of its original beachhead in Western Europe and North America, and has made significant inroads in other parts of the world that do not share the political, religious, and cultural traditions of those areas (1992: 50).

'[T]he creation of a universal consumer culture based on liberal economic principles' 'is capable of linking different societies around the world to one another physically through the creation of global markets, and of creating parallel economic aspirations and practices' (108).

Only 'the Islamic world' keeps resisting (211) the 'glittering material world that modern science has created', this 'true global culture, centering around technologically driven economic growth and the capitalist social relations necessary to produce and sustain it' (126).

Fukuyama's analysis is based on what he calls the 'logic of modern natural science'—'an economic interpretation of historical change, but one which (unlike its Marxist variant) leads to capitalism rather than socialism as its final result' (xv). 'Technology makes possible the limitless accumulation of wealth, and thus the satisfaction of an ever-expanding set of human desires' (xiv).

'Modern consumerism' (83), 'the consumerism of a technological society' (85), 'and the science of marketing that caters to it' (63) have brought about an 'incredible diversity of products and services ..., many of them entirely *de nove*' (92), meeting 'desires that have literally been *created* by man himself' (63), serving 'man's vanity, or what Rousseau calls his *amour-propre*'.

> The problem is that these new wants ... are infinitely elastic and incapable of being fundamentally satisfied. Modern economies, for all of their enormous efficiency and innovation, create a new need for every want they satisfy. Men are made unhappy not because they fail to gratify some fixed set of desires, but by the gap that continually arises between new wants and their fulfillment (83).

'The frivolity of consumerism' (xxi) means that '[u]rban professionals in developed countries ... tend not to volunteer for private armies or death squads simply because someone in a uniform tells them to do so', though they, 'on the other hand, can be recruited to a lot of nutty causes like liquid diets and marathon running' (116–7).

In the political sphere, 'the social changes that accompany advanced industrialization' (xix), people becoming wealthier (206), and in particular the 'tremendous leveling effect' of 'universal education' — '[o]ld class barriers are broken down in favor of a general condition of equality of opportunity' (205) — lead to what Hegel called a '"desire for a desire", or the quest for "recognition"' — individual 'pride', 'self-respect' (155), 'self-esteem' (181), or a 'sense of self-worth' (200; 'when we approve of it'), 'vanity', 'vainglory', or *'amour-propre'* ('when we don't': 155). Thus, in a democracy, '[t]he inherently unequal recognition of masters and slaves is replaced by universal and reciprocal recognition, where every citizen recognizes the dignity and humanity of every other citizen, and where that dignity is recognized in turn by the state through the granting of *rights*' (xvii–xviii).

For Hegel (and Fukuyama), 'liberal society is a reciprocal and equal agreement among citizens to mutually recognize each other'. Democracy meant the abolition of 'the very distinction between masters and slaves ..., and the former slaves became the new masters—not of other slaves, but of themselves'. It was 'the achievement of self-mastery in the form of democratic government' (200-1). 'The fact that modern education teaches the ideas of liberty and equality is not accidental; these are slave ideologies that have been thrown up in reaction to the real situation in which slaves found themselves. Christianity and communism were both slave ideologies' (205).

Liberal democracy 'claims to be the most rational form of government, that is, the state that realizes most fully either rational desire or rational recognition' (211-2). It is by definition *'universal'*, granting 'recognition to all citizens because they are human beings, and not because they are members of some particular national, ethnic, or racial group' (201-2).

> For the foreseeable future, the world will be divided between a post-historical part, and a part that is still stuck in history. Within the post-historical world, the chief axis of interaction between states would be economic, and the old rules of power politics would have decreasing relevance. ... On the other hand, the historical world would still be riven with a variety of religious, national, and ideological conflicts depending on the stage of development of the particular countries concerned, in which the old rules of power politics continue to apply (276).

Fukuyama believes that the post-historical and the historical world will collide over oil, immigration, and 'world order questions' such as 'the spread of certain technologies to the historical world'—e.g. weapons of mass destruction (276-8).

At the individual level, '[t]he revival of religion', religious fundamentalism, 'in some way attests to a broad unhappiness with the impersonality and spiritual vacancy of liberal consumerist societies .... The emptiness at the core of liberalism is most certainly a defect in the ideology' (1989: 14).

Fukuyama's 'last man', 'the vicious slave' (1992: 301) who is '[t]he man of desire, Economic Man, ... will perform an internal "cost-benefit analysis"', put up with it, and work 'within the system'. Fukuyama admits however that the system, come time, could be challenged by a man 'who feels that his worth is constituted by something more than the complex set of desires that make up his physical existence'. A 'man of anger who is jealous of his own dignity' (180) and wishes to be recognized 'not just as equal, but as superior to others'. In short, a new 'master'. 'Does not the satisfaction of certain human beings depend on recognition that is inherently unequal?' (xxiii). A notion that might doom democracy to the fatal destiny that so many writers from Plato and Aristotle to Nietzsche and Spengler have prophesied.

> The end of history will be a very sad time. The struggle for recognition, the willingness to risk one's life for a purely abstract goal, the world-

> wide ideological struggle that called forth daring, courage, imagination, and idealism, will be replaced by economic calculation, the endless solving of technical problems, environmental concerns, and the satisfaction of sophisticated consumer demands. ... Perhaps this very prospect of centuries of boredom at the end of history will serve to get history started once again (1989: 18).

It is fascinating to see how few liberal authors have, in the course of two hundred years, written in favour of the linkage between democracy and capitalism, and how many authors of all political provenance nevertheless found it necessary to write against it — implying that public opinion at all times saw the linkage between democracy and capitalism they opposed. Most people, instinctively, believe that the affirmative liberal authors are right. One might call it common sense.

It is not within the scope of this paper to give an account of everything that has been written against the linkage between democracy and capitalism. Much of what was written from Marx' time onward appears, after the collapse of communism, outdated. Further on, we will look at the arguments of some of the most recent adversaries of the linkage between democracy and capitalism writing in what I called the socialist tradition — exponents of anti- and alter-globalization movements that arose in the second half of the 1990s.

But first, let us look at some empirical evidence for the linkage between democracy and capitalism and at modernization theory.

IV

Modernization theory and empirical evidence

Historically, I submit, democracy always emerged in a 'capitalist' context.

'There is an unquestionable relationship between economic development and liberal democracy, which one can observe simply by looking around the world' (Fukuyama, 1992: 125).

> Traditionally the most economically advanced regions, Western Europe and North America, have also hosted the world's oldest and most stable liberal democracies. ... Right behind Europe economically is Asia, whose nations have democratized (or are in the process of doing so) in strict proportion to their degree of development. Of the formerly communist states in Eastern Europe, the most economically advanced among them — Eastern Germany, Hungary, and Czechoslovakia, followed by Poland — also made the most rapid transitions to full democracy, while less developed Bulgaria, Romania, Serbia, and Albania all elected reform communists in 1990–91 (112).

There is an 'empirical association between capitalism and democracy, both historically and in the contemporary world' (Berger, 1987: 77).

Says Friedman:

> Historical evidence speaks with a single voice on the relation between political freedom and a free market. I know of no example in time or place of a society that has been marked by a large measure of political freedom, and that has not also used something comparable to a free market to organize the bulk of economic activity (1982: 9).

Liberal democracy's 'life began in capitalist market societies' (Macpherson, 1977: 1).

> Historically, a market economy is a necessary but not a sufficient condition for democratic politics. Not all countries with market economies have been democracies, but all modern democracies, without exception, have had market economies. Moreover, modern countries with market economies have found it easier than countries without liberal economic system to adopt democratic practices. The countries of southern Europe in the 1970s and of Latin America in the 1980s, which combined market economies with undemocratic governance, made the transition to political democracy more easily than did the formerly Communist countries of Eastern Europe and Central Asia in the 1990s, in all of which the economy had been centrally planned for at least four decades (Mandelbaum, 2002: 268).

Novak:

> While bastard forms of capitalism do seem able for a time to endure without democracy, the natural logic of capitalism leads to democracy. For economic liberties without political liberties are inherently unstable. Citizens economically free soon demand political freedom (1982: 15).

Peter L. Berger:

> Are there in fact noncapitalist democratic polities? And, to the extent that democracy is empirically linked to capitalism, is this linkage simply the result of historical accidents (such as the fact that both capitalism and democracy are products of Western civilization), or can it be ascribed to built-in structural features of these two institutional configurations? ... In terms of the contemporary world, the empirical correlation can be summed up as follows: *All democracies are capitalist; no democracy is socialist; many capitalist societies are not democracies* (1987: 76).

And Charles E. Lindblom:

> *However poorly the market is harnessed to democratic purposes, only within market-oriented systems does political democracy arise.* Not all market-oriented systems are democratic, but every democratic system is also a market-oriented system. Apparently, for reasons not wholly understood, political democracy has been unable to exist except when cou-

pled with the market. An extraordinary proposition, it has so far held without exception (1977: 116).

'These, then, are the arguments that can be made linking high levels of economic development with liberal democracy. The existence of an *empirical* connection between the two is undeniable' (Fukuyama, 1992: 117).

One year earlier than Lipset (quoted at the beginning of this paper), in an often cited non-empirical study, Daniel Lerner (1958) had already proposed a causal sequence of urbanization leading to literacy and media growth, which in turn would lead to the development of institutions of participatory politics. Karl de Schweinitz (1964) went on to claim that the process of causation runs from industrialization to political democracy and he linked this to people being 'disciplined to the requirements of the industrial order' and therefore more willing to resolve conflicts, arising for example from the distribution of national income, peacefully (33). He affirmed that this form of rationality would only develop 'in a high-income economy', but not in a mere 'subsistence economy' (34).

> It is quite clear, one might say obvious, that extremely poor, traditional societies characterized by illiterate, rural populations in which intergroup communication is barely developed and national identifications and institutions barely extant, will have considerable difficulty in establishing and maintaining political democracy (Neubauer, 1967: 1008–9).

Samuel P. Huntington, an influential author of the neo-liberal revival of modernization theory in the 1980s and 90s, argued that democratization will usually happen 'at the middle levels of economic development. In poor countries democratization is unlikely, in rich countries it has already occurred' (1991: 60). Processes associated with industrialization make it, in his eyes, more difficult for authoritarian regimes to control the population, not least because they promote the growth of an urban middle class (66).

Modernization theory 'supposes that countries develop over a long period, so that all the modernizing consequences have time to accumulate' (Przeworski *et al.*, 2000: 94).

> Because in that view dictatorship would generate development, and development would lead to democracy, the best route to democracy was seen as a circuitous one. The policy prescriptions that resulted from that mode of thinking rationalized support for dictatorships, at least those that were "capable of change," that is, anti-communist ones (3).

Dietrich Rueschemeyer, Evelyne Huber Stephens and John D. Stephens call this 'the assumption of modernization theory — of evolutionism and functional system integration' (1992: 15).

In this structural-functional conception of social order, society, polity, and economy are seen as more or less well-functioning systems integrated primarily by shared values and cultural premises. Democracy arises due to its functional fit with the advanced industrial economy (5).

According to Tatu Vanhanen, modernization theory attempts to offer 'universal explanations for democratization' (1989: 119). No modernization theorist 'doubted that history was directional or that the liberal democracy of the advanced industrial nations lay at its end' (Fukuyama, 1992: 69).

With their writings, authors of modernization theory prepared the theoretical foundations for numerous comparative and cross-cultural studies trying to establish correlations and the causal relationship between capitalism and democracy (for example, Cutright, 1963; Neubauer, 1967; Winham, 1970; Jackman, 1973; Bollen, 1979; Brunk, Caldeira and Lewis-Beck, 1987; Pourgerami, 1988; Vanhanen, 1989; Huntington, 1991; Hadenius, 1992; Rueschemeyer et al., 1992; Burkhart and Lewis-Beck, 1994; Helliwell, 1994; Przeworski et al., 2000).

> Political sociology has few, if any "iron laws." However, certain central hypotheses seem to be so established as to be almost beyond challenge. ... The notion of economic development as a "requisite" to democracy ... has survived increasingly sophisticated statistical tests (Burkhart and Lewis-Beck, 1994: 903).

The authors of these studies would usually include variables such as 'wealth'—operationalized, for example, as 'number of persons per motor vehicle and per physician, and the number of radios, telephones, and newspapers per thousand persons' (Lipset, 1959: 75), and level of per capita (or family/household) income and national income—, 'industrialization'—operationalized as 'the percentage of employed males in agriculture, and the per capita commercially produced "energy" being used in the country' (78)—, 'urbanization', levels of education, communication—'newspaper readers per capita, newsprint consumption per capita, the volume of domestic mail per capita and the number of telephones per capita' (Cutright, 1963: 259–60)—, foreign and domestic investment, organization of labour—'union membership as a percentage of the labor force' (Pourgerami, 1988: 136)—, welfare spending—'expenditure on housing, amenities, social security, and welfare as a percentage of total public expenditure' (136)—, democratic civil liberties—the number of human rights violations (132)—, extent of government control over the economy, and the growth of a middle class.

The task is made more difficult, said Vanhanen, by the fact that there is no agreement as to what constitutes either 'capitalism' or 'democracy' (1989: 96). Also, the proper measures of both remain contested, according to Rueschemeyer *et al.* — which did however not change the fundamental finding of all studies that

> there is a stable positive association between social and economic development and political democracy. This cannot be explained away by problems of operationalization. A whole array of different measures of development and democracy were used in the studies under review, and this did not substantially affect the results (1992: 29).

Independent of their premises and variables, qualitative and quantitative comparative and cross-cultural empirical researchers in Sociology, Political Science, History, and Economics have come to the same conclusion: democracy and capitalism are inextricably linked. The results of empirical studies read thus fairly repetitive and we need not go into too much detail.

Looking at particular studies, we should however take note of the research designs and cases they used. Lipset's path-breaking study, for example, analyzed democracies and dictatorships in Latin America as well as in Europe and the Anglo-Saxon world (1959). Phillips Cutright studied seventy-seven independent nations excluding (for statistical reasons) Africa (1963: 255). Deane E. Neubauer chose a sample of twenty-three democratic (and mostly developed) countries (1967: 1006). Gilbert R. Winham undertook it to verify Lerner's theory and Cutright's study by gathering data on the socio-economic variables (urbanization, education, and communication) and the political development of the United States in the period 1790-1960 (1970: 814). Robert W. Jackman conducted a cross-sectional study of '60 non-communist nations' (1973: 615), while Kenneth A. Bollen took a sample of ninety-nine non-communist countries 'at widely varying levels of development' (1979: 576) and Gregory G. Brunk *et al.* sampled seventy-two nations (1987: 463). Abbas Pourgerami studied ninety-two 'Third World countries which have experienced a cyclical process of alternating autocracy and democracy' (1988: 124, 131). Vanhanen looked at '[t]he 147 states which were independent in 1980 and whose population was more than 200,000 inhabitants .... The period of comparison covers the years 1980-85' (1989: 102). Huntington analyzed what he called *The Third Wave* 'of democratization that began in 1974' (61), while Axel Hadenius included in his study all 132 independent states of the Third World (1992: 2). Rueschemeyer *et al.* did comparative historical studies (1992: 4) and Ross E. Burkhart and Michael S. Lewis-Beck used 'a major, but neglected data set from 131 nations' (1994: 903) to study the development of capitalism and democracy 'over a long period of time (1972-89)' (907). John F. Helliwell employed 'cross-sectional and pooled data for up to 125 countries over the period from 1960 to 1985' (1994: 225) and Przeworski *et al.*, finally, covered '141 countries that we observed for at least some time between 1950 and 1990' and of which '73 were already independent in 1950, and 68 gained sovereignty after 1950' (2000: 36).

Huntington identified 'the extraordinary global economic growth of the 1950s and 1960s' (1991: 311) — 'which raised living standards, increased education, and greatly expanded the urban middle class in many countries' (45) — as the main reason for the third wave of democratization. He found that 'by the early 1970s many countries had achieved overall levels of economic development that provided an economic basis for democracy and that facilitated transition to democracy' (59).

> [S]hifts from authoritarianism to democracy between 1974 and 1990 were heavily concentrated in a "transition zone" at the upper-middle levels of economic development. The conclusion seems clear. Poverty is a principal and probably the principal obstacle to democratic development (311).

Helliwell noted a 'robust positive relation between the level of per capita income and the adoption of democracy' (1994: 246). 'The coefficient of 0.2 on the logarithm of per capita GDP suggests that a 10 per cent increase in per capita income raises the predicted value of the democracy index by 2 points on a 100–point scale' (228). And Przeworski *et al.* are convinced that

> per capita income has a strong impact on the survival of democracies. ... Indeed, no democracy has ever been subverted, not during the period we studied nor ever before nor after, regardless of everything else, in a country with a per capita income higher than that of Argentina in 1975: \$6,055. There is no doubt that democracy is stable in affluent countries. The probability of it collapsing is almost zero (2000: 98).

Critical about some of their findings, Neubauer held that Lipset and Cutright 'are careful to specify that they are speaking of necessary conditions for the achievement of political development (not sufficient conditions)' (1967: 1002). Jackman argued that Lipset and Cutright 'regarded democracy as a *linear* positive function of economic growth' (1973: 611–2), while Neubauer saw it as a 'threshold phenomenon' (613). Jackman's own study found that 'the threshold hypothesis fits the data much more closely than does the linear hypothesis' (1973: 619–20), while Pourgerami mustered evidence that democracy will in turn lead to further economic growth (1988: 136).

It had always been clear that 'economic development' meant capitalism as much as 'political development' meant democracy. However, with the neo-liberal revival of modernization theory in the 1980s, and the fall of communism soon after, many authors of a second wave of comparative and cross-cultural studies spoke more openly of 'market economy' or 'capitalism'. Brunk *et al.* found that 'high levels of democracy coexist with moderate degrees of governmental control over economic life' (1987: 465). In fact, 'democratic political practice reaches a maximum under moderate amounts of public direction of economic affairs' as it is present in European and particularly Scandinavian welfare states (459), while 'under high levels of economic direction, little evidence of democratic practice will materialize' (462; see also Bollen, 1979: 584). This confirmed empirically the 'self-evident' theories of economists such as von Hayek and Friedman who 'have argued that the structure of a nation's economic life (capitalist or socialist) in large part shapes its political institutions' (Brunk *et al.*, 1987: 468). Pourgerami revealed that 'the effect of MARKET on DEMOCRACY is largely direct and partly indirect through its effect on INVESTMENT' and 'EDUCATION' (1988: 132, 139). The effect is 'strong and highly significant' (136). Vanhanen, in a number of studies, elaborated on a market model of democracy — an 'evolutionary theory of politics, according to which politics is principally a struggle for scarce resources' (1989: 95) — and found that '[i]t is true that a high level of GNP per capita is favorable for democratization' (119). Hadenius uncovered that '[a]ll the states which apply markedly socialistic forms of production have low values for democracy (none are above 2.5 on our index), while every country with high values (above 7) is at the other end of the scale (Capitalist or Mixed Capitalist)' (1992: 108).

> In fact, democracy and capitalism are often seen as virtually identical. The East-West confrontation gave this proposition a special quality of proud assertiveness. And the downfall of the state socialist regimes of eastern Europe is celebrated by many as the final proof (Rueschemeyer *et al.*, 1992: 1).

Bollen established that late developing countries are subject to the same sequence of capitalist economic and democratic political development as the countries that developed in the nineteenth century (1979: 581–2). Late developers may even benefit from the experience of others: the 'process of international learning led the upper classes in late developers to perceive that labor was not necessarily a revolutionary threat, it could be integrated into the system' (Rueschemeyer *et al.*, 1992: 283).

My own assumption, in line with most of the cited comparative and cross-cultural empirical studies, is that there is a causal link going from capitalism to democracy, rather than in the opposite direction. This means that democracy becomes sustainable only in circumstances where a certain level of wealth has been reached — usually equalled with a nation achieving the status of a middle-income country. Conversely, this indicates that theoretically a subsistence economy has no chance of sustaining democracy. We can take this as a rule. Logically, this must mean that wherever democracy is introduced in circumstances that are not yet 'capitalist' (as has been tried frequently in post-colonial Africa, notably at independence of Sub-Saharan African states) — that is, where the threshold of wealth of a middle-income country has not been reached — it is bound to fail. Most such attempts in Africa (but also, for example, in our time in Iraq) have indeed failed. That is the theory and it holds, I would estimate, in ninety-five percent of cases. Many countries (even in western Europe: say, France) made this experience more than once.

However, there appear to be some deviant cases in which, against all odds, some form of democracy predated capitalism and nevertheless could be sustained. One might think of Botswana, Senegal, or India. Just why do a few cases appear to deviate from a rule that has been established by so much empirical and theoretical research?

From this previous research we know with sufficient certainty that there are variables inherent in capitalism that sustain democracy once the level of a middle-income country has been reached. This would indicate that the variables that lead to the downfall of democracy in not-yet-capitalist countries cannot be inherent to the process of modernization or the capitalist market system. This is very important to note. We can also assume that the variables leading to the downfall of democracy are not inherent to democracy as in a few cases democracy does survive. There is nothing in the literature to indicate that any combination of or interaction between variables of democracy and capitalism would threaten democratic stability.

My hypothesis is that there are variables outside of democracy or capitalism that commonly lead to the downfall of democracy in not-yet-capitalist societies. Such variables, I suggest, are the same that lead to the downfall of non-democratic regimes in low-income countries. They may include, but are not limited to, ethnic and religious *conflict* (not just diversity), the *struggle* for natural resources (not just their presence), *endemic* corruption, militarization, and war with other countries. I further hypothesize that it must then be the absence of these variables that is responsible for the survival of democracy in a few deviant cases of not-yet-capitalist societies. (In consequence, this might indicate that these variables become of less, or no, importance once a nation is over the wealth threshold.)

The absence of these variables may be due to a variety of reasons. For example, there may be only one ethnic group living in a country, or there is religious tolerance, or the country lacks natural resources. I will go on to hypothesize that steady economic growth (even in nations that have not yet achieved middle-income country status) will tend to mitigate potential sources of conflict too. '[T]he probability that, once established, a democracy will survive increases steeply and monotonically as per capita incomes get larger' (Przeworski et al., 2000: 273).

This would mean that a major reason for the outbreak of violent conflict and the overthrow of democratically elected governments may be the absence of economic growth over a period of time (let us say, a number of years). In light of the economic threshold stipulated by so many authors, it may be speculated that a period of zero growth (or even recession) or of economic turbulence becomes unimportant to the survival of democracy only once a nation has achieved middle-income country status. This could be because at that level citizens will feel less immediately threatened in their livelihoods by economic problems. Even in a time of recession they are not in danger of suffering hunger (unlike the population in a subsistence economy) and therefore less prone to seeking redress by resorting to violent and non-democratic means. Another possible explanation is that a successful and stable market economy may teach people how to negotiate divergent interests non-violently and to mutual benefit.

The objective of such hypothesizing is to improve modernization and democratization theories. Consequently, deviant cases must be submitted to further historical and empirical testing. A study of India, for example, might show that this low-income country avoided a breakdown of democracy, despite the 21–month state of emergency under Indira Gandhi, due to is sheer size and military strength, keeping foreign powers at bay; far-reaching separation of religions on foundation of India and Pakistan in 1947; the caste system that historically and traditionally engrained and mitigated inequality; steady economic growth; and the lack of natural resources and thus limited struggle for national wealth.

> A sociological analysis of any pattern of behavior, whether referring to a small or a large social system, must result in specific hypotheses, empirically testable statements. Thus, in dealing with democracy, one must be able to point to a set of conditions that have actually existed in a number of countries, and say: democracy has emerged out of these conditions, and has become stabilized because of certain supporting institutions and values, as well as because of its own internal self-maintaining processes. ... A deviant case, considered within a context which marshals the evidence on all relevant cases, often may actually strengthen the basic hypothesis if an intensive study of it reveals the special conditions which prevent the usual relationship from appearing (Lipset, 1959: 69–70).

Knowledge of the variables that must be absent from a country in order to allow for democracy to be successfully introduced and sustained in a not-yet-capitalist society would allow for foreign and international interventions to be more targeted and ultimately more successful. Such knowledge would, for example, have made it clear that there was no prospect for democracy in conflict-ridden, ethnically and religiously divided, and economically downtrodden Iraq.

While there may be only a few cases of democracies that have survived in not-yet-capitalist societies, they nevertheless provide us with the basis for an even more intriguing theoretical conclusion for politics of resistance.

It now appears that every form of democracy, if it can just be sustained long enough in not-yet-capitalist circumstances, will lead to the emergence of some form of capitalism.

Moreover, non-capitalist democracies are, as we have seen, prone to being overthrown for a variety of reasons. There is nothing in the literature (nor any evidence from observations we may make ourselves by looking at countries now in existence) to indicate that democracy could sustain itself in the absence of capitalism. Democracy, it appears, needs capitalism for survival. The few deviant cases of not-yet-capitalist democracies just confirm this rule. There is nothing inherent in democracy that will lead to its survival in non-capitalist societies. Rather, it appears to be the absence of threatening variables outside of democracy or capitalism that is responsible for the survival—or, more accurately, the non-downfall—of not-yet-capitalist democracies.

The awareness of this linkage of democracy to capitalism might transform politics once and for all.

V

Fighting Capitalism

Our interest lies with modern-day democracies and modern-day capitalism. It lies with what we have come to call 'globalization'—the global spread of *the two of them*: capitalism and democracy.

And with the fight against them.

The movement against corporate globalization—what came to be known as 'the anti-globalization movement' in the late 1990s (see, for instance, Bello, 2002: 16)—asserts that multinational corporations under capitalism are going further than just to be linked to the democratic state—they replace it. Multinational corporations 'bask in budgets bigger than the gross domestic product of most nations; ... of the top hundred economies, fifty-one are multinationals and only forty-nine are countries' (Klein, 1999: 340). 'At the heart of ... anticorporate activism and research is the recognition that corporations are much more than purveyors of the products we all want; they are also the most powerful political forces of our time' (339).

The movement against corporate globalization is in fact a loose coalition of smaller movements, non-governmental organizations (NGOs), and individuals divided among themselves both in terms of purpose and activities. Actual anti-globalization movements were soon joined by (and sometimes redefined themselves as) movements advocating a different kind of globalization—alter-globalization—, global justice (Monbiot, 2003), global democracy (Danaher and Burbach, 2000: 9), global solidarity, or global accountability (10).

All these terms designate diverse movements favouring peace, human rights, the environment, sustainable development, and debt cancellation for developing countries, fighting free trade agreements and structural adjustment programmes, seeking land reform, explicitly anti-corporate, or in defence of small business and farmers, national sovereignty or culture, and include religious groups, cyberpunks, socialists and Marxists, organized labour, the Mexican 'Zapatistas', anarchists, feminists and gays, libertarians, greens, AIDS activists, community organizers, teachers, and consumer rights activists, among others (Starr, 2000; Burbach, 2001; Monbiot, 2003; Klein, 1999).

According to Amory Starr, who studied the very beginnings of anti- and alter-globalization movements in the 1990s from within (all the authors reviewed here are leading exponents of movements), 'these groups mirror traditional responses to industrialization', '"workers of the world" uniting in a widened framework of dispossession that includes multiple sites of oppression' (2000: xi). This is why it is justified to place anti- and alter-globalization movements into what I called the socialist tradition arguing against an intrinsic linkage between democracy and capitalism, though socialists are only a part of the wider movement.

What unites these disparate movements, NGOs, and activists is a shared feeling of being threatened by corporations' increasing economic and political clout—exercised through unaccountable bodies like the World Trade Organization (WTO), the International Monetary Fund (IMF), and the World Bank—, environmental degradation, social deprivation, human rights abuses, non-enforceability of labour standards, genetic engineering of crops, etc. In response to globalization, a global civil society arose that perceives rural and urban communities in developing and developed countries and people of all races, classes, religions, and nationalities alike as facing problems that are closely linked and require global alliances to be tackled (Starr, 2000). Thus, anti- and alter-globalization movements go beyond the nation state themselves in popularizing their brand of global activism.

Globalized resistance to 'neo-liberal exploitation' (Starr, 2000: 83) was made possible by the new information and communication technologies of the 1980s and 90s—personal computing, the Internet, e-mail, and mobile telephony—as well as cheap air travel. Movements, NGOs, and individuals employ various techniques such as worldwide coalition building, collaborative planning of strategy and events, the organization of an annual World Social Forum, sharing and spreading of information about multinationals, legal actions and legislative initiatives, lobbying and petitioning national and international political bodies and actors, computer hacking and virus attacks, creating alternative (non-corporate) media, training camps for civil disobedience, consumer boycotts, parties and protests held outside stores and stock exchanges or on the rooftops of corporate headquarters, and academic research and education.

Mass protests and demonstrations staged against free trade agreements, the WTO, IMF, World Bank, and other multilateral organizations have disrupted high-level conferences and political summits, for example in Seattle (1999) and Genoa (2001). The use of violence on such occasions has been limited to small groups, particularly young anarchists, although sympathy for it could appear to be more widespread. Demonstrations also continue to occur in developing countries to highlight governments' failure to alleviate poverty and resolve social grievances such as water privatization and lack of health care provision (Starr, 2000; Monbiot, 2003; Burbach, 2001; Danaher and Burbach, 2000; Bello, 2002; Klein, 1999).

Most movements and NGOs refrain from negotiations with corporations so as not to be seen as giving weight to corporate interests (Starr, 2000: 157). Political parties are viewed by many activists as 'no longer relevant or ... under the sway of international capital' (Burbach, 2001: 9).

'Corporate-driven globalization is a process marked by massive corruption', Walden Bello writes (2002: 18). He identifies 'a deepening crisis of democratic governance in Europe', following bribery scandals for example in Germany and at the European Commission, and the rise of billionaire entrepreneurs to highest political office in Italy and Switzerland, which seem to prove the 'increasing captivity of party politics to money' (12). In America, 'liberal democracy' has been 'thoroughly corrupted by corporate money politics' (10). '[P]olitical candidates or parties' are supported by the 'financial contributions' of rich and influential lobby groups (Monbiot, 2003: 121), which

> may also resort to criminal bribery or ... to subtle or less subtle forms of blackmail. The candidates themselves, if they are either extremely

rich or have the backing of someone who is, can effectively buy votes. All these distortions are compounded, on a daily basis, by the media organizations controlled by another special interest group ...: the multi-millionaires who own them (121–2).

All over the globe, 'the governments in power today are those whose policies are acceptable to the financial markets' (75–6).

> The political leaderships of so called democracies have been convinced, and have in turn convinced their constituents to accept corporate hegemony as the best way of organizing the economy. Nations (and localities) can increasingly be counted on to subsidize the costs of corporate projects (Starr, 2000: 16–7).

People are 'lobotomized into believing in one single idea, which is, ultimately, what globalization really is: Life is Profit' (Roy, 2002: 31). This begins in school—'*A democratic system of education ... is one of the surest ways of creating and greatly extending markets for goods of all kinds*' (ex-adman James Rorty in Klein, 1999: 87)—and finds its logical continuation in youth-targeted TV stations: '*MTV is associated with the forces of freedom and democracy around the world*', '*There isn't a lot of angst, it's just unbridled consumerism*' (Viacom CEO Sumner Redstone, owner of MTV, and MTV CEO Tom Freston in Klein, 1999: 129). 'The visible result ... is an army of teen clones marching—in "uniform," as the marketers say—into the global mall' (Klein, 1999: 129).

'Today, thanks to Noam Chomsky and his fellow media analysts, it is almost axiomatic for thousands, possibly millions, of us that public opinion in "free market" democracies is manufactured just like any other mass market product' (Roy, 2003: 78; an insight that, of course, Spengler had decades earlier). The 'mass media systematically' distort 'our perception of the way the world is run', writes George Monbiot, himself a journalist. And the journalist Naomi Klein sees the 'corporate space ... as a fascist state where we all salute the logo and have little opportunity for criticism because our newspapers, television stations, Internet servers, streets and retail spaces are all controlled by multinational corporate interests' (1999: 187).

Neo-liberalism has reduced 'the notion of citizen to that of consumer' (Starr, 2000: 23) and '"consumer choice" replaces citizenship as the pre-eminent right' (17), 'thus the only task for the public sphere is facilitating maximum consumer choice' (23). Neo-liberalism 'promises that free markets will do best at ... procuring the maximum goods for consumption' (17). 'Illusory product diversity replaces the right to know, to participate, to regulate, to govern' (24). Klein even identifies 'the architect of global free trade, Milton Friedman' (1999: 326).

The multilateral lending institutions, the IMF and the World Bank, are seen by anti- and alter-globalization movements as 'the rich world's solution to the poor world's problems' (Monbiot, 2003: 159). In accordance with neo-liberal modernization theory, their 'one-size-fits-all policy matrix' for indebted developing countries, particularly 'structural adjustment', emphasizes 'rapid growth' (Bello, 2002: 83) by

> liberalizing investment policies, privatizing public industries and services, downsizing civil service employment, suppressing labour organizing, lifting costly regulation from business practices, devaluing currency, and cutting social spending and subsidies. All of these changes facilitate corporate entry into the economy and provide opportunities to capture markets. Like free trade agreements, structural adjustment packages undermine national sovereignty ... by shifting authority from national priorities to those of first world neoliberal advisers (Starr, 2000: 46).

While 'among the conditionalities the IMF and World Bank demand of debtor nations are "good governance" and "democratization"' (Monbiot, 2003: 153), corrupt 'governments in poorer countries' help 'to push trough unpopular reforms and quell the mutinies' (Roy, 2003: 106–7). In another instance for '[t]he deeply corrupting role of corporate money in political life' (Bello, 2002: 11), 'corporations purchase politicians in order to protect not only direct subsidies (corporate welfare) but also indirect subsidies (regulatory and deregulatory benefits)' (Starr, 2000: 53). 'Privatization seeks to disengage politics from the market' (Roy, 2002: 51) and is essentially 'the transfer of assets and infrastructure from bribe-taker to bribe-giver, which involves more bribery than ever' and results, for example in India, in the production of 'power at exorbitant rates that no one can afford' (52). 'The real function' of the World Bank and the IMF 'is *not* to promote "development" but rather to integrate the ruling elites of third world countries into the global system of rewards and punishments' (Danaher, 2000: 196).

'[E]lections will become even more of a charade than they already are', Roy fears (2002: 52). 'The effective control of many of the poor nations' economies by the IMF and the speculators ... has dampened public faith in democracy: people know that there is little point in changing the government if you can't change its policies' (Monbiot, 2003: 21).

'[F]ree market rhetoric ... loves to couch itself in the language of efficiency and the ethics of the greatest good for the greatest number, but it is really about promoting corporate power' (Bello, 2002: 18). '"Privatization" is presented as being the only alternative to an inefficient, corrupt state. In fact, it's not a choice at all. It's only made to look like one' (Roy, 2002: 60). '[T]he blatant corporate bias of global rule-making institutions' (Burbach,

2001: 92) is concealed by their 'rhetoric of anti-poverty and human development' beneath which 'the same neo-liberal economic model prevailed' (Bello, 2002: 82). The 'systematic exploitation of dirt-cheap labour' (7) is justified by the 'pursuit of "international competitiveness"' (Starr, 2000: 7).

The linkage between democracy and capitalism works only too well. 'We are left to shout abuse, to hurl ourselves against the lines of police, to seek to smash the fences which stand between us and the decisions being made on our behalf' (Monbiot, 2003: 84). The United States government in Seattle 'behaved as brutally as any anti-people government does in the face of resistance' (Shiva, 2000: 121).

As sound as much of their critique of the world's political economy in general may be, the decentralized structure of the anti- and alter-globalization movements makes it impossible for them to agree on a positive project. They confront corporate power with 'a jumble of contradictory ideas', as activists will readily admit themselves (Monbiot, 2003: 14).

While all of them want to make corporations and governments accountable to common people instead of elites, some of their proposals may seem politically naïve: variously transformation or dismantling and disempowerment of WTO, IMF, and World Bank; either strengthening or abolition of nation states; 'globalization-from-below', a world parliament, and global plebiscites; prohibition of corporate donations to politicians; a new global financial architecture, capital controls, and a tax on foreign exchange transactions; decrying of first-world living standards and separation of citizenship from consumership; coercion of 'the rich' by 'the poor'; destruction of the military-industrial complex and technology in general; stopping trade liberalization and de-emphasizing growth, rejection of 'modernization', and local control over development policies; re-localization, local decision making, re-embedding the economy into communities—cut off from national and global markets—, and co-operative enterprise; abolition of corporations as such (Starr, 2000); 'a more fluid, less structured, more pluralistic world, with multiple checks and balances' (Bello, 2002: 118).

There are however certain convictions all anti- and alter-globalization movements hold in common.

> These movements have a variety of relationships to political economy, formal democracy and existing nations. But none imagines that growth, modernization or technology provide answers to their problems; indeed they see corporate technology as economically and ecologically dangerous (Starr, 2000: 224).

They seek 'a revolution in values as well as in institutions' that would replace 'the money values of the current system with the life values of a truly democratic society' (Danaher and Burbach, 2000: 9), a 'system that venerates life in all its forms' (11) and 'consciously subordinates the logic of the market, the pursuit of cost efficiency, to the values of security, equity and social solidarity' (Bello, 2002: 114). The question then is: 'how can we develop alternative institutions that can make rules for the global economy *democratically*' (11)?

Anti- and alter-globalization movements do not deny that currently democracy and capitalism are linked. They just believe — standing in the socialist tradition arguing against an intrinsic linkage between democracy and capitalism — that they can be separated. They distinguish between liberal democracy and the kind of democracy they strive for. While Starr at one point asserts that most participant movements 'are devotedly democratic, holding Western democratic ideals both as fundamental goals for their movements and as the anvil on which to shatter corporate rule' (2000: 83), at another point she finds: 'Almost all the movements ... are critical of such democracy. They are aware of internal contradictions of liberal democracy and the hypocrisy of American democracy, in particular' (192).

Anti- and alter-globalization movements are grassroots-democratic in their decision making as has been shown above. Furthermore, '[w]hat these various movements have in common is the goal of expanding the practice of democracy to include the economic realm' (Danaher and Burbach, 2000: 10, and Burbach, 2001: 101). 'As everything has been globalized except democracy' (Monbiot, 2003: 83), '[t]here is a crying need for an alternative system of global governance' (Bello, 2002: 112). 'Much of the effort of the ... global justice movement has been devoted to addressing' 'the problem of the migration of power to a realm in which there is no democratic control' (Monbiot, 2003: 51). '[I]t is surely demonstrable that many of the most pressing global and international problems arise from an absence of global and international democracy' (46–7). 'If you consider this distribution of power acceptable, that is your choice, but please do not call yourself a democrat. If you consider yourself a democrat, you must surely acknowledge the need for radical change' (17) and 'if we can — as most people do — agree that democracy is the best way to run a nation, it is hard to think of any reason why it should not be the best way to run the world' (46).

Anti- and alter-globalization activists want to 'construct a world order based on equity and justice' (137), 'integrity, community, greater and more democracy, and sustainability' (Bello, 2002: 114). However:

> The transition from global capitalism to democratized societies and economies will occur much as the transition from feudalism to capitalism occurred — it will be a gradual process in which radical actions and activities, economic as well as social and political, take hold in the midst of the global capitalist order (Burbach, 2001: 92).

Again, there are different and contradictory approaches — plainly naïve, and hardly theorized by their proponents, it appears — on how to achieve this goal.

> Danaher ... proposes to begin "people's globalization" by holding "global plebiscites" in which billions of people would vote on basic economic and human rights issues. Globalization from below movements insist on the possibility of super-participatory, accountable, inclusive democracy, but it is unclear how this is to be achieved. What happens the day after the revolution? How is the new power managed democratically on a global scale? How can massified democracy be participatory and inclusive of difference? ... I worry about the ability of "people's globalization" to develop mechanisms of international democracy (Starr, 2000: 193).

Monbiot, too, is critical of participatory democracy, which is

> the dictatorship of those who turn up. The participants in any global gathering must be — by comparison with most of the world's people — rich, for they can afford to travel and to take time off from work. They must possess passports and enjoy freedom of movement.... Similar constraints govern electronic direct democracy: only the rich or the educated have access to the necessary technology, and only the free are permitted to use it (2003: 119-20).

Monbiot's alternative, a 'world parliament' (83), would 'contain 600 representatives each with a constituency of 10 million people' (87). 'A global election is likely to cost something in the order of $5 billion, while the establishment of a parliament might cost around $300 million, and its annual running costs a further $1 billion or so' (90), funded by 'a global lottery, offering enormous prizes and attracting, as a result, plenty of punters' (92). That far, Monbiot understands capitalism. He rules out taking money from 'states, the international institutions and corporations ... for fear either that they would co-opt the assembly or that we would feel constraint to adjust our plans to their convenience' (91). He proposes 'underground elections' in undemocratic states in order to destabilize them (92-3).

'There is, of course, no guarantee that a democratically elected parliament will make sensible decisions, that people will elect those who best represent their interests or that the battles between them will always be resolved in favour of justice and distribution' (85).

It is worth noting that there would be no 'world government' (93). 'We can hope and expect, moreover, that as our parliament belongs to the people ..., it would differ from, and be an improvement on, the kind of democracy which prevails in the rich world' (109).

According to Monbiot, and only to Monbiot, anarchism is one of 'the alternatives, the two ideologies which, within the global justice movement, compete directly or indirectly with the package of political positions most people recognize as "democracy"' (25). The other, he says, is communism, which 'stands at odds with everything we in the global justice movement claim to value: human freedom, accountability, diversity' (38).

A strange statement if compared to others: 'The reason why democratic governance is more likely to deliver justice ... is that it possesses the capacity for coercion: the rich and powerful can be restrained, by the coercive measures of the state, from oppressing the rest of us' (41). 'For the majority of humankind to be free, we must restrain the freedom of those who would oppress us' (38). Who decides that, anyway—in a grassroots democracy? Wasn't he 'seeking to replace a world order built on coercion with one which emerges from below, built upon democracy' (67–8)?

Having assessed the proposals made by anti- and alter-globalization movements and found them wanting, it is worth noting that a number of socialist and communist writers, critical of the linkage between democracy and capitalism, nevertheless believe that it is inextricable.

Lenin made this point earlier than any liberal author, earlier even then Spengler—five years earlier, in 1917. In his book, *The State and Revolution*, he interpreted Marx and Engels who foresaw, following the communist revolution, a lengthy phase of the state 'withering away' (Lenin, 1975: 18), initiated by the 'dictatorship of the proletariat' (82) imposing 'a series of restrictions on the freedom of the oppressors, the exploiters, the capitalists. We must suppress them in order to free humanity from wage slavery, their resistance must be crushed by force' (84). Ultimately, however, Marx and Engels thought, the dictatorship of the proletariat would lead to a classless communist society. 'Only then', in a society that had rid itself of oppressing classes, 'will a truly complete democracy become possible and be realised, a democracy without any exceptions whatever' (85).

Lenin was critical of this view. In his opinion,

> [a] democratic republic is the best possible political shell for capitalism, and, therefore, once capitalism has gained possession of this very best shell ..., it establishes its power so securely, so firmly, that *no* change of persons, institutions or parties in the bourgeois-democratic republic can shake it (17).

He thought that this is true irrespective of the extent of the franchise (restricted or 'universal suffrage', including or excluding the workers: 17). It can 'be superseded ..., as a general rule, only through a violent revolution' (24). There is an 'omnipotence of wealth in democratic republics of all description' (16), '[d]irect and indirect bribery' of politicians (17, 75), 'the purely capitalist organisation of the daily press'—again! (83)—, and '[i]n reality, the trade unions did not develop "in absolute freedom" *but in absolute capitalist slavery*', making 'concessions to the prevailing evil'—again (109–10)!³ 'The reason why the omnipotence of "wealth" is more *certain* in a democratic republic is that it does not depend' on corrupt individuals, but is systematic (17).

Lenin did not believe that communism, or any system other than capitalism, could be democratic. He was 'in favour of a democratic republic as the best form of state for the proletariat under capitalism' only (22).

> Democracy is of enormous importance to the working class in its struggle against the capitalists for its emancipation. But democracy is by no means a boundary not to be overstepped; it is only one of the stages on the road from feudalism to capitalism, and from capitalism to communism (94).

Ultimately, Lenin aimed at 'overcoming democracy' altogether (77): the withering away, 'the abolition of the state means also the abolition of democracy' (78).

Jean-François Revel, a former Marxist, argued that 'there is not nor ever can be such a thing as a "free communism"' (1977: 38). 'No communist state has ever been other than Stalinist' (39), 'neither democracy as it is understood in the West nor even a flabby sort of "liberalization" can be an essential part of the system. Rather they are its opposite, its mortal enemy' (42). Feeling threatened by deviating political opinions, the communist

---

3 De Schweinitz found that '[o]ddly enough, conflict between labor and management may be a major vehicle for promoting a stabilizing consensus in society, for it can lead to the acceptance by the contending parties of the ground rules under which the contest will be conducted. ... The settlement of the differences of labor and management in the give and take of collective bargaining' (1964: 33–4). The consequence of this mechanism was seen by Lenin as clearly as by Spengler: 'Lenin realized that the trade unions as they developed during the industrialization of the nineteenth century were basically bourgeois institutions. Created to countervail the bargaining power of the private business firms which were leading the advance through the industrial revolution, trade unions took on some of the characteristics of the organizations they originally arose to bedevil. Their leaders became, appropriately enough for a commercial age, cost-benefit calculators, balancing the advantages of higher wages against the advantages of shorter hours and estimating the time that might possibly be lost in strikes in trying to enforce demands for either one. ... The apocalyptic goals of Marxian socialism could not easily be cast in balance and therefore did not loom large in the calculations of trade union leaders. Indeed they were often actively hostile to socialists as they feared that the visions of the latter would lead to precipitous action that could only weaken, or even destroy the organizations which they had worked so hard to form' (Schweinitz, 1964: 73).

'norm is intolerance and its corollary, legitimized violence' (40). 'When communism destroys democracy, it does so because that is its intent. And when it fails to create democracy, that is because it is not in its nature to do so' (50).

> Like it or not, we must face the fact that modern democracy was born in conjunction with industrial capitalism. ... [T]his coincidence between the growth of the free society, resting on political democracy, and the flowering of the capitalist economy is an undeniable if disturbing historical fact (198).

Capitalism 'has always been linked to a critical society', it 'seems unable to function without it, while other societies by contrast seem unable to function with criticism' (198). This is indicated, for example, by '[t]he fact that capitalism gave rise to the labor union movement' (201).

The Marxist Bob Jessop gives a detailed account of the arguments put forward by socialist and communist writers in favour of an intimate linkage between democracy and capitalism (1978). Speaking of 'capitalist democracy' (10), he finds:

> The state is the principle institutional locus of political power in *capitalist societies* and cannot be derived from an abstract consideration of the *pure capitalist mode of production*. Indeed, it is one of the principal difficulties in the capital logic school of analysis of the capitalist state, that it neglects the more concrete problem of *state power in a given social formation* in favour of the *ideal collective capitalist in the CMP*. This makes it impossible for the school to grasp the nature of the capitalist state (11).

He believes that

> the democratic republic can function in the interests of capital in general precisely because it offers opportunities for working class reformism. In short, not only do "normal" forms of capitalist state provide opportunities for the continual adjustment of interests within the power bloc, they also provide continual opportunities for subordinate classes to struggle on behalf of their own interests in a way that favours the continued domination of capital (34).

The 'working class struggle is itself a mechanism of capital accumulation insofar as it forces capital' to reform itself, and thus it is 'instrumental in securing the interests of capital'. '[I]f working class struggles are to be effective moments in the reproduction of capital, it is essential that they be institutionalised. This can be secured through the recognition (and regulation) of trade unions and the extension of the franchise to workers' (33).

Some 'point to the embourgeoisement of working class representatives as a form of political corruption and betrayal of those they represent'

(35–6), but Jessop praises 'the flexibility permitted by democratic forms of representation to working class struggle as well as to the power bloc' (33).

The Marxist Bill Warren, finally, makes it perfectly clear: 'Capitalism and democracy are, I would argue, linked virtually as Siamese twins' (1980: 28).

'Once a certain threshold had been passed in the development of capitalist enterprise and political democracy, the floodgates were opened and the spread of democracy became cumulative'. The 'strengthening of political democracy ... did always accord with' the 'economic interests' of the bourgeoisie (29).

> This connection was maintained and developed over several centuries and has been successfully reinforced, despite the social weaknesses of the bourgeoisie, since the Second World War, with the further extension of democracy under a more planned capitalism. In Western Europe and North America, Australia and Japan there can be no doubt that parliamentary democracy today has more meaning for the individual citizen and gives more scope for the working classes to influence social life than ever before in history. The process of expanding parliamentary democracy, initiated by the bourgeoisie, has been given powerful new impetus by the proletariat and has thus far proved to have a powerful and irresistible momentum *within capitalism* (30).

We just now observe the struggle of anti- and alter-globalization movements *within* the capitalist system, I suggest. It will lead only to a reform and renewed consolidation of capitalism.

As we will see.

VI

Conclusion

What should have become clear from the literature review is that a linkage between democracy and capitalism undeniably exists. The important finding of this paper, and my ongoing argument, is that, independent of their premises, all writers reviewed, except the anti- and alter-globalization activists, have come to the same conclusion: democracy and capitalism are inextricably linked. Democracy, at the national level, stands little chance of survival if not coupled to a capitalist economic system.

'Economic development consistently emerges as a statistically and substantively significant influence on democracy' (Burkhart and Lewis-Beck, 1994: 903). The 'result of the qualitative studies must be considered an established empirical generalization with which all accounts of democratization have to come to terms' (Rueschemeyer *et al.*, 1992: 31). Fukuyama goes as far as to assert that Karl Marx, 'in the preface to the English edition of *Das Kapital*, had stated that "[t]he country that is more developed industrially only shows, to the less developed, the image of its own future." This was, consciously or not, the beginning premise of modernization theory' (1992: 68). Furthermore, as understood by Marx,

> modern democracy was clearly one of the historical achievements of the bourgeoisie, the rising capitalist class ..., and to that extent the phrase "bourgeois democracy", as still commonly used by Marxists, is *historically* valid (even if one puts aside its pejorative connotations and the implication that there is another, better form of democracy under socialism) (Berger, 1987: 73).

I suggested that the few deviant cases in which a democratic constitution that predated capitalism did not fail were sustained by variables external to both capitalism and democracy. While there is disagreement as to whether democratization is a linear or near-linear positive function of economic growth or a threshold phenomenon associated with a country (or its citizens) reaching a particular level of income, either accounts for the fact that capitalism can, and does, exist in countries without democracy. With others, I have argued that only in countries above a certain economic threshold democracy will not be overthrown once it has been introduced. Steady economic growth appears to mitigate the danger of failure of democracy even in circumstances in which such a threshold has not yet been reached. Democracy, in turn, has been shown to stimulate further economic growth.

If indeed democracy and capitalism are linked, more concretely, in the way I hypothesized earlier in this paper, this means that if someone wants to fight capitalism, and maybe sees globalization as today's primary manifestation of it, they need to abandon democracy and its values first.

Radical Islamists, and indeed Islamist terrorists, with their critique of 'Democracy/Capitalism' (British website *Al Muhajiroun*, 2004: par. 7) and 'globalization/Americanization' (al-Hilali, 2002: par. 314), have understood this (see Kofmel, 2009). Terrorists have been known to refer to the writings of anti- and alter-globalization activists such as Bello (al-Qirshi, 2002: par. 191) to point out elements of their socio-political analyses of common concern to both movements. What the non-violent mass protests of 'Seattle' for the anti- and alter-globalization movements, that are the terrorist attacks of September 11, 2001, on the World Trade Center and the Pentagon for the terrorist movements—a major victory over the apparently invincible world power, the United States.

Within their frame of reference, terrorists' actions can only be called consequential and logical, targeting symbols of democratic and economic power alike. Conversely, both theory and empirical evidence suggest that grassroots-democratic anti- and alter-globalization movements are contradictory in themselves and therefore bound to fail. One cannot fight capitalism, it seems, and replace it with some non-liberal democracy because every form of democracy, if sustained long enough, will in turn give rise to some form of capitalism.

Factors associated with a capitalist economic system are among the necessary preconditions for a stable democracy.

Capitalism goes with direct democracy just as well as with representative democracy, as the example of Switzerland illustrates.

This is the deeper meaning of the inextricable linkage of democracy to capitalism: Whoever wants to fight capitalism must be prepared to fight democracy as well.

Being anti-capitalist, one has no choice but to be anti-democratic too.

One has no choice.

That is, if anti-capitalism is to be more than a leftist phrase of the past. If anti-capitalism shall mean to free the human imagination from the coercion of man by money.

This would suggest that what we observe is the struggle of anti- and alter-globalization movements not against, but *within* the capitalist system. Contradictory and under-theorized as that struggle is, it will only lead to a reform and renewed consolidation of capitalism. In the same way that the labour movement, feminism, and green politics caused capitalism to adapt to their concerns, but did not change the economic system fundamentally.

Democracy appears to provide capitalism with a system-immanent opportunity to renew itself whenever a sufficiently strong anti-capitalist, but pro-democratic, movement arises — and to absorb all criticism.

Decades of economic growth under democracy as well as the welfare state, much despised by the neo-liberal Chicago School professors, further consolidated the capitalist economic system in the West by bestowing property and entitlements upon almost every citizen and thus muting fundamental opposition.

The linkage between democracy and capitalism holds many more implications for politics, governance, economic and social policy, and the economy than we can rationally grasp at this stage. There is a whole field of study opening up before our eyes. (Including further elaboration of a theory explaining exceptional cases in which democracy and capitalism may be temporarily de-linked as well as empirical studies into these phenomena).

A proper understanding of the linkage between democracy and capitalism, and its deeper meaning, raises serious issues. While since the fall of communism it has become acceptable to question capitalism, it is, at least in a western context, still a taboo to question democracy. But why? If indeed democracy is the best of all political systems, why should it be dangerous to democracy if we become aware of its intrinsic linkage to capitalism? If however we think that capitalism is the worst of all economic systems, are we prepared to abandon democracy in order to fight capitalism?

Do we prefer to simply avoid the decision?

Whoever wants to fight capitalism has to accept the fact that all indications are that there can be no democracy without capitalism.

The one who really means to fight the system must stand entirely outside of it.

References

al-Hilali, A.A. (2002), 'The real story of the raids on New York and Washington', in *Book commemorates September 11 'raid'*, ed. Majallat al-Ansar/trans. FBIS (retrieved April 17, 2004, from http://www.why-war.com/files/qaeda_celebrate_911.txt)

Al Muhajiroun (2004), *Islam vs. democracy* (retrieved April 17, 2004, from http://www.muhajiroun.com/ [Deen/Link to Islamic Topics/Islam vs Democracy])

al-Qirshi, A.U. (2002), 'The 11 September raid: the impossible becomes possible', in *Book commemorates September 11 'raid'*, ed. Majallat al-Ansar/trans. FBIS (retrieved April 17, 2004, from http://www.why-war.com/files/qaeda_celebrate_911.txt)

Aristotle (1988), *The politics*, ed. S. Everson/trans. B. Jowett and J. Barnes (Cambridge: Cambridge University Press).

Atkinson, C.F. (1971), 'Translator's preface', in *The decline of the West*, by O. Spengler (London: George Allen & Unwin).

Barnard, T. (1982), *The English Republic 1649–1660* (Harlow: Longman).

Bello, W. (2002), *Deglobalization: ideas for a new world economy* (London and New York: Zed Books).

Bentham, J. (1843), *The works of Jeremy Bentham*, ed. J. Bowring (11 vols.; Edinburgh: William Tait).

Berger, P.L. (1987), *The capitalist revolution: fifty propositions about prosperity, equality, and liberty* (Aldershot: Gower).

Bollen, K.A. (1979), 'Political democracy and the timing of development', *American Sociological Review*, 44 (4): 572–8.

Bonjour, E., H.S. Offler and G.R. Potter (1952), *A short history of Switzerland* (Oxford: Clarendon Press).

Brunk, G.G., G.A. Caldeira and M.S. Lewis-Beck (1987), 'Capitalism, socialism, and democracy: an empirical inquiry', *European Journal of Political Research*, 15 (4): 459–70.

Bryce, J. (1921), *Modern democracies* (2 vols.; London: MacMillan and Co.).
Burbach, R. (2001), *Globalization and postmodern politics: from Zapatistas to high-tech robber barons* (London: Pluto Press).
Burkhart, R.E., and M.S. Lewis-Beck (1994), 'Comparative democracy: the economic development thesis', *American Political Science Review*, 88 (4): 903–10.
Cicero (n.d.), *On the commonwealth*, trans. G.H. Sabine and S.B. Smith (Indianapolis, New York and Kansas City: Bobbs-Merrill).
Commentary (1978), 'Capitalism, socialism, and democracy: a symposium', *Commentary*, 65 (4): 29–71.
Cutright, P. (1963), 'National political development: measurement and analysis', *American Sociological Review*, 28 (2): 253–64.
Danaher, K. (2000), 'Why and how to pressure the World Bank', in *Globalize this! The battle against the World Trade Organization and corporate rule*, eds. K. Danaher and R. Burbach (Monroe, ME: Common Courage Press).
Danaher, K., and R. Burbach, eds. (2000), *Globalize this! The battle against the World Trade Organization and corporate rule* (Monroe, ME: Common Courage Press).
Friedman, M. (1982), *Capitalism and freedom* (reissued with a new preface; Chicago and London: University of Chicago Press).
Fukuyama, F. (1989), 'The end of history?', *The National Interest*, 16: 3–18.
Fukuyama, F. (1992), *The end of history and the last man* (New York: The Free Press).
Hadenius, A. (1992), *Democracy and development* (Cambridge: Cambridge University Press).
Hayek, F.A. von (1962), *The road to serfdom* (London: Routledge & Kegan Paul).
Helliwell, J.F. (1994), 'Empirical linkages between democracy and economic growth', *British Journal of Political Science*, 24 (2): 225–48.
Huntington, S.P. (1991), *The third wave: democratization in the late twentieth century* (Norman and London: University of Oklahoma Press).
Jackman, R.W. (1973), 'On the relation of economic development to democratic performance', *American Journal of Political Science*, 17 (3): 611–21.
Jessop, B. (1978), 'Capitalism and democracy: the best possible political shell?', in *Power and the state*, eds. G. Littlejohn, B. Smart, J. Wakeford and N. Yuval-Davis (London: Croom Helm).
Klein, N. (1999), *No logo: taking aim at the brand bullies* (New York: Picador).
Kofmel, E. (2009), 'Comparative political theology', in *Anti-liberalism and political theology*, ed. E. Kofmel (Exeter and Charlottesville: Imprint Academic).
Lenin, V.I. (1975), *The state and revolution: the Marxist theory of the state and the tasks of the proletariat in the revolution*, trans. not named (Moscow: Progress Publishers).
Lerner, D. (1958), *The passing of traditional society: modernizing the Middle East* (New York: Free Press of Glencoe).
Lindblom, C.E. (1977), *Politics and markets: the world's political-economic systems* (New York: Basic Books).
Lipset, S.M. (1959), 'Some social requisites of democracy: economic development and political legitimacy', *American Political Science Review*, 53 (1): 69–105.
Luzzatto, G. (1961), *An economic history of Italy: from the fall of the Roman empire to the beginning of the 16th century*, trans. P. Jones (London: Routledge & Kegan Paul).
Macpherson, C.B. (1977), *The life and times of liberal democracy* (Oxford, London and New York: Oxford University Press).

Mandelbaum, M. (2002), *The ideas that conquered the world: peace, democracy, and free markets in the twenty-first century* (Oxford: Public Affairs Ltd.).

Monbiot, G. (2003), *The age of consent: a manifesto for a new world order* (London: Flamingo).

Neubauer, D.E. (1967), 'Some conditions of democracy', *American Political Science Review*, 61 (4): 1002–9.

Novak, M. (1982), *The spirit of democratic capitalism* (New York: American Enterprise Institute and Simon & Schuster).

Plato (1941), *The republic of Plato*, trans. F.M. Cornford (Oxford: Oxford University Press).

Pourgerami, A. (1988), 'The political economy of development: a cross-national causality test of development-democracy-growth hypothesis', *Public Choice*, 58 (2): 123–41.

Przeworski, A., M.E. Alvarez, J.A. Cheibub and F. Limongi (2000), *Democracy and development: political institutions and well-being in the world, 1950–1990* (Cambridge and New York: Cambridge University Press).

Reagan, R. (1988), *The quest for peace, the cause of freedom: selected speeches on the United States and the world* (Washington, DC: United States Information Agency).

Revel, J.-F. (1977), *The totalitarian temptation*, trans. D. Hapgood (New York: Doubleday).

Roy, A. (2002), *Power politics* (Cambridge, MA: South End Press).

Roy, A. (2003), *War talk* (Cambridge, MA: South End Press).

Rueschemeyer, D., E. Huber Stephens and J.D. Stephens (1992), *Capitalist development and democracy* (Chicago: University of Chicago Press).

Schweinitz, K. de (1964), *Industrialization and democracy: economic necessities and political possibilities* (New York: Free Press of Glencoe).

Shiva, V. (2000), 'Spinning a new mythology: WTO as the protector of the poor', in *Globalize this! The battle against the World Trade Organization and corporate rule*, eds. K. Danaher and R. Burbach (Monroe, ME: Common Courage Press).

Simons, H.C. (1948), *Economic policy for a free society* (Chicago: University of Chicago Press).

Spengler, O. (1971), *The decline of the west*, trans. C.F. Atkinson (London: George Allen & Unwin).

Starr, A. (2000), *Naming the enemy: anti-corporate movements confront globalization* (London and New York: Zed Books).

Tocqueville, A. de (2000), *Democracy in America*, ed./trans. H.C. Mansfield and D. Winthrop (Chicago and London: University of Chicago Press).

Vanhanen, T. (1989), 'The level of democratization related to socioeconomic variables in 147 states in 1980–85', *Scandinavian Political Studies*, 12 (2): 95–127.

Warren, B. (1980), *Imperialism: pioneer of capitalism*, ed. J. Sender (London and New York: Verso).

Winham, G.R. (1970), 'Political development and Lerner's theory: further test of a causal model', *American Political Science Review*, 64 (3): 810–8.

Contributors

Erich Kofmel is Managing Director of the Sussex Centre for the Individual and Society (SCIS) and European Doctorate candidate in Social and Political Thought at the University of Sussex and Sciences Po Paris. He holds Master's degrees in Public and Development Management and Roman-Catholic Theology and has authored numerous long interpretive entries in the *International Encyclopedia of Political Science* (CQ Press, 2009). Besides the present volume, Kofmel is the editor of *Anti-Liberalism and Political Theology* (Imprint Academic, 2009). An edited volume on anti-democratic development and a monograph, *Me Against Mediocrity*, are in preparation. Website: www.scis-calibrate.org; e-mail: e.kofmel@scis-calibrate.org

Jalal Alamgir is Assistant Professor of Political Science at the University of Massachusetts at Boston. His areas of specialty are globalization and democratic politics, perception of rivalry and competition, and violent and non-violent representation, especially through political and economic changes. He has consulted for strategy consulting firms and the United Nations and held research appointments at Brown University and Columbia University. Alamgir's papers have appeared in many peer-reviewed journals and he is the author of *India's Open-Economy Policy: Globalism, Rivalry, Continuity* (Routledge, 2009). E-mail: jalal.alamgir@umb.edu

Thom Brooks is Reader in Political and Legal Philosophy in the Politics Department at the University of Newcastle and the founding editor of the *Journal of Moral Philosophy*. He is the author of *Hegel's Political Philosophy: A Systematic Reading of the Philosophy of Right* (Edinburgh University Press, 2007) and *Punishment* (Routledge, 2009) and editor of *The Legacy of John Rawls* (Continuum, 2005), *Rousseau and Law* (Ashgate, 2005), *Locke and Law* (Ashgate, 2007), and *The Global Justice Reader* (Blackwell, 2008). Brooks is currently working on a book on global justice. E-mail: t.brooks@newcastle.ac.uk

Alexandre J.M.E. Christoyannopoulos has recently submitted his doctoral thesis on Christian anarchist theory at the University of Kent. He is interested in religion and politics broadly defined, but especially in the relation between religion and political theory and philosophy. He has presented papers and convened workshops at several national and international conferences and has published articles in *The Heythrop Journal*, *Anarchist Studies*, and *Politics and Religion*. Christoyannopoulos is also working on the publication of two monographs, one on his doctoral thesis and another on Leo Tolstoy's religious and political writings. E-mail: a.christoyannopoulos@gmail.com

Thomas Crombez is a Research Fellow of the FWO Research Foundation-Flanders. He is currently engaged in a research project at the University of Antwerp on mass spectacle in Flanders during the interbellum period. Crombez studied Philosophy at the Vrije Universiteit Brussel and Theatre Studies at the University of Antwerp and obtained his doctorate in 2006 with a thesis on *The Antitheatre of Antonin Artaud*, published in Dutch (Academia Press, 2008). He is co-editor of *The Locus of Tragedy* (Brill, 2008) and *On the Outlook: Figures of the Messianic* (Cambridge Scholars Publishing, 2007). E-mail: thomas.crombez@ua.ac.be

Wendy C. Hamblet is Assistant Professor in Philosophy at North Carolina A & T State University and a professional ethics coach to the private and public sectors. Her research investigates radical violence from the phenomenological perspective. Hamblet has authored chapters in many edited volumes as well as dozens of articles in peer-reviewed journals and is the author of several books, including *The Sacred Monstrous: A Reflection on Violence in Human Communities* (Lexington Books, 2004), *Savage Constructions: A Theory of Rebounding Violence in Africa* (Lexington Books, 2008) and *The Lesser Good: Plato and Levinas on Ethics and Justice* (Lexington Books, 2008). E-mail: whamblet@ncat.edu

Andy Hamilton is Senior Lecturer in Philosophy at Durham University, specializing in philosophy of mind, aesthetics, political philosophy and history of nineteenth- and twentieth-century philosophy. He also teaches aesthetics and history of jazz and is a music critic and contributor to *The Wire* magazine. Hamilton has published many journal articles, is the author of *Aesthetics and Music* (Continuum, 2007), *Lee Konitz: Conversations on the Improviser's Art* (University of Michigan Press, 2007) and the *Routledge Philosophy GuideBook to Wittgenstein and On Certainty* (2009), and has completed a monograph on philosophy of mind, *Memory and the Body: A Study of Self-Consciousness*. E-mail: a.j.hamilton@durham.ac.uk

Moshe Hellinger is a Lecturer in the Department of Political Studies and in the Faculty of Law at Bar-Ilan University in Ramat-Gan and the Head of the Ernest Schwarcz Institute for Ethics, Judaism and State at Beit Morasha, Jerusalem. His fields of expertise are political theory, Jewish political thought, orthodox Judaism and western culture. He has published numerous journal articles and book chapters both in Hebrew and English and is the editor of *Jewish Political Tradition Throughout the Ages*, published in Hebrew (Bar-Ilan University Press, 2008). E-mail: hellinm1@mail.biu.ac.il

Tuula Vaarakallio is a Postdoctoral Fellow of the Academy of Finland, working in Political Science in the Department of Social Sciences and Philosophy at the University of Jyväskylä, Finland. Her doctoral thesis *Rotten to the Core: Variations of French Nationalist Anti-System Rhetoric* (University of Jyväskylä, 2004) dealt with French nationalism and her ongoing project deals with French anti-parliamentarism. E-mail: tuula.vaarakallio@danpat.fi

Pauline C. Westerman is Professor in Philosophy of Law at the University of Groningen as well as at the Vrije Universiteit Amsterdam. She graduated in Philosophy of Science and wrote her doctoral thesis on *The Disintegration of Natural Law Theory* (Brill, 1998). Westerman is a member of staff of the Academy of Legislation in The Hague and mainly publishes on current changes in regulation and legislation from a legal theoretical perspective. E-mail: p.c.westerman@rug.nl